Ordered Universes

ORDERED UNIVERSES

Approaches to the Anthropology of Religion

Morton Klass

Barnard College

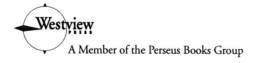

Westview
PRESS

A Member of the Perseus Books Group

Copyright © 1995 by Westview Press, A Member of the Perseus Books Group

Published in 1995 in the United States of America by Westview Press, Inc., 5500 Central Avenue, Boulder, Colorado 80301-2877, and in the United Kingdom by Westview Press, 12 Hid's Copse Road, Cumnor Hill, Oxford OX2 9JJ

Library of Congress Cataloging-in-Publication Data
Klass, Morton, 1927–
   Ordered universes : approaches to the anthropology of religion /
Morton Klass.
      p.   cm.
   Includes bibliographical references and index.
   ISBN 0-8133-1213-2. — ISBN 0-8133-1214-0 (pbk.)
   1. Religion.   2. Ethnology—Religious aspects.   3. Religions.
I. Title.
BL256.K57   1995
306.6—dc20   94-41434
                                                                    CIP

Printed and bound in the United States of America

   The paper used in this publication meets the requirements
   of the American National Standard for Permanence of Paper
   for Printed Library Materials Z39.48-1984.

10

for
Perri
David
Judy
the best there are

I have no hesitation in claiming . . . that though the students of the higher religions may sometimes look down their noses at us anthropologists and our primitive religions—we have no texts—it is we more than anyone who have brought together the vast material on a study of which the science of comparative religion has been, however insecurely, founded. . . .

—E. E. Evans-Pritchard
Theories of Primitive Religion

Contents

Preface

"We have no texts," E. E. Evans-Pritchard admits gamely (1965:3), but of course he is referring to the absence, among the majority of the peoples that anthropologists study, of Bibles and Korans and Mahabharatas and similar sacred books.

It happens, though, that these days we students of the anthropology of religion have no textbooks either. There are excellent readers—collections of papers and chapters of books designed for beginning students of the subject (Lessa and Vogt 1979; Lehmann and Myers 1989; and Middleton's three sourcebooks 1967a, 1967b, 1967c)—but we would have to go back to midcentury and beyond for anything resembling a true introductory text. And in any case most of the introductory texts are out of print.

It seemed to me, therefore, both a necessary and comparatively simple matter to write a book that would introduce all the traditional categories to the anthropological student of religion but would also update them in terms of the research and theorizing of recent decades.

As I worked on the manuscript, however, I began to suspect that there was a good reason no one else had taken on the task in recent years: It was formidable if not indeed impossible. The earlier introductory texts, I discovered, were more than outdated: They approached the anthropological study of religion in terms of theoretical perceptions and assumptions that have long since been jettisoned in most of the other arenas of anthropological concern and activity.

I am of course not the first to make this discovery. Other anthropologists—for example, Clifford Geertz, Melford Spiro, and Victor Turner—have addressed this subject and offered important corrections and alternatives. What is really needed, however, is a thorough housecleaning and then a comprehensive restructuring of the anthropological study of religion.

There are questions we must face and answer: Why, in terms of theoretical sophistication and attention in graduate departments, is the anthropological study of religion lagging behind the study of other dimensions of culture? Has this subdivision of our discipline been effectively co-opted by burgeoning departments of "religious studies"? Given where we are today in anthropology as a total discipline, what do we now mean by the phrase *anthropology of religion*?

In the chapters that follow, I try to respond to questions such as these. Most particularly, I attempt to do this by probing the implications of some of the terms we still use and the assumptions that underlie much of our contemporary categorizing. Why, for example, do we still use words like *myth*? What do we mean by it—what does its use imply about our understanding of the narrative so termed? What are we distinguishing when we refer to some religious leaders as *priests* but to others as *shamans*? Why don't we have one encompassing term for both? What are the significant differences between newly emergent faiths—what we term *revitalization movements* or *cults*—and the ones that, like Buddhism, Judaism, Christianity, and Islam, have been around for a longer time?

I believe that the raising of such questions is overdue in the discipline and vital for any work intended to acquaint new students with the subject matter of the anthropological study of religion. I assume, of course, that the reader has at minimum had a good and reasonably comprehensive introductory course on cultural anthropology and is now ready to look more closely at this particular subdivision.

Inevitably, then, this is a very idiosyncratic work. It is a presentation of my views on the subject, of what I am interested in or have something to say about. And I definitely have points to make.

But not about everything. There is much more to be said, on every subject, than I have here written. There is, for example, much more to be said about spirit possession and altered states of consciousness than is to be found in these pages; the list of what I have not dealt with is long indeed.

The problem is that there is almost no end to the categories and ramifications of religion from an anthropological perspective, and I am not willing to pretend to have something original to say about all of them. Instead, I have tried to introduce what I view as particularly crucial subjects and dimensions of the anthropology of religion, then go on to explore what I see as the problems we, as anthropologists, face in approaching those issues. The interested reader, and particularly the neophyte anthropologist about to go into the field, is urged to go first to the library and do some reading: This book is intended only to start students thinking . . . and arguing.

Indeed, *argument* is the operative word. The even moderately knowledgeable reader will observe immediately that I am arguing with colleagues, past and present, about fundamental issues. The neophyte is warmly invited to follow the arguments, but I am explicit about challenging accepted views and assumptions. It is my fervent hope that others will take up my challenges with a will and respond in kind: It is the arguments, after all, that are really important in any scholarly discipline.

Perhaps I should expand a bit on that last point. All scholars agree on the need for and importance of argument and debate. The terms of the debate, however, may often be circumscribed by the assumptions and perspectives of the debater. Thus, for example, structuralists may express impatience with efforts of human ecologists to explore the relationships between physical environment and social organization—whereas cultural materialists may demand to know what "laws" structuralists have discovered or even sought.

That sort of thing is commonplace in anthropology, as it is in all disciplines, but it constitutes a serious problem for those who would probe religion, which, after all, is the unfolding of underlying, unquestioned assumptions of what is right—indeed, of what *is*. Be aware, therefore, that in this book the theoretical stance is that of eclecticism. That means that without embarrassment I draw upon any theoretical stance that I believe helps illuminate the problem under consideration. And, perhaps more important, I endeavor to expose the assumptions underlying particular kinds of analysis or explanation. I try to explain, for example, why Victor Turner's conception of "liminality" (along with his introduction of such terms as *anti-structure* and *communitas*) constitutes an effort to break some of the bonds imposed by structuralist theory.

Such an approach inevitably generates problems. For me to charge off without preamble into the set of approaches I here champion could serve only to confuse, given the state of most contemporary anthropological references to religion in introductory texts. If, for example, I say (as I do) that the term *supernatural* has no place in contemporary anthropology, then the reader may reasonably inquire why it is used so casually in most introductory anthropology textbooks.

In other words, in order to write a textbook that might help the fledgling anthropologists setting out to observe religion in the field, I found it necessary to wrestle continually and explicitly with terms, notions, assumptions, and even conclusions that would be challenged in any other subdivision of cultural anthropology—and in fact *are* by contemporary scholars of the anthropology of religion—but still find their uncriticized way into all the latest "general" introductory textbooks.

And there is, at least in my view, an even greater problem. Most anthropologists like to think of themselves as scientists, and that of course includes anthropologists who study religion. But science is not only a way of gathering data and testing hypotheses; it is also a belief system in its own right. The testing of hypotheses, for example, reflects an assumption (essentially unprovable) that two experiments will provide the same results if performed in exactly the same manner under the same conditions. I am not challenging this or any other assumption of science; I am merely observing that the study of one belief system by proponents of another belief system is going to raise problems. The term *supernatural* and all that it implies and precipitates is only one example, but, as we shall see, it is an important one.

In the pages that follow, I therefore try to present a series of connected and sequential essays on a set of what I perceive as fundamental issues. In the initial chapters I address problems posed by our "scientistic" assumptions, after which I attempt a value-free operational definition, or delineation, of the subject. In the succeeding chapters I explore, and I hope clarify, important areas of scholarly disagreement and confusion.

To begin with, then, this is an introductory text, but it is in addition a comprehensive and coordinated presentation of my own views on what the anthropology of religion is about (and is not about) and how one might proceed to study it.

Such a book cannot be written in a vacuum or even in an ivory tower. My teachers, colleagues, and students have all contributed to this book—in some ways perhaps more than I have. We have argued incessantly in class, at scholarly symposia, and over beer and coffee late into the night. I suspect I have slighted the views of many who have taught me; I know, too, that I have not cited every book from which I have received knowledge and understanding. It is my hope that this book will challenge some readers to search out all the books and topics I have here neglected—and in turn to challenge me and my interpretations.

I particularly want to thank Herbert S. Lewis, Sidney M. Greenfield, Joan E. Vincent, and Myron L. Cohen for all the insights they have given me over the years. I owe a special debt of gratitude to Alan Segal for his wisdom and his generosity. At a difficult moment during my work on this book, Daniel H. Keyes turned me around and pointed me in the right direction, just as he did more than fifty years ago on a rock off Hoffman Island in New York harbor. Among all the literate, courteous, diligent people at Westview Press, I praise by name only Dean Birkenkamp, who has from our first meeting encouraged and supported my efforts without stint and without hesitation. But my thanks go to everyone at that remarkable publishing house.

I am inexpressibly grateful to all of the above for all they have taught me and done for me, but in the end, of course, I alone am responsible for the interpretations and conclusions set forth here, and for all errors and misstatements to be found in the pages ahead.

And there is one more person deserving of special gratitude for her patience and unending encouragement, without which—truly! truly!—this book could not possibly have been completed.

Thank you, Sheila.

Morton Klass

1

At Play in the Sacred Grove

I hope that after this explicit disclaimer I shall no longer be taxed with embracing a system of mythology which I look upon not merely as false but as preposterous and absurd.

—James G. Frazer
The Golden Bough

To begin with, let us just for a moment pretend that we all know what religion is and even agree on a definition. Religion is . . . well . . . religion, all right? And by the *anthropological study of religion* we mean the enterprise of looking at religion comparatively, or cross-culturally, because, as everyone knows, anthropologists go off to the strangest places, where people believe in the damnedest things.

Before we argue about the definition of *religion,* therefore, I propose to contemplate another and more basic question: Why do anthropologists do such things? What is to be gained by recording and analyzing alien practices and beliefs—things that are frequently disgusting and even more frequently not what we would want to recommend for adoption in our own society?

A lot of people ask such questions, often suspiciously. To take an important case in point, Allan Bloom, in *The Closing of the American Mind,* concludes that "sexual adventurers like Margaret Mead and others" seek to "liberate" our society from its traditional values and restraints (1987:33).[1]

For anthropologists, of course, the reasons we do what we do have been clear since Franz Boas first enunciated them in 1888:

> The data of ethnology prove that not only our knowledge, but also our emotions are the result of our social life and the history of the people to whom we belong. If

---

[1] Nasty, huh? Well, I think so, and I said so in my paper "The Closing of 'the Bazaar of Cultures': Anthropology as Scapegoat" (Klass 1990).

we desire to understand the development of human culture we must try to free ourselves of these shackles. . . . It is impossible to determine a priori those parts of our
mental life that are common to mankind as a whole and those that are due to the
culture in which we live. A knowledge of the data of ethnology enables us to attain
this insight. Therefore it enables us to view our own civilization objectively.
(1940:636)

Pursuing this noble (to us, anyway) objective, we anthropologists have fanned
out over the globe, striving to reach every island, every village, every urban
neighborhood—in short, every distinctive gathering of humans, counting each
(whether it be a conglomeration of 10,000 computer specialists or an encamp-
ment of twenty foragers) as one example of a human attempt to address the
problems of life on this planet.

Nothing people do or think while engaged in that endeavor escapes the attention of the anthropologist, and one would assume that particular attention
would be addressed to the body of beliefs and practices that are to be subsumed
in the anthropologist's notebook under the rubric *religion*.

There are problems here, however. Religion seems to give the anthropologist
more grief than does technology or social organization or practically anything
else. It seems to be harder to define, for one thing, and for another almost any
contemplation of belief systems appears to precipitate intellectual discomfort,
almost indigestion: The observer is, after all, for the most part examining the
minutiae of complex practices that—the observer believes—have no effect on
anything; no practical utility whatever.

And that is only the beginning. Of all the practices on which the anthropologist reports (with the possible exception of sex, *pace* Bloom), religion is most
likely to raise suspicions that the anthropologist has gone native. Consider the
implications of Frazer's pained disclaimer in his preface to the 1922 edition of *The
Golden Bough:* "I hope . . . I shall no longer be taxed with embracing a system of
mythology which I look upon not merely as false but as preposterous and absurd" (1958:vii). One implication, of course, is that Frazer has been thoroughly
embarrassed by being "taxed"; people have been whispering or perhaps even
writing about Frazer's morbid fascination with Kings of the Wood, temple prostitutes, eunuch priests, and other such un-Christian and morally dubious matters.

There are even more troublesome implications to be noted in Frazer's disclaimer, as we shall see, and in my view they illuminate a serious and continuing
problem: For some time many have seen the anthropological study of religion as
essentially dead in the water. Clifford Geertz has argued that the subdiscipline
"has made no theoretical advances of major importance" since the end of World
War II. He adds that "it is living off the conceptual capital of its ancestors" and
suggests that "the anthropological study of religion is in fact in a state of general
stagnation" (Geertz 1971:1).

Now it is true that Geertz wrote this particular paper in 1963 (and first published it in 1966), and clearly much has been written since then—by Geertz him-

self, among many others. Nevertheless, it could convincingly be argued that much of Geertz's criticism is still valid. Certainly, we have not progressed in the area of the anthropology of religion with anything like the theoretical sophistication that has been achieved in the study of social organization or political systems.

Furthermore, in the same volume (Michael Banton's *Anthropological Approaches to the Study of Religion,* 1971), Melford Spiro—essentially in agreement with Geertz that such a problem exists—attributes much of the difficulty to inadequate definition, and I intend to argue in Chapter 3 that we have hardly moved at all in that regard.

Well, one might ask, is the topic really of great importance? I would argue that it is more than that: It is of *central* importance. After all, anthropologists study culture, and if there is one perception about the nature of culture that contemporary anthropologists (whatever their theoretical allegiances) share, it is the awareness of the interrelatedness, the inseparability, of what we once thought of as distinct categories: social organization, economic relationships, symbol systems, and the like.

This is because *a* culture (exactly like *a* language) is a system of systems of rules determining what is "right," what is "good," what is "the way we do it." These rules, we all know, encompass all aspects of behavior and belief, and therefore what we categorize as social organization (the ordering of human relationships) or religion (the ordering of the universe) are aspects of the same thing: There are values and beliefs that underlie all social relationships, just as there are social relationships (between human and human and between human and other-than-human) inextricably entwined with beliefs about the nature of the universe and with the practices that devolve from those beliefs.

In every human society (I have no way of knowing about the nonhuman ones), then, there is an ordered system of values, beliefs, relationships, and rules about such matters as death, meaning, sanctioned actions, and control of events. Anthropologists study culture, and culture—by way of what we label religion— orders the universe, thereby eliminating (or at least walling off) chaos, meaninglessness, and human helplessness.

Anthropologists, it therefore follows, must not only study religion but must give the subject *at least* as much attention, and particularly theoretical attention, as they would give to any other dimension of culture. In fact I think they should give it even more.

But back to Frazer and his embarrassed disclaimer. He was, he says, "taxed with embracing" the body of beliefs he had described and analyzed in his compendious work, admittedly an awesome charge. But consider: He might, in reply, have done no more than remind the reader that, in the words of Herodotus (written about 430 B.C.E.), "My duty is to report all that is said, but I am not obliged to believe it all" (1942:556). That dignified observation by the father of the social sciences was apparently not enough for Sir James G. Frazer, though; he wanted the world to be in no doubt that he regarded *everything* he studied to be "not merely as false but as preposterous and absurd"!

It seems to me self-evident that the scholar who works with material he or she considers "false" and "preposterous" and "absurd" is in serious trouble—not just from mocking readers, but from the iron rules of research. A rather dramatic statement, that: Let me try to defend it.

I began with the most fundamental of questions, Why should anthropologists study religion? The obvious response, one that is implicit in Frazer's disclaimer, is that we are simply gathering data about beliefs just as we might gather data about kinship or gardening techniques. Well, yes, but note that the issue of truth or reality never enters the discussion when one is considering mother's brother's daughter marriage or slash-and-burn horticulture. Those are things people do; I myself may neither do them nor even admire them, but I am perfectly comfortable observing them, much as an astronomer would be when contemplating blue giants or a paleontologist while considering the bones of a possible ichthyosaur.

None of these scholars—and no student of horticultural techniques—ever felt compelled to make a disclaimer such as Frazer's, and I don't mean to ignorant readers, but to himself or herself. Indeed, suppose a physicist did in fact offer a Frazerian disclaimer about her work or a geneticist about his or historians about theirs. Wouldn't that raise questions in your mind? You might accept their findings, if with a touch of uncertainty, but you would certainly worry about their interpretations and conclusions.

One may study slash-and-burn horticulture in West Irian whether one is a gardener oneself or has never touched a hoe; all that we ask or expect is that personal experience and personal beliefs play no part in the research or the later analysis. We require of the student of horticultural techniques only accuracy and meticulous attention to detail. We require the same of the student of religious beliefs and practices, of course, but here we observe a disturbingly ubiquitous penetration of the study by the student's private beliefs. Might this significantly affect both research and analysis?

For example, suppose, on the one hand, you are a "religious" person. In that case, you accept without doubt, or at least without serious question, a set of specific teachings about the nature of the universe, about the constitution of the divine, and about much else. Since you *know* the *truth,* and since other accounts—to the extent that they differ from your *truth*—must by definition constitute *error,* are you not aware (indeed, can you ever forget?) that you are spending your time studying *error?*

Or, suppose, on the other hand, you are "nonreligious." That would mean, presumably, that you reject all dogma as suspect, and—as a rationalist, perhaps even a scientist—you invariably accept only that which is capable of being either validated or proved false, and even such things only provisionally. Well, if you reject as intellectually unacceptable even the belief systems of your *own* society, what is really to be gained from studies of the even more unacceptable belief systems of other societies?

This is not a frivolous matter. The issue I raise is that of the beliefs of the student of beliefs: For the student to ignore that issue is to imperil the study. I suggest (and I hope to demonstrate) that this single issue has been a major source of the problems of the field: problems of definition, problems of comparison, problems of explanation, and more. After all, almost all of our data and analyses derive from the writings of people (such as Christian missionaries) who adhere firmly to a particular Western belief system or from proponents of Western scientific rationalism—and also from those who manage to adhere to both systems.

Am I then challenging the entire discipline, calling into question all its findings and interpretations? Not necessarily. I am simply suggesting that the traditional scholarly, even scientific, approach to the study and analysis of religion has uniquely disturbing aspects. I therefore propose to examine the traditional set of approaches to determine whether this peculiarity—what we might call the presence of a "belief factor"—has in any way contaminated the findings. Since I think that it has and expect to be able to demonstrate that, I believe we need alternative approaches to the anthropological study of religion, and I propose to offer them.

First, of course, I must present evidence that the belief factor adversely affects research or analysis. Let us therefore begin by returning one last time to Frazer's observation that the beliefs and practices to which he had devoted so much scholarly attention were, in his view, "false" and "preposterous" and "absurd."

Such an observation reflects a disturbingly negative view of the people who hold such beliefs and engage in such practices. Now, it goes without saying that you and I and Frazer and all good scholars scrupulously try to avoid making value judgments. Of course we all do. But let's pull down the window shade and have some privacy: Really, now, what sort of people continue—*generation after generation!*—to believe in, to devote their lives to, beliefs and practices that you, I, and James G. Frazer all know to be "false" and "preposterous" and "absurd"?

Dumb people, right?

At the very least they must be woefully ignorant, but maybe they are even mentally deficient, or maybe they are just liars. Surely, if they had even a bit of the sense and discrimination that *we* have, they would perceive the total wrongness of what they have been doing and believing and would turn away from it. But they don't. Well, if that is what they are like, how are we to explain what they continue to do and believe? Does it not follow that we must seek explanation in such things as the inability to think logically; the inability to observe accurately; severe mental imbalance; or, worst of all, the intent to deceive the gullible for gain?

Of course, we can be nicer than that. We can explain that these people are not really stupid or crazy or crooked; the meaningless practices they engage in have meaning or function on a deeper level. That is, they may be "instrumentally" worthless, but they have value or significance in some "symbolic" dimension. Or maybe the seemingly silly practices and explanations do have *some* instrumental value: Though it goes without saying that their "god" does not exist, nevertheless the evocation of the nonexistent deity provides them with a sense of community.

Or when the witch doctor goes into a state resembling schizophrenia and thinks he is communing with "ghosts" or "spirits" (none of which actually exist, as *we* never forget), it may well be that his impotent and even crazy maunderings serve to provide his people with an ecologically advantageous element of chance.[2]

The alert reader will have noted that I have just encompassed an awful lot of traditional anthropological thinking and explanation about religion. The "thinking," I would point out, seems to involve a lot of "explanation"—of why people engage in activities that clearly lack instrumental validity and do not relate to objective reality. To put it another way, such people spend a lot of time spinning wheels, apparently without ever noticing (as *we* do) that nothing is moving. Without exception the "explanations" either imply that there is something wrong with such people or that there *really is,* somewhere, a level of objective and instrumental validity even though those people are totally unaware of it. What explanations might we come up with if we successfully jettison these two implications? We can never know until we try.

I therefore propose that anthropologists once and for all table the issue of whether the things a given people believe in or do in the way of religion are true or false, wise or stupid, just as we would when we study their cousin terminology or their pottery designs.

I am not asking anyone to accept or admire any beliefs and practices other than his or her own. Rather, I ask the anthropologist to look upon the content of a given religious system—beliefs, practices, myths, and whatever—as things in themselves. We must never ask whether they are "true," whether they really "work." We must avoid all explanations, definitions, methodologies, and even terms that carry judgmental baggage. Thus, for that reason alone, we cannot continue to use the term *supernatural,* and, as we shall see, we are even going to have problems with *myth* and *shaman.*

Won't this tie our hands? I think it will free our minds. What assumptions are left to us? I suggest the following:

• The people who believe in and do the things anthropologists study under the rubric of *religion* are perfectly intelligent, as well as unintelligent, humans (in other words, they are just like us). If so, then it follows that they are endowed with exactly as much perception, insight, and critical capacity as we are—no more, maybe, but no less.

• For such people, therefore, the things they do and believe in are fully— *fully*—as "true" and as "verifiable" as are *all* the things *we* do and believe in.

---

[2] "My ghosts say there is water to the north!"
   "*My* ghosts say to the south!"
   With that much confusion and disagreement, one of the groups in the drought area might just make it.

These are, of course, the basic assumptions of all anthropological research; why, then, should we have so much difficulty extending them to the anthropological study of religion? A good question, that, and one to which we will return from time to time, but for now I would observe that if we can really achieve such objectivity, if we can really introduce some of the badly needed advantages of the phenomenological approach (in which one avoids addressing the issues of objective reality and subjective response), then the anthropological study of religion can indeed be as useful for our growing comprehension of human flexibility, variability, and potential for change as are our anthropological studies of art forms and child-rearing practices.

And maybe if we can agree on how to approach the study of religion, we might even be able to agree on what we mean by the term itself.

2

The Noisome Bog

It is always hazardous to set forth in search of the headwaters of human institutions. The unwary scholar is all too apt to find himself soon mired in a noisome bog of speculations, unable to extricate himself with dignity and subject to stoning by his more prudent colleagues on the bank. Nonetheless. . . .

—Anthony F.C. Wallace
Religion: An Anthropological View

I began the previous chapter with the proposal that we pretend we all agree on what we mean by *religion*. It should go without saying that we don't agree; indeed, we most profoundly disagree on what we consider to be our subject matter and on how we distinguish it from other rubrics or categories anthropologists study. More than that: Anthropologists even disagree on the importance of seeking a commonly acceptable definition!

Melford Spiro, in fact, stands almost alone in urging us to contemplate definition itself, as well as the consequences for the enterprise of anthropological inquiry of the definitional choices one makes.[1] The majority of writers on the subject tend to provide some terse, take-it-or-leave-it definition (e.g., "It is the premise of every religion—and this premise is religion's defining characteristic—that souls, supernatural beings, and supernatural forces exist" [Wallace 1966:52]) so that they may move swiftly to the aspects of religion they really want to discuss.

Is it not astonishing to reflect that since the very beginning of the anthropological (and sociological) study of religion, we have been in continuous and fundamental disagreement about what we are talking about? Is it not curious that most

---

[1] See "Religion: Problems of Definition and Explanation" (Spiro 1971). These issues and Spiro's arguments are subjects of discussion in the next chapter.

writers on the subject prefer to give much more attention to the disputes over how religion came into existence than to the disputes over what religion *is*, as a category of culture?

In this book I propose to reverse the customary pattern. Instead of beginning with a brief definition, I here attend briefly to views on the origins of religion, relying in large measure on the summary provided by Edward Norbeck (1961). In succeeding chapters I move to the issues encompassed in any effort to define *religion*—from the consequences of seeking definition to such things as the implications of the use of a term such as *supernatural*. After all that, and given all that, I offer what I perceive as an operationally meaningful and anthropologically acceptable definition or delimitation of the cultural rubric we have labeled *religion*.

First let us review some of the traditional theories about how and why religion originated. This issue is not without its own special pitfalls; efforts to explain origins are almost universally considered to be fraught with danger. Anthony Wallace's observation (cited as the epigraph to this chapter) points to the hazards (and also provides me with a chapter title). In addition, however, he poignantly expresses the frustration we anthropologists feel about being warned away from the subject. After dutifully posting the warning, he begins his own excursion into the danger zone with a quietly heroic "nonetheless": "Nonetheless, in this section we shall, in as gingerly a fashion as possible, consider the problem of the origin of religion. We shall seek the beginnings, not of any particular religion, but of religious behavior *sui generis*. We do this, not merely from antiquarian interest, but because a consideration of origins is prerequisite to a theory of ritual process" (1966:216–217).[2]

Here, then, we have another example of the seemingly intractable conflicts that beset the anthropological study of religion: We *must* "consider the problem of the origin of religion," Wallace instructs us—it is, he says, a "prerequisite"—but if we do, we soon "become mired in a noisome bog" and are even "subject to stoning" by our anthropological colleagues.

Why should such a problem exist? After all, Claude Lévi-Strauss could speculate about the origins of kinship systems without fear of being stoned, and scholars to this very day, confidently and without trepidation, speculate in print about the origins of technology. Why should similar speculation about the origins of religion so particularly constitute "a noisome bog"?

The question—How did the human institution of religion begin?—seems at first glance both innocent and reasonable, but all too often what is really being asked is:

When early humans, emerging from the primeval slime, became aware of the universe around them and began to consider it, why did they have to come up with such absolutely silly

---

[2] "The most obvious candidate [for a 'formal-functional property of animal behavior that is intrinsic to religious behavior in man'] is the phenomenon of ritual" (Wallace 1966:218).

conclusions, ones without basis in reality and studded with outlandish notions and even more outlandish nonexistent beings?

The "bog," I am suggesting, is of our own devising: We try, even as we ask such a question, to distance ourselves from any implication that we personally subscribe to the phenomenon whose origin we seek. We do this, of course, not out of Frazer-like embarrassment but because we are *scientists*, and we know that religious views and practices not only have no place in science but are antithetical to the scientific enterprise.

Emerging as they do from such an uncompromisingly scientistic[3] view of religion itself, therefore, a lot of the classic explanations of the *origin* of religion almost begin to make sense—at least in their own terms. The underlying assumptions in these explanations are that early humans turned to religion (read: nonsense) because the early humans were stupid, desperate, confused, or misled or for any reason other than because religion was accurate or instrumentally effective. Those latter reasons, every sensible person knows, were out of the question.

Recognizing the mind-set of the majority of scholars who have wrestled with the question of the origin of the institution of religion, we should not be surprised that most of the explanations of origin have been shot down almost as fast as they were launched into the air. This in turn has contributed to the bad name that any search for origins has today—rather than to any serious questioning of the mind-set that produced the unacceptable solutions.

One unfortunate consequence is that in recent decades there has been no close review of the "unacceptable" explanations themselves. Are there perhaps some meaningful perceptions to be extracted from them, unsatisfactory in toto though they may be? And there is another unfortunate consequence: Many of these supposedly discarded explanations, laughed at and dismissed by anthropologists, are often considered quite acceptable by members of the larger nonanthropological world.

Some writers on the sociology and anthropology of religion refer to these early explanations of the origin of religion apparently for the sole purpose of indicating how hopeless a task it is to make such inquiries. Others (see Goode [1951] 1964, Norbeck 1961) are interested in cataloging or assorting them for us. Norbeck, for example (1961:16–24), proposes that theories of the origin of religion seem to sort themselves into three basic categories: (1) theological, which posit some divine or beyond-human source for religion; (2) psychological, which assume that religion derived from some "need" of the human mind or psyche; and (3) sociological, which assume that religion is in some way a consequence of the human propensity to live in structured social groups.

---

[3] I use this term frequently throughout the text. It implies an approach based upon an assumption that a *scientific* explanation or interpretation invariably takes priority over, or is superior to, all others; compare Beattie's usage (1964b:203), also cited in this text in Chapter 4.

One could approach these categories from many points of view,[4] but I want to concentrate chiefly on some of the implications for our understanding of the nature of religion of these now exploded and neglected theories of origin. Let us turn first to the most widely held theory of the origin of religion—oddly, the one that social scientists give the smallest amount of attention. I refer of course to what is usually termed the theological explanation, that religion exists among us because we humans have been the fortunate beneficiaries of divine revelation. It may seem odd that such a widespread human belief should have received short shrift from those most interested in studying human belief, but such is in fact the case:

> Among the nonscholarly population of at least the civilized world surely the most common idea is that religion, if it be "true," has been divinely revealed. Divine revelation as an explanation of religious genesis has no place in this book, and under ordinary circumstances all theological interpretations of the origins of religion would be dismissed from consideration as irrelevant or prejudicial. (Norbeck 1961:22)

What are the special circumstances that impel Norbeck at least to acknowledge the existence of theological explanations of origin? Only that "theologians who are also social scientists have contributed empirical data relevant to an understanding of primitive religions and bearing directly upon theories of origin" (1961:22–23).

Here, of course, Norbeck is referring to the research and theoretical contributions of clerics such as Wilhelm Schmidt ([1908] 1954) and others who pointed to the presence of monotheism among peoples otherwise exhibiting the supposedly simplest ways of life on earth. This evidence contributed to the ultimate collapse of simplistic "unilineal evolutionary" approaches in anthropology. That consideration aside, however, we are advised that theological explanations "have no place" in a scholarly text (even one on religion) because they are "irrelevant" and "prejudicial."

What Norbeck means, of course, is that from a scientific (shall we say "rational"?) point of view, such explanations are clearly "wrong." This may be "good science," but in my view it raises problems for anthropology. We are, after all, anthropologists as well as generic scientists. From the days of Edward B. Tylor to the present, we have urged our students never to ignore the perspectives, insights, and explanations of our hosts, the people we are studying. The "native sociologist" may lack the benefits of a Western university education, but he or she has

---

[4] Why only three? Why not eight or nine, so that the psychoanalytic and rational and materialistic and so on could each occupy appropriately separate pigeonholes? Three is certainly a magic number in our society and therefore in our social sciences (three classes, three stages of social evolution, three human races, etc.). To be fair, I come up with such triplets myself, as the reader will see. In any event, I have enough problems in this work without unnecessarily ruffling culturally embedded cognitive categories, so let it stay three for all of me.

the advantage of a lifetime of observation. The linguistic researcher is usually pathetically grateful for an informant's views on categories of sound and grammar, and even the scholar who ultimately modifies or even rejects the insights provided by the informant knows that it is always necessary to consider the implications of the way the member of the society orders the universe.

Gregory Bateson ([1936] 1958) urged us to seek the "eidos," the characteristic or systemic cognitive processes, of a society, and much fruitful anthropological research, such as that under the heading of ethnoscience, depends directly upon this awareness that *all* people order and analyze. To be compleat anthropologists, therefore, we must—at very least to begin with—give respectful attention to our informants' views.

What, then, might we learn from theological views about religion? Consider again the dispute, referred to earlier, that raged at the end of the nineteenth century and the beginning of the twentieth about whether or not human society can be said to have evolved. In the latter half of the nineteenth century (and in the early decades of the twentieth), it was widely assumed in Europe, and in societies deriving from Europe, that "evolution," or at least continuing "progress," characterized the universe in all its component dimensions, including that of human society.

Many (particularly among the religious) contested this view, and the *Kulturkreis*[5] school of anthropology reflected this opposition. The position many espoused was that religion was God's gift and that it was a straightforward and unambiguous gift: Humans *began* with a true and complete knowledge of the one God. If some societies today have no such knowledge, it is because they have lost it through human error and confusion. Since from this perspective God's revelation is always perfect to begin with, it follows that if we perceive any confusion or contradiction—or even any "progress"—it is solely because of human imperfection.

For many anthropologists, this dispute among members of our discipline is, as we have seen, significant only in that it illuminates the early theoretical controversy about cultural evolution. What interests me, at least for the purposes of the present discussion, is that the above controversy is also one between adherents to different belief systems: between those in nineteenth-century Europe who believed in Progress and Evolution and those who believed in God and Revelation. For, clearly, when we talk of universal progress or perfect revelation, we are in fact exposing fundamental assumptions (or a worldview) about the nature of the universe, about the meaning of meaning—not just of individuals but of societies

---

[5] A theoretical school or approach to the emergence of culture, popular in Germany (and some other European countries) in the 1920s and 1930s. The proponents argued that in ancient times a series of isolated populations somewhere in Asia had developed distinctive cultures (*Kulturkreise*) and that these had then spread to other parts of the world as the carriers of the cultures migrated. This series of distinctive cultures accounted, in the view of proponents, for the differences that other anthropologists attributed to cultural evolution. (See Lowie 1937:175–195.)

or of societal subdivisions, and these are appropriate subjects for anthropological analysis.

In South Asia, to return to the question of progress, there have emerged a cluster of religions (including such major ones as Hinduism, Jainism, and the many divisions of Buddhism) that exhibit axioms quite different from those of European belief systems. Jains, for example, perceive the universe as exhibiting continual and inescapable degeneration, so that each generation is more unhappy (and further from a merger with divine Godhood) than the previous one. As proof, they point to the ever decreasing number of Jains in the world and look forward with resignation to the inevitable demise of their faith, when the world has simply become too degenerate for it.

Hindus, in contrast, perceive revelation as something incremental, capable of change and refinement over time, something in fact essentially evolutionary: Vishnu (who represents the preservation/maintenance aspect of divinity) is believed to appear among humans in many guises and in many different places and times. But are not the teachings of the Buddha somewhat in conflict with those of Krishna? And what of Moses, Christ, Mohammed? If, as some Hindus would aver, these, too, were avatars of Vishnu, why do we see such differences in revelation?

According to Hinduism, revelation preserves and uplifts, but it would fail if it became too revolutionary, if it stepped too far beyond the comprehension of its listeners. To be successful, it must be couched in familiar terms and call for rituals and practices that are intelligible and acceptable to the people of the time and place. For some, this might mean animal sacrifice and propitiation of terrifying divinities; for others, the revelation might demand only prayer or only meditation and the relinquishment of any graphic representation of divinity.

Norbeck, we have seen, rejects any consideration of theological explanations because such considerations imply granting to those explanations a degree of respectability, a concession however grudging that they might be true or at least might be evaluated along with the nonreligious explanations of scholars. In the foregoing paragraphs I have tried to (1) examine such beliefs in a way that sidesteps the issue of whether or not they are ultimately "correct" and (2) consider (briefly, of course) what we, as students of society and religion, might learn from an examination of such explanations.

What, then, can we learn from the array of *non*theological theories of how, why, and when religion came into existence in human society? A great deal, I would argue in much the same vein, irrespective of whether the particular theory (or the body of them) has any factual basis.

By *sociological theories* Norbeck really means only the proposal advanced by Émile Durkheim that religion emerged—during the emergence of human society itself—as a symbolic expression or representation of the social organism, of the "sense of unity" among those who make up a human society, and by means of which, as Norbeck puts it, they "uphold and reaffirm at regular intervals through collective ritual the sentiments and values of the society" (Norbeck 1961:22). One could certainly argue, however, that the category might also serve as the home for otherwise orphaned materialist explanations, such as the view that once humans began to assort themselves into structured societies, religion arose as a device of natural selection: a pathway for occasionally necessary chance to be reintroduced as a counterweight to human ignorance and folly.[6]

Norbeck's category of psychological theories is more crowded, for he subsumes under it rationalistic, emotionalistic, and psychoanalytic theories. Rationalistic theories, in his view, are those that see religion as "cognitive attempts of primitive man to interpret and adjust to his external environment"—those, in other words, that seek the source of religion in the flowering of human reason (Why is there death? What happens to the individual after death? Will the sun rise tomorrow?). Thus, Norbeck includes under this rubric Tylor's proposal that religion came into existence when "primitive philosophers" attempted to explain the phenomena of dreams, disease, death, and so on. He also includes here Frazer's view that religion grew out of magic. Both of these descriptions, believes Norbeck, reflect pseudoscientific efforts to control the universe in general and in particular the events taking place and about to take place.

Norbeck's emotionalistic theories are ones that imply that "religion ultimately sprang from various affective or emotional states automatically evoked in man in the events of daily life"—those, in other words, that propose that religion came into existence as a coalescence of the awe and fear early humans experienced as they became aware of time, death, and a universe outside themselves.

Norbeck includes in this category Herbert Spencer's suggestion that religion began as the propitiation, after death and out of fear, of departed ancestors—and Max Müller's view that, in Norbeck's words, "religion sprang from spontaneous emotional reactions of wonder, awe, and fear evoked in man by natural phenomena such as the sun and the moon" (Norbeck 1961:19, and see Müller 1878). Norbeck does not mention Bronislaw Malinowski's views on the origin of religion, but they probably also belong here: Religion emerges not simply from fear of the dead but as a response to death itself.

> The whole event breaks the normal course of life and shakes the moral foundations of society. The strong tendency . . . to give way to fear and horror, to abandon the corpse, to run away . . . all these impulses exist, and if given way to would be extremely dangerous. . . . Religion counteracts the centrifugal forces of fear, dismay, demoralization, and provides the most powerful means of reintegration of the group's shaken solidarity and of the re-establishment of its morale. (Malinowski [1948] 1954:52–53)

---

[6] Of course, if we believe materialist explanations can never be bedded down with sociological ones, the need for at least a fourth category becomes pressing.

Under his final subheading, psychoanalytic theories, Norbeck subsumes the views of only one scholar: Sigmund Freud. For Freud, Norbeck reports, religion—perceived as an expression of the internal complexities and contradictions of the human mind—emerged as a response to the need to avoid confronting such urges as the desire to kill one's father and have sex with one's mother. In other words, for Freud, Norbeck argues, religion emerged as a mechanism for sublimation, transference, and other forms of release from too painful psychological stress.

Now, as we know, Norbeck and others have dismissed as unacceptable all of the foregoing theories of how and why religion came into existence, and I have no intention of resuscitating them as such. We can look at them another way, however: as intimations of various scholars' conclusions regarding what religion *is*, on the basis of which they could then speculate about how an institution with such concerns and such scope might have come into existence.

From this perspective, then, we observe that a number of scholars universally hailed as brilliant have variously suggested that

- religion encompasses human attempts to explain, interpret, predict, and control phenomena and events and provides an avenue for the manifestations of chance;
- religion encompasses human emotional responses to the awesomeness of the universe and to the impact of illness, the death of loved ones, and one's own mortality;
- religion encompasses mechanisms for the release of psychological stress and internal conflict, utilizing inherent tendencies to ritual behavior;
- religion serves both to symbolize and to express the sense of unity in a society and its sense of separation or distinction from other human groups.

If we accept the foregoing (and surely it is hard to quarrel with the combined views of Tylor, Spencer, Frazer, Malinowski, Müller, Durkheim, and Freud, among others), we must to begin with acknowledge the overwhelming importance of religion as an institution and as a subject of study.

But in addition we may observe that though when presented as a theory of origin, each view seemed to be in contention with all the others, when taken together they constitute a most impressive exploration not simply of why religion emerged among humans but of what religion *is* and *does*.

In other words, although we may never know how or why or when religion as a category of human culture first came into existence, we have it on the best of authorities that—having come into existence for whatever reason—religions serve to satisfy our need for explanation; they provide channels for our emotional responses along with our fears and projections; they provide the sense of unity inherent in a cultural system. In short, in the ongoing drama that is any culture, the institution of religion provides meaning and purpose and satisfaction and order to an otherwise chaotic universe.

Those, then, are things that religions do, and surely they are important enough! But are we not continuing to sidestep the question of definition? How shall we, as anthropologists, distinguish religion from all other human cultural institutions? How shall we know it when we see it, so we can study it?

3

The Definitional Daisy Chain

When I mention religion I mean the Christian religion; and not only the Christian religion, but the Protestant religion; and not only the Protestant religion, but the Church of England.

—Parson Thwackum in Henry Fielding's
The History of Tom Jones

The problem with Parson Thwackum is not simply that he was opinionated and prejudiced; worse than all that, for our enterprise, is that he didn't understand the nature and importance of definition. In this regard, unhappily, he does not differ from many in the discipline of anthropology, where definitions are in remarkably short supply.

The number of anthropologists who have written on the clan, for example, is large, but only a tiny fraction of those writers have paused in their work to say exactly what they mean by the term or even to compare their own usage to that of other scholars. The word *tribe* is ineradicably embedded in the ethnographic literature, but what it means or whether it should be used at all was never a subject of discussion until Morton Fried raised the issue (1975).

Therefore, although I am aware that some impatient readers would prefer that I provide, as tersely as possible, the particular definition of *religion* I prefer above all others, so that we may move swiftly to "more important" matters, I cannot do that. In my view, the issue of definition may well be the most important topic I cover in this book, at least for those who are embarking for the first time upon an inquiry into the anthropology of religion.

The term *religion*, it is true, has been the subject of scholarly pondering both within anthropology and without. Some anthropologists have taken what might be termed a generic approach, accepting without debate the dictionary definition as applicable to anthropology as to any other discipline. Others have seen a need for a discipline-specific definition. It turns out, however, that there are really only two such to choose between; some scholars opt for one, some for the other, and many uncaringly meld the two.

In this chapter, therefore, I propose to bring definition front and center. Happily, Spiro has blazed an easy trail for us to follow, and through his efforts we will gain insight into the reasons why some scholars genuflect to Durkheim's definition and then proceed to ignore it. Spiro not only explores some aspects of the nature and consequences of definition itself; he makes it clear why he finds it necessary to reject Durkheim's classic definition of religion. But, as we shall see, Durkheim anticipated Spiro's arguments and rejected them even earlier. After a review of the debate between Spiro and Durkheim, we turn to Geertz in an effort to determine whether he has, with his very different approach, finally solved the problem of definition for us.

In our exploration of the problem of defining our subject matter, we shall inevitably observe that perhaps the most commonly held definition of *religion* is that it deals with the supernatural. I therefore touch on this topic in this chapter, but I argue that it is sufficiently momentous an issue to deserve separate consideration in a chapter of its own. After that, however, I promise to conclude the subject with what I hope will serve as an operationally meaningful delineation of religion as a panhuman, cross-culturally valid, nonethnocentric cultural rubric.

Though I am arguing that there are currently really only two significant and widely held positions on the definition of religion as a panhuman phenomenon—as a rubric or institution of culture—there are, of course, significant differences, often of some substance, among those who hold to a particular definition. The first step on the path through the disputational complexity, it seems to me, must be taken in the dictionary.

The *American Heritage Dictionary* offers an array of definitions, and I cite only the two that relate to the concerns of anthropology: "1. The expression of man's belief in and reverence for a superhuman power recognized as the creator and governor of the universe. 2. Any particular integrated system of this expression: the Hindu religion" (*AHD* 1969:1099). The *American Heritage Dictionary* goes on to advise that the word religion derives from the Latin term *religio*, which it defines as "the bond between man and the gods," an observation of some relevance to our discussion.

The compilers of the *Oxford Universal Dictionary* are in essential agreement with those of the *American Heritage Dictionary* on definitions of the contemporary English word (though they appear unwilling to commit themselves on the matter of etymology[1]). Thus: "3. Action or conduct indicating a belief in, reverence for, and a desire to please, a divine ruling power; the exercise or practice of

---

[1] The *OUD* notes only "etym. obsc." (*OUD* 1955:1697). This is somewhat odd, since the *OUD* is specifically offered as an abridgement of the full *Oxford English Dictionary*, and the latter (*OED* 1989:568–569) does in fact mention, as a possible derivation, the etymology offered by the *AHD*.

rites or observances implying this. . . . 4. A particular system of faith and worship" (*OUD* 1955:1697). One tends to quail before such authoritative pronouncements, but they do present problems. We observe, for example, that the *American Heritage Dictionary* cites Hinduism as its example of a religious system. Well, it happens that there is a difference of opinion about whether Hinduism may fairly be described as a faith primarily (or even significantly) concerned with superhuman or divine powers (see Klass 1991a, Radhakrishnan 1939).

In any case, there are of course many scholars who subscribe to the view that a belief in some superhuman power is the defining feature of religion. Tylor phrased it as "the belief in Spiritual Beings" ([1871] 1970:8), Frazer as "a propitiation or conciliation of powers superior to man which are believed to direct and control the course of nature and of human life" ([1922] 1958:58–59). A. R. Radcliffe-Brown apparently accepted Frazer's definition, for it is the only one *he* ever offers (1965:137; first given as the lecture "Taboo" in 1939); William James called religion "the feelings, acts, and experiences of individual men in their solitude, so far as they apprehend themselves to stand in relation to whatever they may consider the divine" ([1902] 1985:34).

Yet there have been those who disagreed completely with this definition, most particularly Durkheim, who, writing in the early twentieth century, observed quite forcefully: "In the first place, there are great religions from which the idea of gods and spirits is absent, or at least, where it plays only a secondary or minor role" ([1912] 1965:45). He went on to discuss Buddhism and Jainism as clear and specific examples and concluded: "Thus there are rites without gods, and even rites from which gods are derived. All religious powers do not emanate from divine personalities, and there are relations of cult which have other objects than uniting man to a deity. Religion is more than the idea of gods and spirits, and consequently cannot be defined exclusively in relation to these latter" ([1912] 1965:50).

Many (perhaps most) scholars who subscribe to the "superhuman" definition simply ignore Durkheim's argument.[2] Thus, Paul Radin begins his book *Primitive Religion* ([1937] 1957) by acknowledging that "to describe the nature of religion is extremely difficult." He then proposes:

> We may safely insist, however, that it consists of two parts: the first an easily definable, if not precisely specific feeling; and the second certain acts, customs, beliefs, and conceptions associated with this feeling. The belief most inextricably connected with the specific feeling is a belief in spirits outside of man, conceived of as more powerful than man and as controlling all those elements in life upon which he lays most stress. ([1937] 1957:3)

Radin, apparently overwhelmed by the difficulty of the task, has contented

---

[2] Spiro, as we shall soon see, is a most honorable exception.

himself with what is simply a rephrasing of the common dictionary definition, for him the "safest" of all.

Radin's evocation of safety provokes me to inquire why scholars find the problem of definition of *religion* so dangerous, or at least difficult, in itself. Robert H. Lowie observed that any attempt at definition at the outset of consideration of the subject of religion "would be as futile . . . as a corresponding definition of consciousness in a textbook of psychology, or of electricity in a treatise on physics" (1924:x). It may well be that Radcliffe-Brown shared this view of Lowie's; in any event, apart from the aforementioned citation of Frazer (in his paper "Taboo"), Radcliffe-Brown avoids the issue of definition, as, for example, in his seminal essay "Religion and Society," where he makes no attempt whatever to define the institution whose functions he is setting out to delineate (Radcliffe-Brown 1965:153–177).

Spiro, however, not only offers his own definition of religion (and explains why he rejects Durkheim's arguments) but suggests why such definitions are so hard to come by: "An examination of the endemic definitional controversies concerning religion leads to the conclusion that they are not so much controversies over the meaning of the term 'religion' or of the concept which it expresses, as they are jurisdictional disputes over the phenomenon or range of phenomena which are considered to constitute legitimately the empirical referent of the term" (1971:87). It may well be that Durkheim himself was making much the same point when he described the efforts of "philosophers" to "know what religion in general is." As he observed, "Unfortunately, the method which they generally employ is purely dialectic: they confine themselves to analysing the idea which they make for themselves of religion, except as they illustrate the results of this mental analysis by examples borrowed from the religions which best realize their ideal" ([1912] 1965:16).

Whatever the extent of the agreement between Durkheim and Spiro about the difficulties of definition, they disagree thoroughly about what constitutes an acceptable definition of religion. For Durkheim, "all religious beliefs, whether simple or complex, present one common characteristic: they presuppose a classification of all the things, real and ideal, of which men think, into two classes or opposed groups, generally designated by two distinct terms which are translated well enough by the words *profane* and *sacred*" ([1912] 1965:52). With this he arrives at his now classic definition:

> *A religion is a unified system of beliefs and practices relative to sacred things, that is to say, things set aside and forbidden—beliefs and practices which unite into one single moral community called a Church, all those who adhere to them* ([1912] 1965:62) [italics his].

Spiro reviews Durkheim's definition and then absolutely rejects it: "What, for example, does Durkheim's 'sacred'—which he stipulates as the essential nature of religion—really mean? How useful is it, not in religious or poetic, but in scientific discourse? It is much too vague to be taken as a primitive term in a definitional chain, and it is useless to define it by equally vague terms such as 'holy' or 'set apart'" (1971:89).

For Spiro, any acceptable definition must, to begin with, constitute a hypothesis "susceptible to cross-cultural testing." He goes on, however, to argue that it must do more:

> But this criterion of cross-cultural applicability does not entail ... universality. Since "religion" is a term with historically rooted meanings, a definition must satisfy not only the criterion of cross-cultural applicability but also the criterion of intra-cultural intuitivity; at least, it should not be counter-intuitive. For me, therefore, any definition of "religion" which does not include, as a key variable, the belief in superhuman—I won't muddy the metaphysical waters with "supernatural"—beings who have the power to help or harm man is counter-intuitive. (1971:91)

Thus Spiro, after surveying the possibilities, returns like Radin to the classic (historically rooted?) definition, one I would insist is not too far from the one Parson Thwackum "intuited" in Fielding's novel. In any event, the "metaphysical waters" remain muddy, at least for many anthropologists. One common solution, therefore, is to combine Durkheim's definition with what Spiro calls the "intra-cultural intuitive" one: "'All mankind, Greeks and non-Greeks alike, believe in the existence of gods.' So said Plato more than two thousand years ago. Few would deny that some form of religion is universal among mankind. We have yet to discover any society that does not articulate some notions about the sacred and about spiritual beings" (B. Morris 1987:1).[3]

Another solution (the very one Spiro tries to avoid)—is to absorb the notion of the superhuman into what is perceived as a more comfortable and perhaps seemingly less controversial category, that of the supernatural—wherein, if we listen carefully, we may even hear muted echoes of Durkheim:

> The least constricting terms our vocabulary provides to enable us to set off the realm of religion from the rest of culture are the natural and the supernatural. Most if not all peoples make some sort of distinction between the objects, beliefs, and events of the everyday, workaday, ordinary world and those which transcend the ordinary world. Using this distinction, as others have done, we shall define religion as ideas, attitudes, creeds and acts of supernaturalism. (Norbeck 1961:11)

Norbeck then goes on to define *supernaturalism,* but if we go into that now we shall find ourselves in a new place on what Spiro has termed "the definitional chain." Let us therefore postpone a contemplation of the supernatural for a few pages and stay with religion.

---

[3] Was Plato a Thwackum? Is belief in gods the same as belief in God? Monotheists are likely to say that there is a most profound difference, but one that might well escape the polytheists (and of course the atheists, among whom Brian Morris—perhaps in a Frazer-like disclaimer—specifically includes himself [B. Morris 1987:4]).

Spiro, you will remember, complains that Durkheim's sacred-profane dichotomy is "much too vague"; even "holy" and "set apart," he argues, do not meet the need for a clear and acceptable definition of *sacred*. Norbeck deals with this problem by attempting, in effect, to define *profane:* "the objects, beliefs, and events of the everyday, workaday, ordinary world." Presumably, all other "objects, beliefs, and events" reflect the other, "nonordinary," world and are thus in the province of religion.

Perhaps. But perhaps, also, this seems so reasonable merely because it appeals to the Parson Thwackum within us; it exactly fits the experience of those who have grown up in a European milieu characterized by participation in one of the component sects of Christianity or Judaism, where the Sabbath, the seventh day, is set off distinctly from the rest of the week. In Yiddish, a language of the Jews of northern Europe, this distinction is in fact embodied in two words, *shabosdik*—all that characterizes behavior and concern on the Jewish Sabbath—and *vokhedik*—all that pertains, as in Norbeck's words, to the "everyday, workaday, ordinary" other six days of the week (Weinreich 1968:279, 163).

It may be that such a sacred-profane distinction characterizes other religions, even those that know nothing of weekly or even congregational assemblies, or it may be that it doesn't. What clearly emerges, however, is that Durkheim's sacred-profane distinction, even as sharpened by Norbeck, is not a definition but rather a hypothesis, to be investigated and tested in the field.

Norbeck, it must in fairness be noted, is quite aware that his definition of *religion* "undoubtedly represents the extension to the primitive world of ideas of Western society," but he offers an excuse: "Unfortunately, we can never be certain that we know native viewpoints" (1961:11). Although this is often true enough despite all the efforts of anthropologists and anthropology, we cannot therefore simply give up the struggle to find universally applicable definitions.

Happily, Geertz did refuse to give up that struggle, and he has successfully liberated those of us who want to be from the endless definitional daisy chain of *superhuman* to *sacred-profane* to *supernatural* to some combination of them all, and then back to *superhuman,* and so on. He briskly proposes:

> Without further ado, then, a *religion* is: (1) a system of symbols which acts to (2) establish powerful, pervasive, and long-lasting motivations in men by (3) formulating conceptions of a general order of existence and (4) clothing these conceptions with such an aura of factuality that (5) the moods and motivations seem uniquely realistic. (Geertz 1971:4)

It will be clear throughout this text that I am indebted to Geertz for these (and many other) insights. The very title of this book echoes Geertz's "conceptions of a general order of existence." Nevertheless, there are problems with Geertz's formulation when we approach it as a definition. For one thing, he is in fact not defining *religion* as a rubric but rather telling us what *a* religion is. From the perspective of contemporary anthropology, as we noted earlier, this is a most laudable approach: The field ethnographer studies *a* culture in terms of its institutional subdivisions. Still, with all the controversy about what religion is and is not, it would certainly be helpful if the young ethnographer could go into the field armed with some generally accepted notion of what religion is in any and every human society.

Another, and major, problem with Geertz's proposed approach is that he places what he himself terms "a tremendous weight" upon the term *symbol*. Spiro reminds us that definitions fall if they depend upon vague and imprecise terms, and *symbol* is surely one of the most difficult to delineate. The best that Geertz can do is to fall back upon Suzanne Langer, and he cites her as urging that the term be used for "any object, act, event, quality, or relation which serves as a vehicle for a conception—the conception is the symbol's 'meaning'" (Geertz 1971:5, and see Langer 1960).

Given the nature of culture—particularly as Geertz himself perceives that nature—what features of the human enterprise can we exclude from the category of symbol as it is so defined? What can we even differentiate? Geertz suggests, "There is something to be said for not confusing our traffic with symbols with objects or human beings, for these latter are not in themselves symbols, however often they may function as such" (1971:6). Nevertheless, his original definition (see above) includes "object" and "relation" as "symbols," and the distinction he wants to make is certainly difficult to keep in mind in any kind of analysis.

Therefore, although I in no way reject Geertz's approach, I do think there are more effective ways to delineate the anthropological enterprise of studying religion in all its manifestations. For one thing, religion in all the human societies we know about is concerned with issues—what Geertz in fact refers to as "conceptions of a general order of existence"—and our definition must enable us to penetrate these issues or "conceptions."

Religion, for example, is concerned with causality: Are events invariably consequential, derivative from previous events? Are events inevitable, potentially predictable (e.g., if we control all the variables, will the experiment replicate exactly?)? Or is there some power or being or principle with the capacity to interfere, to cause an unpredictable result (a "miracle")?

Religion is concerned with reality: Is the universe "real" or "material," or is it in some sense "immaterial"? Is it, for example, a figment of some divine imagination, some divinity's dream? If it is real, what does that *mean*? Of what elements is it composed? Is the universe finite, and if so, how and why did it come into existence and by whose agency? How and why and by whose agency will it end?

There are, as we shall see, many more such issues with which religion wrestles. Is there human existence after death? Why *is* there death? If divinities exist, are they moral (assuming whatever it is we mean by *moral*)? We require, in short, a definition that encompasses such issues not only as they are exhibited in particular religions but in *religion* as a rubric of *culture*.

Before offering such a definition, however, I want to turn, as promised, to a consideration of the term *supernatural.* In that effort, I suggest, we not only perceive more clearly the pitfalls that await the anthropologist who would study religion, but we meet Parson Thwackum in new habiliments: He will have put off the clerical collar and have assumed the laboratory smock (or tweed jacket) of the scientist and modern rationalist.

4

The Problem with *Supernatural*

This view that belief in the supernatural is universal has been completely confirmed by modern anthropology.

—Talcott Parsons
Introduction to Max Weber's
Sociology of Religion

What I find most intriguing about Talcott Parsons's assertion is not that he says that "belief in the supernatural is universal" but that he is so confident that it "has been completely confirmed by modern anthropology." As we have already observed, anthropologists (and sociologists) both modern and old-fashioned have expressed discomfort with many of the implications of the term. I doubt that Parsons was unaware of the discomfort; I can only conclude that his need for the term—his sense of its utility and importance—made it necessary for him to dismiss all objections to its use.

Well, what, after all, is so terrible about defining *religion* in terms of belief in the supernatural? Surely the concept is easier to delineate and bound than is the term *sacred*. As Spiro observes, *sacred* is vague and in the end perhaps undefinable. True, but it doesn't carry the remorselessly unavoidable ethnocentric judgment of *supernatural*: that there is on the one hand a natural—real—universe, and on the other hand there are notions about aspects of the universe that are situated outside the natural and real and are therefore labeled supernatural by the person who *knows* what belongs in which category.

How does one know? Science investigates the natural world; that which is not amenable to scientific (or at least scholarly/rational) investigation is beyond the bounds of the natural or real. If there were any way to test the particular assertion about the nature of the universe, any way to measure or objectively verify, we would immediately move it to the natural; failing all of that, however, such an assertion belongs to the realm of the supernatural.

Consider, for example, Norbeck's quite straightforward definition of the term *supernaturalism*:[1]

> By "supernaturalism" we mean to include all that is not natural, that which is regarded as extraordinary, not of the ordinary world, mysterious, and unexplained or unexplainable in ordinary terms. Being extraordinary, mysterious, and unknown or unexplainable in terms of natural or ordinary things or events of the world, the supernatural may evoke various other attitudes. It may be associated with awe, veneration, wonder, or fear. A common denominator in subjective states which the supernatural evokes is an attitude of *apartness* from the mundane. (Norbeck 1961: 11)

Norbeck is remarkably explicit about many of the problems and limitations posed by his own definitions. He notes, for example, that in "our own society . . . it is often regarded as a mark of militant atheism to refer to our religious faiths as supernaturalism," and he goes on to observe that "man interprets his universe in two principal and different ways and on the basis of these interpretations he is afforded patterns of behavior with relation to the universe so that he may know how to act. One of these kinds of interpretation we call naturalistic, the other supernaturalistic. Naturalism and supernaturalism are both ways of adjusting to the universe" (1961:12, 13). And it is with these last two observations, it seems to me, that Norbeck provides us with grounds for concluding that his definition of *religion*—as "supernaturalism"—is really an unacceptable one for anthropologists, though it may be perfectly acceptable for students of other disciplines.

For it is not only a "mark of militant atheism" to refer to religious belief systems—ours or anyone's—as supernaturalism; it is also, as we have begun to note, a mark of rational scholarship, of science, of *any* discipline that rejects religious revelation as an acceptable source of accurate information. Why does the historian reject Homer's account of the Trojan War and the Bible's account of the battle of Jericho? The answer, as we all know, is that because they both include references to supernatural events and personages, neither can be considered an acceptable account of an event in history and therefore evidence of the actual existence of either city. We now believe there was indeed a historical Troy but *only* because Heinrich Schliemann uncovered the archeological site, just as the walls of Jericho are attested to *only* by the archeological research of K. M. Kenyon and others.

The chemist, the physicist, the geologist, the astronomer all reject—as indeed all scientists *must* reject by the rules of their respective disciplines—all explanations of natural phenomena that involve extrasensory perceptions or reflect the actions or interests of divinities or spirits. For the extrasensory, like the spiritual, moves us beyond the realm of natural into that of supernatural, and there, I have

---

[1] As we have already observed, Norbeck began by defining *religion* itself as "ideas, attitudes, creeds and acts of 'supernaturalism.'"

argued, science cannot tread, unless it be to demonstrate that what is seemingly supernatural can in fact be explained in natural terms.

Thus, the biologist, following Charles Darwin, *must* exclude any divine plan from an explication of the development of life on earth: There is no place for such a thing in natural selection. For many religious people, though, Darwin's theory of evolution would be perfectly acceptable if only it encompassed, or at least permitted the possibility of, some kind of divine guidance of events.

All of this, as Norbeck intimates, is reflected in the conflict encapsulated in the terms *naturalism* and *supernaturalism.* It is a distinction born in Europe and fundamental to all European (or European-derived) scholarly and scientific disciplines. Only anthropology, as far as I know, has had a serious and continuing problem with this distinction.[2]

The reason for that is not hard to find. Anthropology deals with the crosscultural, the panhuman, and most particularly with that which is not Western— not derived from or related to European culture. Not every anthropologist does so, of course, but the discipline does. From such a perspective and for such concerns, the term *supernatural* and its antonym, *natural,* become exceedingly troublesome.

This observation may surprise scholars of other disciplines and indeed may irritate some anthropologists. Is anthropology not entitled to a place among the scholarly disciplines? Am I a closet supernaturalist intent on confusing the necessary distinction between natural and supernatural explanation? I can only plead, with Frazer-like humility, that my opposition to the term *supernatural* and to the *natural-supernatural* dichotomy has nothing to do with my personal beliefs about the nature of the universe nor with any feeling that anthropology is not subject to the same rules of analysis and explanation that govern other scholarly disciplines.

Because a primary concern of our discipline, however, is with cross-cultural comparision, our analysis will inevitably flounder in confusion whenever our definitions of the matters we wish to compare cross-culturally are ethnocentric: Terms such as *barbaric, savage, primitive, civilized, preliterate,* and even *leader* (as in "Take me to your leader") have had to be excised from the ethnographic vocabulary, though they continue to be used quite comfortably in the discourse of other disciplines. Thus, those who wish are certainly entitled to speak of "a savage beating," "primitive living conditions," "preliterate children," and so on. But in the anthropological discourse there are no longer any savage (or primitive or barbaric) *societies;* check the appropriate contemporary texts for yourself.

The reason such terms cannot be used in the anthropological enterprise is that they are irremediably ethnocentric and thus lead inevitably to confusion and

---

[2] Some medical researchers, however, are peering uncomfortably at "holistic" and other nonscientific healing systems and have begun to question some of their own assumptions about what is natural.

misinterpretation. "Take me to your leader" implies that every human group *has* a leader, some one person empowered by members of a group to represent them or speak for them. This turns out not to be true for many hunting-and-gathering societies and indeed for some components of sedentary agricultural societies. The field ethnographer, therefore, must phrase an inquiry into politics and social control in a way that will reveal—not distort—the actual situation. For, as every anthropologist knows to his or her grief, if you ask them to take you to their leader, they *will*—even if they never had one until that moment![3]

Supernatural is another such term. It is perfectly acceptable in certain contexts (say, "tales of the supernatural," references to "supernatural strength," and most of all for discussions of "natural" as against "supernatural" explanations). It is, however, too ethnocentric to be of use for cross-cultural study: Serious problems arise when an ethnographer attempts to distinguish the natural from the supernatural in a society in which no such distinction is made or in which instead significantly different ones are made.

My own first experience of the danger of using such a term occurred while I was conducting research among people of South Asian descent (commonly referred to, then, as East Indians) on the island of Trinidad in the West Indies in 1957 (Klass [1961] 1988). Most of the villagers with whom I lived raised rice, primarily for home consumption, in small fields which they rented from a few wealthy absentee landowners. During my first participation in a rice harvest, I observed the farmer performing a brief ceremony in a corner of his field: He killed a cockerel and sprinkled its blood on the ground and on a plate containing an oil lamp, some flowers, biscuits, and a cigarette. In response to my inquiry, he explained that these constituted an offering to the *di*[4] of the field, his term for the spirit of the first owner of the field. For, as the farmer and his fellows saw it, every field everywhere under cultivation must have had an original owner or cultivator whose spirit would remain associated with that field forever more and could affect the quality and quantity of the harvest. A propitiated *di* could arrange for a good harvest; an angry one could precipitate a poor one or no harvest at all. The wise farmer, therefore, before harvesting a good crop, showed his thanks to the *di* in material terms, with an appropriate offering.

I entered all this in my notebook but of course in a section other than that devoted to the details of harvesting procedures. When we arrived back at the farmer's house with the loaded carts at the end of the day, my final observation

---

[3] See, for example, Kathleen Gough's account of what happened when such requests were made in south India by British officials in the early nineteenth century. The problem here was not so much the absence of permanent leadership; it existed but was vested in a *panchayat*, a committee of autonomous equals. The request for "a leader" therefore precipitated decades of struggle for supremacy in the *panchayat* (Gough 1962).

[4] Some Indo-Trinidadians, and some scholars, prefer to spell the term *dee* or *dih*, to avoid possible confusion about pronunciation.

was of the farmer segregating and separately storing a substantial quantity of rice. This, he explained, was the portion of his harvest that must go to his landlord as rent.

Now, given the distinction we make between the natural and supernatural, we must of necessity categorize the propitiation of the *di* as a supernatural act (for *we* know there is no *di*, no spirit capable of affecting the harvest for good or evil), and we must categorize the payment of rent as a natural act, part of the local economy (for there is, unquestionably, an absentee landlord who will never permit the farmer to plant another crop if the rent is not paid).

We are of course aware that from the perspective of the farmer the foregoing categorization is inappropriate: For him, the *di* exists as much as does the landlord, and he is certain that the slighting of either one will endanger the rice harvest of the following year. For him, both actions (propitiation and payment) are fully natural ones. We, however, are constrained to ignore his view in our analysis, for his categories, or lack of them, reflect what some would term *native* perceptions—what many anthropologists have come to call *emic* (culture-bound, subjective) as opposed to *etic* (cross-cultural, objective) conceptualizations. After all, though I spoke up earlier for *awareness* of native categories, I, too, "must never forget" that if my study is to have any merit, it must in the end be objective, scholarly, etic. In short, supernatural phenomena must be clearly distinguished from natural phenomena, or the discipline totters.

Or so it would seem. I would argue that by imposing the supposedly etic and supposedly necessary natural-supernatural distinction on the above data, we have not only distorted it but have significantly impaired our chances of comprehending cultural dynamics and interpreting—let alone predicting—culture change.

Consider: The farmer in the above account has never met or seen the *di* but neither has he ever met the absentee landlord! An agent, or bailiff, of the landlord has always come to the village to collect the rice owed. True, the farmer knows what will happen if he withholds the rent; he has seen or heard about what happened to neighbors who tried to do that. But it is also true that he has known or heard about farmers who suffered poor crops because they failed to propitiate the *di*s of their fields. From the farmer's perspective, therefore, he has in fact solid reasons to believe in the reality—the naturalness—of both *di* and landlord, and it imperils our study if we ignore or dismiss that solidity.

For consider further: Suppose the farmer has a son who goes off to the university and there encounters the writings of anarchists and others who have challenged notions such as that of private ownership of property, and let us further suppose that the son adopts those views. Consequently, the son, now a revolutionary, returns home and tells his father that the landlord has no right to the land. Comes the revolution, he says, the fields will belong to the people who till them.

The son's statement, we observe, constitutes a denial of the existence (in the natural universe that *he* believes in) of the right of someone to share in a crop he has not personally planted: In principle, it is therefore a denial of the existence of landlords in a proper (natural) universe. Dare we term the landlord a supernatural entity, from the son's perspective? Dare we not? After all, if the revolution succeeds, the landlord will in fact cease to exist as such—though the farmer (and his son after him) may continue to propitiate the *di* whose existence they continue to accept.

I challenge the anthropologist who would insist on assigning the *di* to the supernatural universe and the landlord to the natural universe to set forth how, from such an ethnocentric perspective, one might cope with such a sequence of events and with the underlying shifts in perception about the nature of reality.

This unintended but nevertheless intrinsic ethnocentrism precipitates distortion and disturbance for students of the anthropology of religion not only in the matter of the dichotomy of the natural versus the supernatural but in all aspects and ramifications of the term *supernatural*. Norbeck, we observed, proposes that the term encompasses (in addition to all that is not natural) "that which is regarded as extraordinary, not of the ordinary world, mysterious, and unexplained or unexplainable in ordinary terms" (1961:11).

Ordinary and *extraordinary* are in this context essentially equivalent to *natural* and *supernatural* and precipitate the same kind of difficulties. But why is a *di* more "mysterious" than an absentee landlord one has never met? Again, if *you* believed in transmigration of souls or benevolence of ancestral spirits, what would be "unexplained" or "unexplainable" ("in ordinary terms") about such matters?

In sum, the term *supernatural* predisposes the data: It remorselessly, inescapably categorizes all the information the ethnographer collects in terms of one consideration only—what the *ethnographer* considers to be part of reality and what the *ethnographer* personally excludes from reality.

Other scholars have of course noted this problem. Geertz suggests that it derives not so much from the anthropological enterprise as from what he calls the "religious perspective," which, in his view

> moves beyond the realities of everyday life to wider ones which correct and complete them, and its defining concern is not action upon those wider realities but acceptance of them, faith in them. It differs from the scientific perspective in that it questions the realities of everyday life not out of an institutionalized scepticism which dissolves the world's givenness into a swirl of probabilistic hypotheses, but in terms of what it takes to be wider, non-hypothetical truths. (1971:27)

For Geertz, therefore, a religion is "a model *of*"[5] reality, that is, an imposition of order, a system for staving off chaos (1971:8, 13, 14). Apart from Geertz, how-

---

[5] In addition, of course, to being a model *for* reality.

ever, it must be noted that the natural-supernatural dichotomy is so attractive (so "intuitive"?) for Western scholars that even those who recognize its shortcomings tend more often to prefer replacement to total rejection. Thus, John Beattie advanced (long before I did, and I herewith acknowledge my debt to him) a strong argument about the essential and unacceptable ethnocentricity of such terms as *supernatural* (and *magic*, and even *sacred* and *profane*). He concludes his critique with the following observation, one to which, as I have already indicated, I subscribe without reservation: "The trouble with such distinctions is that very often they commit the cardinal sin of social anthropology, by imputing to another culture a kind of category-making which is characteristic of our own practically oriented, 'scientistic' society" (Beattie 1964b:203).

But then Beattie goes on to propose a solution that, in his view, makes it possible to *maintain* the old distinction on a more modern and acceptable basis:

> There is, none the less, a distinction between these two kinds of activities [natural and supernatural], even though both of these may be regarded as equally "natural", and although the distinction cannot always be clearly formulated by the members of the cultures concerned. It rests simply on the presence or absence in what is done of a symbolic element, in which something is standing for something else. This means that the whole procedure, or rite, has an essentially expressive aspect, whether or not it is thought to be effective instrumentally as well. In every rite something is being said as well as done. The man who consults a rain-maker, and the rain-maker who carries out a rain-making ceremony, are stating something: they are asserting symbolically the importance they attach to rain and their earnest desire that it shall fall when it is required. (1964b:203)

In my view Beattie's new dichotomy is indistinguishable from the one it is supposed to replace. Geertz, after all, has reminded us, if indeed we needed reminding, of the ubiquity of symbolism in the human cultural enterprise. Thus, when Beattie draws our attention to the symbolic content of consulting a rainmaker, are we not compelled to observe that there is an exactly equivalent symbolic content to the act of consulting an agricultural expert? In both cases we see "an expressive aspect," in one reflective of the desire for rain and in the other of the desire for healthy plants. What "is being said" symbolically in both cases is that the farmer is concerned about his crop and engages in the action taken (the consultation with an expert) in the hope that it will contribute to an eventual successful crop.

It is true that in both cases (that of the rainmaker and that of the agricultural expert) we anthropologists can detect symbolic content—but it is equally true that in both cases the farmer believes the action will be "instrumentally effective."[6] We come remorselessly down to one difference: *We* know there is nothing instru-

---

[6] Or he may be equally skeptical about both but in his desperation equally willing to give both a chance.

mentally effective about the rainmaker's actions—it is, after all, nothing more than a rite—whereas *we* are sure (perhaps surer than the farmer) that the agricultural expert's advice and materials will indeed be instrumentally effective.

Has not Beattie fallen into the very trap from which he was trying to extricate himself? Is he not himself guilty of what he has termed "the cardinal sin of social anthropology"? The only solution, at least as far I can see, is to give up, once and for all, the effort to maintain the dubious dichotomy. With that in mind, I urge a simple substitution—*cultural activity* for *rite*—so that one of Beattie's sentences in the passage cited above be changed to read, "In every cultural activity something is being said as well as done."

The dichotomizing of natural as against supernatural—whether it be expressed in terms of "explainable" as against "unexplainable," "ordinary" as against "extraordinary," "sacred" as against "profane," or even "symbolically expressive" as against "instrumentally effective"—remains invincibly ethnocentric and therefore unsuitable for anthropological analysis.

Happily, anthropological students of religion are not alone in their plight; anthropologists, as we have had occasion to observe, have had to wrestle with ethnocentrism since the discipline began and no matter what institution was under consideration. I propose, therefore, that we seek advice and strategy from those who were successful in earlier struggles.

For example, although it is only fair to give full credit to Lewis Henry Morgan for introducing to anthropology the importance of the study of kinship systems (Morgan 1870), it was not until 1909, when Alfred A. Kroeber published his article "Classificatory Systems of Relationships" (Kroeber 1909), that anthropologists were able to embark on meaningful research and analysis on the subject. The problem in that case was that Morgan had distinguished only two types of kinship terminological systems: "descriptive," in which distinct relationships are terminologically distinguished from each other,[7] and "classificatory," in which a number of different relationships are classified under one term.[8]

Following Morgan, we would have to label a given "system of consanguinity" either descriptive or classificatory; he provided no other choice. Why were these categories so limited in number and so subjective? For Morgan, of course, they served to buttress a concern entirely apart from the study of kinship: He saw the kinship categories as another demonstration of the stages of the evolution of human societies. Thus, European societies—in his view at the top of the evolutionary ladder—were characterized by descriptive systems, whereas more "primitive" societies were characterized by classificatory systems.

As we know, however, European kinship systems, like those of all societies, ex-

---

[7] For example, the term *mother* in English, which may be properly applied only to one relative (apart from special gestures of affection or respect): an individual's female parent.

[8] For example, the term *uncle* in English, which lumps together such disparate relations as mother's brother, father's brother, mother's sister's husband, and father's sister's husband.

hibit both kinds of terms: Morgan's dichotomous distinction, therefore, is not only ethnocentric but essentially useless for comparative study. Kroeber put it this way:

> The single fact that another people group together various relationships which our language distinguishes does not make their system classificatory. If there is a general and fundamental difference between the systems of civilized and uncivilized people, its basis must be looked for in something more exact than the rough and ready expressions of subjective point of view that have been customary.
>
> It is apparent that what we should try to deal with is not the hundreds or thousands of slightly varying relationships that are expressed or can be expressed by the various languages of man, but the principles or categories of relationship which underlie these. (1909:78)

Kroeber then went on to propose eight categories of relationship (e.g., "the difference between persons of the same and of separate generations," "the sex of the relative," etc.) that have been noted as underlying kinship terminological differences in all societies for which information is available. Not every society makes use of all the categories, he noted, but all use some, and no other categories have as yet been detected.

Kroeber was not necessarily correct in all his observations and conclusions; the study of kinship has gone off in directions he could not have predicted in 1909. What is important about his approach, however, is that it freed the study of kinship from the ethnocentric and subjective imprisonment imposed by Morgan's categories and for the first time offered objective and cross-culturally applicable categories to the student of kinship—ones that could be sought for and identified and most of all ones that could be added to or replaced if need be.

I would argue that Kroeber's approach is an *operational* one; that is, it is concerned exclusively with effectiveness in research and analysis, exhibiting a minimum of prior assumptions, and is in no regard an effort (conscious or otherwise) to advance or buttress an extrinsic belief or system of beliefs (such as, in this case, the position of a society on an evolutionary scale).

In my view the anthropological study of religion desperately requires a similar approach and therefore, to begin with, an operational definition. Neither the approach nor the definition is easily come by. There is another branch of anthropology, however, that has wrestled long and most painfully with the twin problems of definition and approach: the branch commonly referred to as economic anthropology.

There is by no means general agreement among economic anthropologists on these questions, but the debate is illuminating in itself and, in my view, very relevant for those of us wrestling with the anthropology of religion. So I propose to turn now to that debate, and to use it as a guide in my effort to construct an operational definition of *religion*.

5

An Operational Definition of *Religion*

A social arrangement, a culture trait, an institution is not defined exclusively or even primarily by its function, and the first thing to know about is not what it does for men or society. The first thing to know is how it operates within itself and how it came to be. . . .

—Conrad M. Arensberg
"Anthropology as History"
in Karl Polanyi et al., eds.,
Trade and Market in the Early Empires

The problem for anthropologists interested in the institution of economy has been that economics is a distinct and important academic discipline in its own right, one that not only antedates anthropology but that clearly overshadows it in academia as well as in the world at large. Economists have not only successfully unraveled the workings of the marketplace and been able to predict the fortunes of price and employment, but they have devoted much scholarly attention to the terms and even the philosophical underpinnings of their discipline.

All of this was very fine, but it didn't seem to help the poor field ethnographer who, armed with textbooks in economics, was out in the world trying to comprehend the economic system of some bewildering society without money, without specialization, and most of all without any sign of a market.

To be fair, some anthropologists, and particularly those with training in economic theory, have been quite content to use the terms and concepts of classical economics: If a man builds a canoe, he is an artisan; if he then assembles a group of relatives and friends and goes out on a fishing trip, he has become an entrepreneur; and if he returns and distributes his catch, he is obviously engaged in some kind of market activity whether or not money exists and changes hands.[1]

Other anthropologists, however, have reported problems. In his book *Economic Anthropology* (1952), originally published in 1940 as *The Economic Life of Primitive Peoples,* Melville J. Herskovits reviewed the problems of field ethnographers who wanted to understand the economic behavior of the people they were studying, and he petitioned the economists to provide much-needed conceptual assistance:

> In the absence of pecuniary mechanisms and the element of profit in the transactions of the market, it follows that the problem of the relation between supply and demand takes on unexpected turns. The West African woman trader who will not lower the price of the commodity she sells when business is dull—and this is an economy where values have for centuries been expressed in the quantitative terms of the prevalent form of money—presents a difficult enough problem. But where the total supply of commodities, even of subsistence goods, available to the members of a given society is severely limited, the question of fluctuations in value becomes pointless.
>
> Economic theory, on the whole, is not geared to consider the problem of demand schedules where the alternatives are so restricted that there is no margin between utility and disutility—or to put it in other terms, where the choices are so few that no curve of indifference can be drawn between satisfactions and costs. (Herskovits [1940] 1952:15)

Herskovits's book brought forth a response from the economist Frank H. Knight (1941) that Herskovits incorporated into the later volume along with his reply ([1940] 1952:507–531). Knight's reaction to the anthropologist's cry for help was dismissive: "The principles of economy are known intuitively; it is not possible to discriminate the economic character of behavior by sense observation; and the anthropologist, sociologist, or historian seeking to discover or validate economic laws by inductive investigation has embarked on a 'wild goose chase'" (Herskovits [1940] 1952:512).

Herskovits, of course, was not so much interested in "validating" economic laws as he was in trying to make sense of economic behavior in the societies anthropologists were studying. Knight apparently saw little point in conducting such research into *any* aspect of life in such societies, since in his view we already knew all the answers, as "intuitively" as Knight knew the principles of economics: "Any social scientist should early learn to recognize the fact that 'man' (in our culture, if not universally) including himself and his fellow scientists, is a competitive, contentious, and combative animal, given to self-aggrandizement, and inclined to make this end justify nearly any means" (Herskovits [1940] 1952:513).

Happily, at least one economist, Karl Polanyi, was willing to consider the implications of the findings of anthropologists and to join with them in a search for

---

[1] See, for example, Raymond Firth (1946), Scott Cook (1966), and others.

a definition of *economic* that would be less narrow and, most particularly, more inclusive. What eventually emerged from his effort to deal with this issue was a collection of papers written by economists, anthropologists, sociologists, and others (Polanyi et al. 1957).

Polanyi's "substantive" definition of *economic* is an informative example of what I have called an operational approach to the study of a social institution. Specifically, Polanyi observes that there are in fact two ways of defining the term *economic:* He labels them the "formal" and the "substantive." By "formal" he means the definition underlying the discipline of economics itself:

> Formal economics refers ... to a situation of choice that arises out of an insufficiency of means. This is the so-called scarcity postulate. It requires, first, insufficiency of means; second, that choice be induced by that insufficiency. ... For the insufficiency to induce choice there must be given more than one use to the means, as well as graded ends, i.e., at least two ends ordered in sequence of preference. (1957:246)

Note that the formal definition implies a large number of underlying assumptions (for Knight, "intuitions"), most particularly that in economic matters humans must and will make choices in their allocation and acquisition of goods and services. But suppose the anthropologist observes that in a given culture choice is not possible: Goods *must* be given first to specific relatives and in a specific order; or (in another case) the most desirable goods *must* be given to the chief or to the temple, regardless of any offers of recompense made by others. In such cases one must conclude either that such a society does not exhibit economy or that the formal definition is limited in applicability.

Polanyi believes that the latter is indeed the case, and he therefore proposes a second and alternative definition of *economic:* "The fount of the substantive concept is the empirical economy. It can be briefly (if not engagingly) defined as an instituted process of interaction between man and his environment, which results in a continuous supply of want satisfying material means" (1957:248).

Are there not assumptions underlying Polanyi's "substantive" definition? What, for example, of "instituted process," "interaction between man and his environment," "continuous supply of want satisfying material means"? Yes, but these are very different from Knight's "intuitions." Polanyi's substantive definition unquestionably reflects assumptions about the nature of humans and their societies: that humans interact with their environment, that humans require a continuous supply of material goods from that environment, that the interaction is in the form of an instituted process—that is, that it exhibits rules and system.

These statements, therefore, may perhaps more properly be termed *conclusions* rather than *assumptions:* They reflect, after all, the observations of anthropologists and other students of human societies. All human societies *do* interact with their environments for the purpose of supplying their material needs; no one has ever observed a society that does not. All such interaction is in the form of "instituted process"; no one has ever observed a society characterized by random and unregulated grabbing from one another, something Knight's vision of "man's" nature would surely lead us to expect to find.[2]

The assumption, however, that is most clearly missing from Polanyi's substantive definition is that in economic transactions individual humans must invariably *make choices:* choices among the things they will extract from their environment, choices in the allocation of goods in hand, and choices among the goods others offer to them.

But suppose, then, that in a given society—approached for the first time by any ethnographer—it is observed that choice plays as much of a role in economic affairs as it does on the New York stock exchange? No problem: The approach made possible by the substantive definition does not rule out the possibility of ever using the formal definition; the latter (the one that underlies the discipline of economics) now becomes clearly applicable to the society being studied. In effect, Polanyi has encompassed formal economics within the wider rubric of economic behavior as defined under the substantive definition. It is important to emphasize here that although the substantive definition and resultant approach in no way inhibit the application of formal economics where appropriate, the formal definition makes it almost impossible to study economic behavior in any society where choice is not present.

One could easily find other examples of operational definitions and approaches in the anthropological literature, but surely the above is sufficient for our purposes here. We must—in religion as in economics—seek nonrestrictive, nonforeclosing definitions and categories, ones that, like the "substantive" definition in economics and like Kroeber's eight rules of kinship, make it possible to perceive and therefore analyze the unexpected rather than doom the unexpected to be fitted into a Procrustean bed of prior assumption and categorization.

It does seem to me there is a particularly apt parallel to be drawn between the dispute about the definition of *economy* and the dispute about the definition of *religion.* In the first instance we observe anthropologists in contention with people (economists) who believe that formal economics is true—or, at minimum, that it is the only valid avenue for studying and evaluating economy. In the second our problem is with people (ourselves!) who believe that the natural-supernatural distinction is true and provides the only valid avenue for studying and interpreting religion. In both cases we free ourselves by realizing that our assumption of what is true and therefore universally applicable must be converted, for the purposes of cross-cultural research, into a hypothesis: Is the distinction, which is so valid and so important for us, at all important or even at all present in the particular case under consideration?

---

[2] There is of course the case of the Ik of East Africa, as described by Colin Turnbull (1972). Even if they do in fact lack instituted economic exchange, however, it is clear from Turnbull's account that this is a very special case; the traditional (and instituted) way of life has comparatively recently been demolished by famine and other major adversities.

How, then, may we, avoiding all scientistic bias and prior assumption, develop an operational definition of *religion* equivalent to Polanyi's substantive definition of *economics*? I propose to proceed cautiously: Before we define, let us try to encompass the scope of our subject.

Earlier I attempted to amalgamate the views on the nature and scope of religion proposed by some of the most illustrious scholars in the fields of anthropology, sociology, psychology, and more. Drawing upon the insights of this assemblage of scholars, we may conclude that a religion constitutes the total set of beliefs, practices, associated symbols, and interactions (among and between humans and between humans and other entities those humans recognize as being capable of such interaction) that are concerned with the following:

> Explanation, understanding, coherence; relief from psychological stress; release and channeling of emotions; social cohesiveness; sense of effectiveness and ability to cope with death, illness, and misfortune in general; maintenance of a sense of order by continual counteraction of powerlessness, randomness, meaninglessness, chaos.

The subject matter is enormous in scope if we are to accept the proposals of these scholars. But we do not yet have a definition. Let us therefore move to the next step: We anthropologists know that religion, as an institution, is manifested in specific systems of values, beliefs, and practices. Given that, and in order to hew closely to Polanyi's model—as well as to provide a guide for the anthropologist in the field—I offer the following as an operational definition of *religion* as cultural category:

> Religion in a given society will be that instituted process of interaction among the members of that society—and between them and the universe at large as they conceive it to be constituted—which provides them with meaning, coherence, direction, unity, easement, and whatever degree of control over events they perceive as possible.

Now that I've done it, how useful is it? In what ways does my operational definition provide new insights or help us to settle disputes arising from the earlier attempts at definition?

Let us take as a first consideration the ongoing controversy, reviewed earlier, over using the term *supernatural* to define *religion*. The greatest difficulty, we observed, was that like the formal definition of economics, the use of the term *supernatural* forecloses the examination of societies that do not share (and exhibit, in their belief systems) the assumptions implicit in the term. Nevertheless, although we may therefore refuse to make a belief in supernatural phenomena our fundamental defining feature, we would not want to ignore the importance, in so many belief systems, of the phenomena subsumed under the labels *supernatural* or *superhuman*.

Let us observe, then, that the above operational definition in no way excludes the possibility of determining that a particular belief system reflects the fundamental importance of the supernatural or superhuman—but at the same time it does not require us to *impose* the presence of superhuman power or powers upon a system where such are either not present or not of fundamental importance. In other words this operational definition encompasses supernatural belief systems as easily as substantive encompasses formal.

To turn to another issue touched on earlier, I would argue that the operational definition leads us to the observation that a belief system—a religion as defined above—provides an explanation of events, but it does much more; most importantly, it provides the basic understanding about the nature of the universe and the events that take place in it that makes it possible for those who adhere to the belief system to *seek* and *find* explanations. Thus, the anthropological student of the society may ask of the religious practitioner, "Why is there death in the world?" The question may be answered politely, but both question and answer in fact subtly serve to distort the issue: Adherents of the system do not need to ask why there is death; they *know*. Their question, rather, tends to be some variant of, "Given the reason why death occurs (touch of a ghost, anger of an ancestor, spell of a sorcerer, deity's whim, or whatever), why did this particular individual recently die?"

The distinction between the two questions is made particularly clear in the Book of Job. Job's comforters explain that suffering is punishment for sin, and Job replies, almost impatiently, that he is as aware of that as they are; but since he knows that he has been as sinless as a man can be, he wants to know why he has been made to suffer so awfully. In all their debate neither he nor his interlocutors, as they seek answers, ever challenge the fundamental assumption that misfortune is punishment administered by a just God. Others (readers of the Book of Job) of course may raise such questions; they may even conclude that the work itself constitutes such a challenge, but the actual personages in the account do not.

We will return to the implications of the Book of Job for issues raised in this book. My point here is that—as in the case of Job—in every belief system the fundamental assumptions are normally never challenged; instead, they form the basis for finding explanations and solutions. Thus, from the perspective of a given belief system, there is nothing inexplicable, nothing mysterious, except in the imperfect mind of the human actor. Rather, somewhere, at the core of the universe or in the mind of God or wherever, it all makes sense. Of course, the assumptions and fundamental beliefs may indeed sometimes be challenged, but we might be interested in determining whether the challenge reflects the presence of someone who comes from (or has been) outside the system or actually represents an indigenous effort to move beyond the system.

The proposed definition does not solve all the problems the anthropological student of religion faces. How shall we, for example, set boundaries between religion on one side and, on the other sides, science, philosophy, medicine, psychology, and so on? Do we indeed need boundaries? May it not be that in some human societies such specializations simply do not exist, and the religious practitioner is also the doctor, the psychiatrist, the philosopher, the scientist, and perhaps even the poet?

Other questions arise, unresolved by the proposed definition: What does *coher-*

ence mean? What constitutes control over events? What are values? What is meaninglessness—indeed, what do we mean by *meaning*? Such questions—such calls for definition—are of course important, but they require us to move to different places on the definitional chain, as we shall, for example, in the next chapter.

The point is that the operational definition is not offered as an answer to all questions. It is offered, rather, in the hope that it will serve as a useful and even necessary basis for tackling the problems and questions that have been and continue to be of interest in the anthropological study of religion in all of its cross-cultural manifestations.

Armed with the above operational definition, the field ethnographer should now find it easier to go on to examine, in a particular religious system, values (or underlying principles), symbol and belief structures, personnel (both living humans and other-than-living-humans), and all the activities and events relating to the areas of concern noted in the definition, and all of this without ever having to impose upon the data categories and assumptions deriving from other belief systems—including, of course, that of the ethnographer.

6
The Value of *Values*

The knowledge that many cultures possess deep-seated guiding principles governing the lives of its members is of the greatest importance to the understanding of cultural behavior in general and religious behavior in particular. Benedict stressed the necessity for studying human behavior in its cultural context, and this is particularly important for the study of religious behavior, because religion—more, perhaps, than any other institution—helps to express, uphold, and reinforce the cultural configuration and its dominant values.

—Annemarie de Waal Malefijt
Religion and Culture

In the previous chapter I observed that "we anthropologists know that religion . . . is manifested in specific systems of values, beliefs, and practices." We may "know" that, but do we really "know" what we *mean* when we use terms such as *values?*

No one, of course, would contest the importance, indeed the centrality, of contemplating values when studying a religion or religion itself. Max Weber, in his classic work *The Sociology of Religion* ([1922] 1963), refers to values no less than thirteen times (if we may trust the index) and even distinguishes between "esthetic," "eternal," "ethical," "religious," and "ultimate" values. But never once does he pause to explain exactly what he means by the term or why he feels justified in using it with all those qualifying adjectives.

Am I making heavy weather? Consider, then: Are "artistic" values in any way like "economic" values? If so, what is it that they have in common? The dictionary (*OUD* 1955:2332) does not help us with this last question; it defines *value*, to begin with, in terms of "worth"[1] ("material or monetary worth . . . that which is

---

[1] And then defines *worth* (*OUD* 1955:2453) in terms of *value!*

worthy of esteem," etc.) but reports other, rather different usages (e.g., "*Math.*
The number or quantity represented by a figure or symbol . . . *Mus.* The relative
length or duration of a tone signified by a note . . . *Painting* . . . relative tone of
colour in each distinct section of a picture," etc.). Values, it would therefore seem,
reflect worth and/or the quality of relativity among elements in a particular category.

In any case for the anthropologist interested in social or cultural values, perhaps "that which generates degrees of esteem" is the most useful definition. A bit
of modification is in order, however, to avoid the usual ethnocentric trap and to
promote cross-cultural comparisons. I suggest the following as an anthropological definition of *value:*

> A sentiment or principle, noted in and characteristic of a given culture, that reflects or
> expresses what is generally perceived by the members of the culture as being worthy, desirable,
> or proper. Such sentiments will be observed to precipitate relative levels of esteem for actions
> taken or views expressed and therefore serve as guides for, or even determinants of, behavior.

If that definition is at all acceptable, it is clear that values (as de Waal Malefijt
has observed) underlie *all* cultural concerns and activities. Still, how are we to
distinguish (if indeed we should) values related to religion from values (in art,
say) that presumably have little or nothing to do with religion? And when we
have successfully distinguished religious values from all others, what is the nature
of the interaction between values and beliefs? That is, do values generate beliefs
or does religion set and maintain values or both?

In my view those are important questions and deserve much more analysis
and, particularly, much more cross-cultural research than they have received to
date. We can be happy that field ethnographers have not entirely neglected the
study of values, and so there are some observations to be made, preliminary
though they are.

How do we detect the values (all the values, any of the values) of a given culture under study? There are no doubt many ways. One could certainly inquire
directly, since in any society individuals are aware of what is proper, what is good,
what is "the way we do it." Still (again, in any society), there are important values
that never surface to the point where people are fully conscious of them—
perhaps because they seem so fundamental, so intrinsic to the nature of reality
itself. The observer must infer their presence from behavior, as in the choices individuals make. Values, most fundamentally, are choice determinants: They serve
to guide individuals in situations where more than one response is (in that society) conceived of as possible.[2]

How, more or less exactly, do values determine or even influence choices? The

---

[2] We have seen that the presence or absence of choice is an important issue for economics; it is of
course a major issue for social organization. See, for example, Klass 1966.

ethnographic literature on this topic is scanty but not empty. An important (and early) exception to the general neglect is to be found in the writings of Gregory Bateson—specifically, in *Naven,* his classic study of the religion and culture of the Iatmul, who live in the Sepik River region of what is today Papua New Guinea (Bateson [1936] 1958). In this study Bateson deliberated on two concepts of particular relevance for the anthropological study of values: *ethos* and *eidos.*

Bateson began by accepting the *OED* definition of *ethos* as "the characteristic spirit, prevalent tone of sentiment of a people or a community" ([1936] 1958:2) but went on to propose that "ethological relationships" may be observed to exist "between emotional aspects of details of cultural behavior and the emotional aspects of the culture as a whole." Thus, in Bateson's view, such ethological relationships constitute "affective relationships, between details of cultural behaviour and the basic or derived emotional needs and desires of the individuals: *the affective motivation of details of behaviour*" ([1936] 1958:29–30; italics mine).

Iatmul men (but not women), Bateson observed, are characteristically "occupied with the spectacular, dramatic, and violent activities which have their centre in the ceremonial house" ([1936] 1958:123). In Bateson's view the ceremonial house in fact expresses this male ethos:

> The ceremonial house is a splendid building, as much as a hundred and twenty feet in length, with towering gables at the ends. . . . Inside the building, there is a long vista from end to end down the series of supporting posts as in the nave of a darkened church. . . . There is a series of taboos on any sort of desecration. . . . A man should not walk right through the building and out at the other end; he should turn aside and pass out by one of the side entrances. ([1936] 1958:123)

As Bateson saw it, however, the Iatmul men's ceremonial house is in certain particulars very different from a church: It stands as a symbol of their pride in headhunting and thus reflects "the violence and killing which were necessary for its building and consecration," and it is, in addition to a place of ritual, "a clubhouse where men meet and gossip and . . . an assembly room where they debate and brawl" ([1936] 1958:123–124).

Thus we see the playing out of Iatmul male ethos: The building that serves as ceremonial center is as spectacular as Iatmul technology can devise; within it the Iatmul men continually combine their penchants for both dramatic and violent behavior. Bateson argued, in fact, that similar behavior is to be noted in even mundane activities like hunting, fishing, and canoe cutting: "The completion of every considerable task is marked by the performance of some spectacular dance or ceremony" ([1936] 1958:129). He concluded that "the whole culture is moulded by the continual emphasis upon the spectacular, and by the pride of the male ethos" and then showed expressions of this "male ethos" in initiation rites, headhunting, and ceremonial life ([1936] 1958:129).

In contrast, Bateson argued, the ethos of Iatmul women is totally different:

"There is no such emphasis on pride and spectacular achievement" but rather on quiet activities privately carried out ([1936] 1958:142).[3]

Eidos, for Bateson, is also a source of motivation, but it is something very different from ethos; it has little or nothing to do with emotion or affect but refers instead to "structural or logical relationships between the cognitive aspects of the various details of cultural behaviour: the cognitive reasons for behaviour" ([1936] 1958:29). Thus there are to be observed what he referred to as "eidological relationships between the cognitive aspects of details of cultural behaviour and the general patterning of the cultural structure" ([1936] 1958:30).

Two terms Bateson used call for some attention: *cognitive* and *patterning.* The latter term of course calls to mind Ruth Benedict's *Patterns of Culture* ([1934] 1959), and we will come back to her work and to the subject of patterning in a moment. *Cognition* refers to "the action or faculty of knowing; knowledge, consciousness . . . *a product of such an action*" (*OUD* 1955:337; italics mine). Bateson has thus raised a significant question: Do members of a particular culture exhibit a standardized way of "knowing," of perception and interpretation and ordering of phenomena and events? Is there a culturally specific way in which they "choose" what to "know"? If indeed there is, then the central issue of this book—how culture orders the universe—will be seen to be a subcategory of how culture orders cognition.[4]

According to Bateson, Iatmul cognition reflects a "hypertrophic eidos," one characterized by a tendency to structural complexity or multiplicity of premises, to be noted in religion, in social structure, and much else. Thus, "vast and detailed erudition is a quality which is cultivated among the Iatmul. This is most dramatically shown in the debating about names and totems, and I have stated that a learned man carries in his head between ten and twenty thousand names" ([1936] 1958:222). This "erudition," Bateson insisted, is not at all "rote memory" but rather demonstrates the refinement of "higher processes" of thought. The Iatmul eidos has the effect of "stimulating memory" in general, most specifically in the area of "visual or kinaesthetic imagery." This is true, he argued, not just for a "small minority of specialists" but for Iatmul males in general, constituting a "patterning of the standardised thought and the sorts of logic which are characteristic of it" ([1936] 1958:223–224).

Both ethos and eidos, according to both Bateson and Benedict, may indeed be encompassed by Benedict's more general concept of "fundamental and distinc-

---

[3] This may be an accurate summation of Iatmul women's ethos (Bateson was there, and I wasn't), but it does sound a bit thin and oversimplified. There is always the possibility that his abiding interest in male ethos left that of the Iatmul women somewhat out of focus.

[4] The interested reader is urged to consult the growing literature on metaphor, beginning with Stephen Pepper's *World Hypotheses* (1942). Two important anthropological volumes are *On Metaphor* (1979), edited by Sheldon Sacks, and *The Social Use of Metaphor* (1977), edited by J. David Sapir and J. Christopher Crocker. In Chapter 16 I explore some aspects of myth approached as metaphor.

tive cultural configurations that pattern existence and condition the thoughts and emotions of the individuals who participate in those cultures" (Benedict 1959:55).

Whatever the merits of the terms *configuration, eidos,* and *ethos,* all have fallen under the same pall of neglect. Bateson's terms are certainly worthy of more attention than they have received. Consider, for example, those phenomena of European-derived societies commonly referred to as machismo and fair play: Can we not in both cases detect "ethological" (i.e., "affective") relationships "between details of cultural behaviour and the basic or derived emotional needs and desires of the individuals"?

Fair play, specifically, is usually considered to be particularly characteristic of Britain and British-derived societies, including the United States.[5] It could indeed be argued that the fair play value derives from a wider European value placed on equality. Louis Dumont (1970), in fact, has proposed that European societies are populated by what he calls *Homo aequalis*—people whose fundamental value is equality—as opposed to those who people India, which he sees as the home of *Homo hierarchicus,* his term for those who perceive only a gradated or hierarchical social structure.

In any event it would certainly seem that especially in the United States, the fair play value takes the form of an equalitarian ethos that is expressed and even exhibited in many different dimensions of the society. The point here is not that everyone—or indeed the society itself—responds in all situations in ways reflective of this ethos, but rather that it is an ideal principle that almost everyone accepts as the way things should be. Thus, on the one hand, a charge that one is being unfair or elitist cannot be shrugged off but must be refuted. In other words one must either demonstrate the "fairness" of one's action or excuse it by arguing that in the particular case "fairness" is not possible or appropriate. On the other hand, a response that acknowledges unfairness and actually glories in it (e.g., "We have the power and we don't want to share it with others!") is usually rejected as improper and unacceptable by *all* members of the society.

When, for example, the right to vote was restricted to males, the demand for women's suffrage was met with the argument that women were by nature too emotional or pacifistic to be able to participate in the electoral process: Presumably, if it could have been conclusively demonstrated that they were not, there would have been no reason for denying them the vote.

Similarly, the argument for continuing segregated education in the United States took the form of insisting that people having any ancestors deriving from Africa south of the Sahara lacked the ability to be educated to the level attainable by people whose ancestors (at least as far as anyone knew) had come only from

---

[5] Such at least is the commonly held opinion in those countries. People in places in the world that have come under the military and economic attention of Britain and the United States have been known to express other views.

Europe (see, for example, Putnam 1961). Whites (those of putatively European ancestry) would never say publicly that they enjoyed being separate and wished to keep it that way, no matter *what* the capacity of people of African descent.

Those readers who have followed the discussion this far are now invited to try their hands at ethological analysis. Is machismo an example of the ethos of peoples of Mediterranean derivation? What other examples might be advanced? Myself, I will move on to eidos, for though this concept of Bateson's has (as far as I can determine) received even less attention than ethos, yet it also has, or should have, its attractions for students of values in religion.

My own attention to eidos was set in motion many years ago in a conversation with Nancy Munn, who had then returned from her first fieldwork among the native peoples of Australia and who had found Bateson's concept of eidos useful and stimulating. Following her lead, I attempted to see if I could apply it to the communities in or derived from South Asia among which I had lived and conducted research.

It seems to me that one might apply the label *analytic eidos* to the culturally conditioned cognitive dimensions of many of the peoples of the South Asian subcontinent. I mean by this a tendency to analyze or dissect in a constant concern for ever finer distinctions and ultimate subdivisions. This eidos finds constant expression in the writings of Hinduism, almost from the very beginning. There is, for example, an early Vedic "Hymn of Creation" that begins and ends (in A. L. Basham's translation, 1954:247–248):

> Then even nothingness was not, nor existence.
>   There was no air then, nor the heavens beyond it.
> What covered it? Where was it? In whose keeping?
>   Was there then cosmic water, in depths unfathomed?
>
> Then there were neither death nor immortality,
>   nor was there then the torch of night and day.
> The One breathed windlessly and self-sustaining.
>   There was that One then, and there was no other.
>
>   . . . .
>
> But, after all, who knows, and who can say
>   Whence it all came, and how creation happened?
> The gods themselves are later than creation,
>   so who knows truly whence it has arisen?
>
> Whence all creation had its origin,
>   he, whether he fashioned it or whether he did not,
> he, who surveys it all from highest heaven,
>   he knows—or maybe even he does not know.

Basham calls this "one of the oldest surviving records of philosophic doubt in the history of the world," and so it may be. But another way of looking at it would be to argue that the hymn was intended not so much to express doubt but to consider—when contemplating the awesomeness of creation—all the possibilities: Before creation was there nothingness or not even nothingness? Did a creator create creation or everything but creation? Is it possible that the "One" who knows all does not know the answers to this question?

This kind of analysis—in my terms, seeking out possibilities, not expressing doubt—pervades the religious literature of South Asia. For example:

"He is not a male, He is not a female, He is not a neuter; He is not to be seen; He neither is nor is not; when He is sought, He will take the form in which He is sought, and again He will not come in such a form. It is indeed difficult to describe the nature of the Lord" (de Bary et al. 1958:356). And from the Buddhist *Sutta* 63:

> Now it happened to the venerable Malunkyaputta, being in seclusion and plunged in meditation, that a consideration presented itself to his mind, as follows:
> "These theories which the Blessed One has left unexplained, has set aside and rejected—that the world is eternal, that the world is not eternal, that the world is finite, that the world is infinite, that the soul and the body are identical, that the soul is one thing and the body another, that the saint exists after death, that the saint does not exist after death, that the saint both exists and does not exist after death, that the saint neither exists nor does not exist after death—these the Blessed One does not explain to me." (Burtt 1955:32–33)

Again, as in the case of the "Hymn of Creation," this musing may certainly be interpreted as doubt, but I see it as another example of the analytic eidos at work: There are, after all, so many possibilities to consider.

And I would further argue (following Bateson's lead) that this analytic eidos can be observed in many dimensions of South Asian culture, particularly in social structure, the most obvious example of which is the caste system. How many castes are there? Well, according to Hindu tradition, in the beginning there were only four: the classic *varnas* (Brahman, Kshatriya, Vaishya, and Shudra). There are thousands of castes now, however, and the traditional explanation is that they are all the result first of matings between members of the original four and then the complex interweaving of descendant castes. Thus, the Chandela caste, rated as one of the lowest of untouchables, derived from the mating of Brahman (the highest *varna*) women with Shudra (the lowest *varna*) men. The alternatives become endless, of course.

Even more: the rules of avoidance and association for members of different castes also express this analytic eidos. In certain parts of south India, for example, there are (or were) strict rules governing how close members of specific castes may come to Brahmans. The caste closest in rank may approach within 8 feet of a Brahman, members of the next only within 16 feet, the next 32, and so on. Far at the bottom is the caste whose members must not allow their shadows to touch a Brahman. Below them is the caste whose members must continually tinkle warning bells, for the mere sight of one of them striking a Brahman's eyeball would render the Brahman unclean.

Consider, finally, the reputed aptitude of South Asians for mathematics: Could this reflect the analytic eidos? Indeed, South Asia is the source of what are usually referred to as Arabic numerals, for many reasons the essential tools of modern mathematics but most particularly because they include the zero. And so consider the zero: With all the mathematical concerns and developments attributable to Europe, Southwest Asia, and East Asia, the notion of taking nothingness and converting it to a computable quantity occurred only once in all the history of the Old World,[6] and that was in South Asia. Analytic eidos?

We should in all fairness turn to Benedict's neglected work for a summation of the issues addressed in this chapter:

> A culture, like an individual, is a more or less consistent pattern of thought and action. Within each culture there come into being characteristic purposes not necessarily shared by other types of society. In obedience to these purposes, each people further and further consolidates its experience, and in proportion to the urgency of these drives the heterogeneous items of behaviour take more and more congruous shape. ... The form that these acts take we can understand only by understanding first the emotional and intellectual mainsprings of that society. ([1934] 1959:46)

Another word for those "mainsprings," of course, is *values.*

---

[6] It also occurred in the New World in the case of the Maya, but that is another story.

7

Assumptions, Beliefs, and Facts

Faith may be defined briefly as an illogical belief in the occurrence of the improbable.

—H. L. Mencken
Prejudices

Even apart from *faith* itself, there are many terms in use in the discourse on religion with which we could wrestle (*premise, proposition, tenet, truth,* just to mention a few), but this is neither an essay in logic nor an effort to create a lexicon. With a minimal clarification of the three listed in the heading (plus a few brief nods to other terms), I hope we can move significantly in the direction of the nonethnocentric distinctions so necessary for any meaningful anthropological study of religion.

With this aim in mind, let us note the tendency in anthropology to lump values and beliefs together: I here urge they be kept conceptually separate. For one thing, there is a region of seemingly impenetrable haziness right at the border between the two, in the area occupied by assumption. For another thing, it is difficult enough to study the categories of another culture; we must, at least to begin with, be clear about our own categories.

By *assumption,* then, I mean something so fundamental that it is usually simply taken for granted; essentially, it is *unquestioned* rather than *unquestionable*—it rarely even rises to the surface of awareness, let alone discourse. *Belief,* in contrast, definitely implies awareness: It is an opinion about what is true or real. This does not mean that assumptions can *never* be brought into the conscious purview of those who hold them but that when they are, it frequently means the assumptions are in the process of being transformed into beliefs—opinions, views, interpretations, conclusions that are (potentially) subject to challenge or at least discussion.

If both *assumption* and *belief* seem slippery and sometimes hard to distinguish, *fact* seems easy enough to define: that which really happened, that which really *is*. Unfortunately, however, fact is abysmally difficult to demonstrate. Given that, some would assert that perhaps there is no such thing as objective reality, that the very notion that there is, or could be, is just another emic, culture-bound assertion of our scientistic sociocultural system.

Well, if the debate between proponents of the real and ideal, between those who care whether the universe actually exists or is only a convenient fiction, has not been resolved for us by our philosophers, dare we assume that we know what is fact and what is not as we try to penetrate what members of other societies think they know?

The issue is important but of course irresolvable, at least at the moment. A way out of the dilemma is to view fact (in our society, scientistically) as an ideal condition, one that can be approximated—if never fully attained—by careful experiment and meticulous observation. Put another way, assumption and belief are emic categories (i.e., reflective of a given cultural system), whereas fact is etic (i.e., objective, suprasystemic, "scientific"). Fact may be all of those things in principle, but it is nevertheless frequently impossible to determine what *is* actually a fact.

When studying religion, the best we can (or should) do, therefore, is to observe that though members of a given society may consider their assumptions and even beliefs to be facts, they are not necessarily such (and of course not necessarily *not* such). In short, cross-culturally speaking, the concept of fact represents any culture's particular understanding (if it has one) of reality, of ultimate truth.

The significance, at least for me, of the foregoing definitions and distinctions lies in the following derivative observations. Intelligent, thoughtful members of any social system are likely to be able to state their beliefs—which they may very well describe as statements of fact. Such beliefs, however, invariably reflect the existence of underlying assumptions, themselves reflective of the values of that society and particularly of ethos and eidos. Such assumptions are usually not easily accessible to the member of that system (though if faced with one, a person may well respond—as Knight did to Herskovits—that such a statement is so self-evidently true that it would be silly to discuss it).

We observe, then, that *fact* has two meanings: In an etic sense it refers to true or objective reality. From an emic perspective, it refers to that which, in a given human society, is understood to be reality. The anthropologist engaged in cross-cultural research must never ignore the distinction or dismiss the implications of the two meanings. There is (presumably) true reality in the universe, but there is also the emic reality of every cultural system (including ours). I urge anthropological students of religion to focus upon the emic categories and leave the etic debate to philosophers and such.[1]

To the equally knotty distinctions between *assumption* and *belief*: Is it possible

---

[1] The philosopher Arthur W. Collins urges us to be aware of the differences between *belief* and *truth* (1987:23) on the one hand and *belief* and *knowledge* on the other (1987:32–35). He notes, for example, "It is one thing for S to believe that p is true and another thing for p to be true" (1987:45).

for the anthropologist to distinguish, both consistently and comparatively, between these two, using the definitions I have proposed above? I offer herewith a test case, deriving, as in the previous chapter, from my own area of research, South Asia.

In classical India about the sixth century B.C.E., there was apparently much religious debate and turmoil, much reexamination of traditional beliefs, all followed eventually by the emergence of new religions. Specifically, the tenets of what until then had been traditional Brahmanical Hinduism came under attack by the founders of what we now call Buddhism and Jainism: Siddhartha (who came to be called the Buddha) and Vardhamana (who came to be called Mahavira). And there were indeed others who were challenging Brahmanical Hinduism (and one another) at that time, though their teachings have unfortunately survived only in fragments and often only in the suspect citations of other faiths (see de Bary 1958:42–44).

A Hindu tenet that underwent particular attack was that of the special purity or other superiority of the atman, or "soul," of the Brahman.[2] Hinduism taught (and still teaches) that after the physical death of a person, that individual's atman is almost invariably fated to migrate to another living entity (human or otherwise) about to be born—and not simply to any newborn, for there exists a cosmically decreed hierarchy of positions—a ladder if you will—that every atman is fated to climb or to slip down. Behavior is the determinant: One's position in the scheme of things (animal, servant, farmer, warrior, priest, or other) is the result of one's behavior in previous lifetimes, and that is true also of the events that befall one during life (particularly fortune or misfortune). All of this is summed up by the term *karma,* the burden of good and ill each human carries. Whatever one's karma, however, every individual (according to Brahmanical Hinduism) is free to respond in any way to the experiences and events of life (pious acceptance of one's duties and fates, say, or impious railings against fate, or full sensual enjoyment of good fortune, or sharing one's good fortune with the less fortunate). Thus, at the time of the Buddha and other founders of new South Asian religions, Brahmanical Hinduism taught that what one *does* determines what one will *become* in one's next life and the human social-structural ladder, known as the *varnas,* represents the playing out of this system of rewards and punishments. At the bottom of the human system were the Shudras, those fated by their previous behavior to perform menial labor for others.[3] Above these were the Vaishyas, the yeoman farmers and solid merchants. Above them were the

---

[2] Both terms need explication, but this is not the place. See Chapter 13 for further discussion (and Klass 1991a:86–89).

[3] Beliefs apparently varied, and still do, as to who or what constitutes categories below even the Shudras: Are those who are guilty of particularly unacceptable behavior reborn as members of communities completely outside the hierarchy (i.e., "tribals," "untouchables," foreigners), or may they even be reborn as animals? There are of course also Hindus, particularly in recent times, who argue that although one's behavior will determine the circumstances of one's next life, a life of misery or happiness need not necessarily take place only in the context of the caste system.

Kshatriyas, the warrior/noble category, and highest of all were the Brahmans, priestly folk whose atmans were as pure as it was possible for those of humans to be.

According to this belief system, then, all humans (but most particularly those in India) exhibited and reflected—in their present positions on the *varna* ladder—the behavior of their atmans in previous lives. Further, just as an atman could, by being wicked enough, drop below the human line to animal existence, the atman could, by being good enough, rise beyond Brahman to ultimate merger with the universal Godhood (let us call it *brahmana* to distinguish it from the human Brahman who partakes of, or represents, it) and thus cessation of continual rebirth. This ending of the cycle of continual rebirth, with all its inevitability of human suffering, was the desire of all, from the purest of Brahmans to the most polluted of Shudras—or so the Brahmans taught, for we have no record of the views of anyone else, at least until the coming of the Buddha and the others who questioned and challenged the Brahmanical formulations.

Siddhartha Gautama, the man who was to be known as the Buddha, set out to understand, his followers have told us, the ultimate meaning of life and death, along with the source of human suffering and the means of assuaging it. He arrived at an understanding that diverged significantly from the teachings of the Brahmans. As he saw it, "desire" was the root of the problem, most of all the desire to live, despite one's understanding that life—rebirth—meant only renewed misery and nothing else.

From this perspective it follows that existence has no point; it is nothing but the crystallization of human desire to maintain things as they are and most particularly of the human desire to continue to live. Further, it is this desire that creates karma: If one but relinquishes desire, one's karma diminishes until in the end all desire has been eliminated and along with it the very atman itself, and therefore rebirth and the attendant inevitable suffering will all blessedly come to an end.

According to the Buddha, therefore, nothing really exists in the universe but desire and the manifestations of desire. Since all of these offer nothing but continued suffering, each person should strive to relinquish desire in all its forms and by doing so achieve nirvana, which, for the Buddhist,[4] means the blessedness of nonexistence.

---

[4] Buddhism is by no means a monolithic religion. Some Buddhists would certainly challenge this particular definition of *nirvana*, for the term is unquestionably difficult to define. Edwin A. Burtt, for example, noting on the one hand that the "goal is entrance into Nirvana instead of union with Brahman" (1955:19), on the other hand cautions that "Nirvana . . . is to be conceived not as sheer extinction but as the state . . . marked on the positive side by a sense of liberation, inward peace and strength, insight into truth, the joy of complete oneness with reality, and love toward all creatures in the universe (1955:29). Exactly how this differs from "union with Brahman" or accords with the notion of "paranirvana" ("utter extinction—no longer participating in any describable form of existence nor, indeed, of non-existence"; 1955:85) is not entirely clear. The reader interested in the problem is urged to consult the literature; for our purposes here, I think it adequate to term nirvana as something approximating, if not entirely identical with, extinction.

Mahavira, who lived at approximately the same time as the Buddha, proposed (or championed) an alternative non-Brahmanical position, that of what has come to be called Jainism. For Mahavira and the Jains, there *is* a universal something; there is Godhood (equivalent to the *brahmana* of Brahmanical Hinduism). This Godhood is for Jains the true underlying reality of the universe: all encompassing, noncorporeal, immaterial, perfect. Unhappily, at least as the Jains see it, fragments of the Godhood separate themselves, become coated with the tarnish of materiality—which is what they perceive karma to be—and thus manifest themselves in the material universe as supposed separate entities, everything from humans through all life forms to rocks and other manifestations of materiality.

This patina of materiality, karma, thus prevents the separated fragments from merging back into Godhood, and for humans this results in endless rebirth of the soul (the *jiva*). Again, as in Brahmanical Hinduism and in Buddhism, the objective in Jainism is to end the cycle of rebirth for the individual soul; in the case of Jainism this is accomplished by diminishing karma to the point where the separated *jiva* can merge back into Godhood.

How? On the one hand, one's karma increases when one causes suffering to another *jiva*: hurting a human, killing an animal (even an insect), kicking a rock out of the way. On the other hand, one's karma decreases as one mortifies one's own *jiva*. Thus, the Jain might most speedily attain nirvana by sitting unmoving in one spot (thereby in no way inflicting suffering on another *jiva*) and quietly starving to death (a combination of self-mortification and avoidance of taking any life, plant or animal).

As I have indicated, the Buddha and Mahavira were by no means the only ones to dispute with Brahmans and with each other, though they were the most successful—not only in founding religious movements that have survived to the present but in having their views, in full complexity, come down to us.[5]

In the literature (particularly the Buddhist literature) there are fragmentary references to other disputants of the period. There was, for example, one Gosala, whose views gave rise to the movement known as *ajivika:* He taught (or his followers believed or are said to have believed) that there was little or no place for free will in the universe; everything that happened or would ever happen (including rebirth of humans) was predestined from the beginning, and so humans must bow to the workings of *niyati* (fate).

In any event that is what the Buddhists claim Gosala taught, and they gleefully report the Buddha's refutation of Gosala's views and criticism of the behavior of *ajivika* monks. We lack the responses of Gosala and his followers, as we do the responses of the other, now nameless philosophers whom the Buddha is said to have refuted in debate.

The issue for us in all this, let us remember, is the significant difference, if such

---

[5] Again, for the full complexity of Jainism, Hinduism, Buddhism, and the other, more obscure and now extinct systems of belief, the reader should go to the appropriate literature. I present here only a summary.

there be, between assumption and belief. We have observed that the Buddha, Mahavira, Gosala, and the others disagreed profoundly with one another on certain issues—such as the fundamental nature or reality of the universe, the nature or reality of the soul, the reasons for transmigration or continual rebirth, and most of all about what one could or should do to end the endless cycle of rebirth.

Still, they all (including the much beset Brahmans) appear to have been in agreement about—or at least never disputed—certain other issues. Not one of the disputants, as far as we can now tell, suggested that perhaps transmigration or rebirth did *not* occur: that perhaps the soul's experience of the material universe began and ended with the birth and death of *one single human*. Indeed, this particular assumption so crucial to the Western religions makes no appearance at all in the South Asian disputes. Nor indeed does any suggestion that perhaps there are no souls of any kind, only animate humans (and animals) in an otherwise inanimate universe.

There are other assumptions to be found in other societies that are also missing in South Asian thought, such as that death constitutes only loss of corporeality, that after death one merely becomes invisible but otherwise continues to be a member of one's family or lineage and to be involved in the affairs of one's descendants. My point is that despite all disputes, the Buddhist, the Jain, the Brahman, the Ajivikist, and everyone else engaged in the debate adhered to a common set of unchallenged, *unstated* assumptions. Among these assumptions, we may particularly distinguish the following:

- Humans are mortal, but their souls are immortal and thus condemned to continuing, perhaps endless, rebirth.
- The word *condemned* is appropriate because such rebirth inescapably constitutes misfortune whatever form it takes, and the only good fortune consists of somehow ending the cycle of rebirth.
- The universe exhibits a *law of karma* that prescribes what awaits the souls of humans in their next lives.
- The gods, whether they exist or not, cannot interfere with the workings of the law of karma.

Everyone shared these assumptions; where the debaters disagreed with one another was in their beliefs. Did the universe really exist or not? Could fate, or karma, be changed or modified—and if so, how? Granted the "soul" was "reborn" after "death," what exactly was the soul? What was rebirth? What was death?

Given my views on whether the student of religion should become involved in questions of truth or fact, I shall not even speculate whether any or all of the above assumptions and beliefs have any objective (or etic) validity. Surely the number of people in the world who hold or have held these ideas suggests that they are powerful, pervasive, and convincing.

I do want to reiterate, however, my contention that belief is an opinion about some aspect of the universe—and it reflects the presence, usually below the level of consciousness and therefore consideration, of assumptions about the fundamental nature of the universe. Our job, as anthropologists, is of course to analyze and record beliefs and belief systems. But it is also our job, and a much more difficult one, to seek out the underlying assumption system upon which the beliefs rest—even when the latter seem to be in furious contention.

8

Exploring *Explanation:*
Why Do People Die?

Remember, I pray thee, who ever perished, being innocent?
Or where were the upright cut off?

—**Eliphaz the Temanite**
Job 4:7

Religion, as we have surely seen, offers many things to the pious. In the previous chapter we considered, albeit briefly, religion as a wellspring of both values and beliefs. One of the most important things religion provides, almost everyone agrees, is explanation. For chaos, religion substitutes order; for seeming point-lessness, religion gives us meaning. But most comfortingly, many insist, religion provides answers to questions beginning with *why.* Why is there suffering and death? Why is there injustice? Why is there evil?

In presenting my operational definition, I have argued that although religion—seen as a rubric of culture, as a universal institution—may provide explanations or answers to such questions, specific belief systems (religions as manifested in particular sociocultural systems) do not necessarily do so. My point is that a given believer knows why there is evil: because of the Fall, because there are witches, and so on.

In a footnote in the previous chapter, I cited the philosopher Arthur W. Collins on the distinction between *belief* and *truth* (1987:23). For members of a given be-lief system, however, the distinction is slippery, if indeed it even exists. To believe is to know the truth. The observer (the philosopher, the anthropologist) per-ceives the distinction and, similarly, assumes that the believer (like the observer) is seeking explanations or answers to the cosmic questions, such as why there is death or how the universe came into existence.

We therefore sorely need greater clarity about *explanation* if the concept is to be used in the cross-cultural study of religion and religions. I suggest, to begin with, that we be aware that in most cases the believer does not ask (or asks only rhetorically) why death or illness or other misfortunes occur. Naturally, if the observer, the field ethnographer, asks why people die, the informant will explain, but the need for explanation exists primarily, perhaps even only, in the mind of the questioner.

The believer, for his part, secure in the knowledge of why there is death or misfortune in general, is preoccupied with a different set of questions: Why did *my* brother, a good man, die in such pain? Why is *my* wife barren? Why did *our* cow stop giving milk?

David G. Mandelbaum (1964) suggested that the variations in practice and belief that anthropologists had noted in South Asian villages might not be due, as many had supposed, to the presence of conflicting religious traditions (i.e., "Great Tradition" versus "Little" or "Local Traditions") but reflected instead two distinctive but complementary sets of concerns and derivative practices and practitioners. He proposed that one set reflected a concern with "transcendental" issues: the nature and maintenance of the universe, the relationships between humans and the divine, and so on. The second set reflected concerns about "pragmatic" issues: the mundane problems of living persons confronting illness, barrenness, poverty, natural disasters, and so on.

Mandelbaum's observations are helpful, I would argue, for more than an explication of religious practices in Hindu villages in India. They may also serve to explain variations and seeming contradictions in many other societies. I find them particularly enlightening for a cross-cultural study of explanation in religion.

Religions vary not only in beliefs and practices but in complexity. Those like Hinduism with full-time religious specialists, an ancient tradition of theological debate and exploration, and (above all) a body of written religious literature must obviously differ in scope and subtlety of argument as well as in complexity and variation of practice from the belief systems of societies lacking all that.

For all of that, even sophisticated inquiries, within a belief system, into transcendent issues—such as why there is suffering in the universe—come up against the boundaries of what is self-evident, known to be true.

And in all societies the pragmatic issues—why *this* specific disaster occurred *now*, to *us*—must be addressed continually. It is the need to ask such questions, deriving as it usually does from nonhypothetical anguish and fear, that tends to precipitate trepidation, awe, and uncertainty. People are in pain, the belief system and its underlying assumptions seem to hang in the balance, but the challenge is implicit, not explicit—and the high drama lies in how the challenge is met, for it must be.

I suggested earlier (see Chapter 5) that a classic example of this is to be found in the Book of Job.[1] We observe that a fundamental assumption of the belief system—that death and other misfortunes are divine punishments for wrongful behavior—is in fact expressed in the words of the first of Job's comforters, Eliphaz the Temanite: "Who ever perished, being innocent?"

But Job's problem, of course, is that although he *knows* that he himself is innocent and upright, he has nevertheless been subjected to horrendous misfortunes. The issues—derivative of and therefore reflective of the fundamental assumptions—are starkly set forth, but always by implication, never in so many words. For example, even if it is assumed that death and misery are divine punishments, could not a whimsical or unfair divinity punish good people just as much as wicked people?

Impossible: This thought never surfaces as Job and his friends search for explanations for what has befallen him—even though the story begins with an account of a wager between God and Satan. Thus, it would seem that one fundamental assumption of this belief system (at least as it is portrayed in this particular work) about the cause of suffering and death is linked to another assumption—about the nature of divinity. That is, although illness, death, and all forms of misfortune constitute divine punishment, such things can never happen to the innocent and upright because over all there is a moral divinity: omnipotent and omniscient but above all *fair*.[2]

But of course bad things do happen to good people, and so the Book of Job can be taken to represent an effort to deal with what believers must view as an impossible contradiction: The omnipotent divinity who inflicts illness, death, and misfortune upon humans *is never*—can *never be*—either whimsical or unfair; but it is also perfectly apparent to any but the most closed-minded of Temanites that misfortune strikes the innocent and upright about as frequently as it strikes the wicked.

It follows that *we* (the aforementioned believers: the personae in the Book of Job; the author thereof; the readers) might be tempted to ask whether one or another of the fundamental assumptions is incorrect. Can God indeed behave whimsically or unfairly? Do illness, death, and misfortune stem from some source other than divine displeasure?

---

[1] Here I must confess to my own feelings of trepidation. Scholars of Judaism, Christianity, and Islam have debated the meanings and implications of this book for hundreds, perhaps even thousands, of years. I would not presume to join that debate, and my comments should not be interpreted as such a presumption. My concern, rather, is to attempt a cross-cultural comparison: How do some of the issues and concerns touched on in the Book of Job relate to areas of concern in very different and totally unrelated belief systems? To that end, I have simplified, but I hope not trivialized, some of the issues and elements.

[2] Or as later Hasidic Jewish rabbis speculated, naively but perceptively, when God is not unavoidably busy administering the affairs of the universe, he studies the Torah, the book of laws and law that he himself gave to humans.

The very possibility that such questions could be asked forms part of the power of the text, but none of those questions is in fact ever set forth in so many words within the text itself, nor are the fundamental assumptions ever phrased any more clearly than they are in the cited words of Eliphaz the Temanite. Yet the implications of the unstated assumptions and the unasked questions pervade the entire text.

Lévi-Strauss has alerted us to the tremendous problems posed by inherent unresolvable contradictions in belief systems.[3] It is certainly possible to argue that the Book of Job represents another example of an irresolvable conflict between fundamental assumption and practical experience. We have observed that the problem facing Job and all his interlocutors is never, Why do people die? They all (and again we must include both author and readers among the "they") *know* the answer to that question: Death, along with illness and other misfortunes, is visited upon people by God as punishment. It must be apparent, therefore, that only naive (perhaps ignorant) anthropologists or people lacking faith would ask such a foolish question. In every society the sensible, knowledgeable person begins the debate about death with the next question: Taking as given the reason why people *in general* die, why did *this particular* person just die?

The question posed in the Book of Job reflects an assumption—what we might term a *given.* A similar given underlies, as we have seen, the questions of the Buddha and Mahavira: Taking as given that souls transmigrate after death and that such transmigration is undesirable, what can we do to end the process? The anthropologist, therefore, must seek the assumption, the given, in the pragmatic response to crisis.

The inhabitants of the Andaman Islands, Radcliffe-Brown reported, *know* the source of illness and death: Spirits of the already dead come into contact with a living person, intentionally or inadvertently. By their presence (or touch) they cause that person to fall sick or die:

> At the death of an individual his social personality . . . is not annihilated, but is suddenly changed. This continuance after death is a fact of immediate experience to the Andaman Islanders and not in any way a deduction. The person has not ceased to exist. . . .
>
> The spirits are feared or regarded as dangerous. The basis of this fear is the fact that the spirit . . . is obviously a source of weakness and disruption to the community. . . .
>
> If the Andamanese are asked what they fear from the spirit of a dead man they reply that they fear sickness or death, and if the burial and mourning customs are not properly observed the relatives of the dead person will fall sick and perhaps die. (Radcliffe-Brown [1932] 1964:297–298)

"But," an Andamanese Job might observe, "we fulfilled all the burial and

---

[3] "The purpose of myth is to provide a logical model capable of overcoming a contradiction (an impossible achievement if, as it happens, the contradiction is real)" (Lévi-Strauss 1967:226).

mourning customs meticulously, and still other members of our family continued to sicken and die. Why?" To seek an answer to this very reasonable question,
we turn to the Andamanese explanation of the origin of death—and let us note
that the Andamanese urgently need such an explanation to cope with a most profoundly Lévi-Straussian inherent contradiction: If death is caused by the touch of
a spirit of someone who is already dead, how did the first person die?

> *Yaramurud,* having died through an accident, self-caused, becomes a spirit. . . . The
> spirit then comes back to see his brother and by this contact causes his brother's
> death. The story implies that it was not because *Yaramurud* was evilly disposed to-
> wards his brother that he killed him, but on the contrary it was his attachment to
> his relative that caused him to return to visit him, and death followed as a result of
> this contact of the living man with the spirit. Since that time deaths have continued
> to occur in the same way. (Radcliffe-Brown [1932] 1964:299)

Thus, the answer to the Andamanese Job's question must be: Given that death
occurs when the spirit of someone who has died comes into contact with a living
person, and given that though the spirits may mean no harm, they can nevertheless precipitate illness and death by mere propinquity, it follows that the reason
death is continuing to occur among us despite all proper burial ceremonies is
because the spirits are continuing to move among us.

Let us consider still one more example, that of the Saulteaux, a Canadian
branch of the Ojibwa people. According to A. Irving Hallowell, the Saulteaux
have certain a priori, unchallengeable assumptions about illness: "Disease situations of any seriousness carry the implication that something wrong has been
done. Illness is the penalty" (Hallowell 1949:377). To be more specific:

> In Saulteaux belief, one of the major causes of illness arises from what they term
> "bad conduct". . . . "Because a person does bad things, that is where sickness . . .
> starts," is the way one informant phrased it. In other words, a person may fall ill
> because of some transgression he has committed in the past. It is also possible that
> an individual may be suffering because of the bad conduct of his parents. . . . Con-
> sequently, if a child falls seriously ill, it is often attributed to the transgression of a
> parent. (Hallowell 1949:380)

Thus, for the Saulteaux, life-threatening illness is caused by "bad conduct" on
the part of the ill individual or (and in anticipation of a query from a Saulteaux
Job who is certain *he* is not guilty of any "bad conduct") on the part of some close
relative: Illness is present because *someone* is behaving improperly. Not an unusual assumption, perhaps; we are reminded of the problems the citizens of
Thebes experienced when their king, Oedipus, was sleeping with his mother. Of
course, Oedipus had no idea he was engaging in bad conduct until the seer Tiresias pointed it out to him. The Saulteaux, however, focus on more conscious
transgressions because of another of their fundamental assumptions:

Now one of the distinctive features of the Saulteaux belief system is this: if one who is ill because of "bad conduct" *confesses* his transgression, the medicine will then do its work and the patient will recover. ... It means that deviant behavior may not only lead to subsequent illness but that in order to get well one has to suffer the shame of self-exposure involved in confession. This is part of the punishment. (Hallowell 1949:383)

But suppose someone is ill, and no one confesses to "bad conduct"? Obviously, the medicine will not work, and the patient's condition will deteriorate. But—as we Saulteaux *know*—someone has in fact transgressed: How are we to find the culprit and get him or her to confess?

Happily, that is within the powers of the Saulteaux religious officiant: "Since it is also believed that the medicine man's guardian spirits ... will inform him of the cause of the trouble, there is no use withholding anything" (Hallowell 1949:383). And there is one more element built into the belief system:

Among these Indians the notion is held that the very secrecy of the transgressions is one of the things that make them particularly bad. This explains why it is that when one person confesses a sexual transgression in which he or she participated with a second person, the latter will not become ill subsequently or have to confess. Once the transgression has been publicized, it is washed away or, as the Saulteaux phrase it, "bad conduct will not follow you any more." (Hallowell 1949:384)

The Saulteaux belief system thus encompasses the source of illness and death, the powers of the religious officiant (and healer), and the techniques for dealing with illness. If there is illness, someone has misbehaved; therefore someone must make a public confession. If no one does, the religious officiant will uncover the deed through "conjuring":

When anyone is sick, there is no isolation of the patient; on the contrary, the wigwam is always full of people. Any statement on the part of the patient, although it may be made to the doctor, is not only public but also very quickly may become a matter of common gossip. Where conjuring is resorted to in cases where all other efforts have failed to reveal the hidden cause of the malady, the whole community may be present en masse. Under these conditions, to confess a transgression is to reveal publically a secret "sin." Consequently, the resistance to self-exposure is very great and the shame experienced by the individual extremely poignant. (Hallowell 1949:384)

The healer, after consulting his guardian spirits or seeking information in other ways, challenges an individual to confess his or her transgression (usually, though not invariably, of Saulteaux sexual mores). Obviously, when the healer finds you out he finds you out, and you may as well confess.

The point I pursue in this chapter is that although a belief system, a "religion," certainly seeks answers, it is not always to the questions outsiders would pose. That is, the religion is based upon a substantial set of fundamental assumptions, things everybody knows—everybody but the nonbeliever who is describing the system.

Thus, I would argue, no religion in actuality seeks to know the answers to such questions as: Why do people die? Are there souls? Does something live on after death? Are divinities whimsical or invariably morally just? How can we penetrate the significance of events? Rather, the answers to such questions are *givens,* fundamental assumptions, the bedrock upon which the real questions of the system are based:

- We *know* why there is death and illness in general; why in *this* particular case?
- We *know* what the possibilities are for the soul after death; what can we do to effect the best eventuality?
- We *know* the nature of divinity; what can we do to influence divine action?
- A frightening, even inexplicable, event has occurred; given our assumptions, though, how can we interpret it and deal with it?

Such questions, of course, imply not only a backdrop of prior assumptions and beliefs but an actual *system* of assumptions, beliefs, practices, and relationships within which questions can be asked—and answered.

9
Clerical Orders

[Meyer Fortes] once invited a rainmaker to perform the ceremony for him for an attractive fee, and the officiant in question replied, "Don't be a fool, whoever makes a rain-making ceremony in the dry season?"

—Stanley Jeyaraja Tambiah
Magic, Science, Religion, and the Scope of Rationality

As I hope we have begun to see, religion—like much else of human culture—is something you think. But (and, again, like culture in general) it is also something you do (or someone or something does). And, of course, it is something being done, but we'll get to that later. The concern for the moment is with the personnel of, the participants in, religion: *who* is doing what.

One might think that the participants in religious events would draw a great deal of attention, and indeed they do—but mainly from observers. Theorists, for their part, those whose primary concern is with religion as something you *think*, tend to dismiss as fools or charlatans those who actually *do* religion. Rarely indeed do the theorists accord such people the dignity of being colleagues, of considering them to be engaged in the very same enterprise.

I am thinking here primarily, of course, of early writers on the anthropology of religion (Frazer, Durkheim, etc.), but even many of the more contemporary or ethnographically oriented anthropologists (Malinowski, Radcliffe-Brown, Lévi-Strauss, etc.) who describe religious participants in considerable detail in their accounts pay remarkably little attention to them in their theoretical writings. This is a much too sweeping condemnation, I realize, but it at least has the merit of noting a possible source of the problem.

For there most definitely is a problem: The student about to go into the field has a vague understanding that he or she will likely encounter "shamans" of one sort or another and should watch carefully what they do and say, but that is about it. The religious officiant is not perceived as a theologian but simply as one of the more active participants in religious activities. And in addition the term *partici-pants* is usually narrowly interpreted to encompass only *human* participants, and most attention is given to the participants who act as religious officiants.

Well, who else is there? To begin with, there are, almost invariably, a number of humans participating in a given ceremony (congregation, petitioners, and others) who are very definitely not officiating at anything. Perhaps even more to the point, there are important participants in religious events who are not human at all: Some, such as ancestors, were so once but are no longer; others, such as gods and demons, never were and never will be. To those who believe in them, werewolves are of course as real as priests, and therefore the category of *partici-pants* should include every participant, human or whatever.

But then the category of participants suddenly becomes so large that it is in danger of being unmanageable. I therefore propose to focus for a time on *human* participants, leaving other types for later consideration. The larger category to which all belong, however, remains (at least in my mind) one and indivisible: This subdivisioning should not be understood to imply a distinction reflecting a view that one subdivision is necessarily more real or more actual than another.

I might easily have titled this chapter "Religious Officiants" (because that is what I propose to discuss here), but *officiant* is unquestionably an off-putting term. What, then, shall we call the persons in charge of religious events or cere-monies? It would seem sensible that we use one term for all such, with provision for appropriate differences or subtypes. One might, for example, assume that *priest* would be the easiest and most obvious cross-culturally applicable label for religious officiants, but we seem to be prevented from using it by some of the connotations and reverberations connected with the term. For example, shall we categorize Jewish rabbis as priests, since they certainly officiate religiously? If so, how shall we distinguish the contemporary rabbi from the biblical *kohen,* a term usually translated as "priest"?

Again, may we (comfortably) class as a priest an old woman who casts bones to peer into the future or a man who goes into a trance and sucks illness out of the bodies of sick people? This latter question is, I suspect, of more moment to people who are reluctant to use *priest* generically than is the problem of the rabbi and the kohen. The reluctance may perhaps stem from a widespread feeling that a priest is a dignified male[1] religious personage, someone who commands a corpus of formal (that is, *written*) religious knowledge and practice. Even more specifi-

---

[1] The word *priestess* raises additional difficulties, perhaps because female priests were not tradition-ally present in "Western" (Jewish, Christian, Muslim) religions and, when observed among other reli-gions, were much disapproved of because they were often associated with rituals involving sexual acts. Nevertheless, there are indeed today female ministers and rabbis, though as yet no female Catholic (or Eastern Orthodox) priests and no female imams or mullahs.

cally, priestly religious behavior is generally assumed not to encompass altered states of consciousness, such as possession, ecstasy, and visions. The priest as we know him may on occasion be called upon to cure someone who is possessed, but he does it in a businesslike, nonecstatic way.

Thus, in the common view priests may be found in the major religions of complex, literate societies: There are priests in the Eastern Orthodox and Roman Catholic churches; in Buddhist, Jain, and Hindu temples; and so on. Protestant ministers, Jewish rabbis, and Muslim imams and mullahs may not *exactly* be priests, perhaps because they are not formal enough. Nevertheless, most people (including scholars) would not object too strenuously to including ministers, rabbis, and mullahs under the broad rubric of *priest*,[2] whereas there might be considerable objection to the use of *priest* for other kinds of religious practitioners.

The other kinds are those who in popular (or at least nonanthropological writings) are commonly called such things as *witch doctors* and *medicine men*: in other words, those religious officiants increasingly referred to in scholarly literature by the supposedly neutral term *shamans*. These people may be male or female, they may go into trance or undergo possession, they may kill at a distance or suck evil substances from the bodies of their devotees—but they may *not* easily be called priests.

The issue of a priest-shaman distinction is obviously important, but it is also important that we cannot seem to find a nonjudgmental, nonopprobrious, non-culture-bound term for the larger category, that of the leader or supervisor or instigator of religious activities, as well as the instructor or authority on religious matters (meanings, morals, rituals, etc.) in general. I suggest, in fact, that a major reason that we who would study religion cross-culturally continually find ourselves bogged down by ethnocentrism is that most of the terminology upon which we must draw is heavily weighted with ethnocentric, or at least culturally specific, baggage.

There is another possibility, of course: No such term is appropriate. Some scholars see the differences between *priest* on the one hand and *sorcerer, magician, medicine man, witch doctor,* or *shaman* on the other as so great that *no* encompassing term is possible or advisable (see, for example, Radin [1937] 1957, Weber [1922] 1963, and Goode [1951] 1964). Even such writers, however, find themselves forced on occasion to refer, if fumblingly, to practitioners and officiants. Whatever the degrees of difference one sees among the officiants, therefore, an encompassing term would seem to be called for.

Short of creating an entirely new term (something I do find myself constrained to do, in a later chapter, for the hopelessly ethnocentric *soul* and all its soulmates), I think there is a word in fairly common use that might do. I propose we

---

[2] In the U.S. military services, Roman Catholic and Eastern Orthodox priests, along with Protestant ministers and Jewish rabbis, are all referred to as chaplains.

use *cleric* as the term encompassing religious practitioners, officiants, leaders, and authorities wherever and whenever we find them.

The term does have some minimal baggage,[3] but it also has the peculiar advantage of an ambiguous or disputed origin.[4] It was first applied, some argue, to the biblical tribe of Levites and was intended to signify that they, in contrast to the other tribes, received as their inheritance no portion of territory but only the right to conduct religious services. Or, still others say, it reflects the arbitrariness of being chosen (by God, by "lot") to enter upon a life of religious service. From either perspective, I would argue that we may, without too much discomfort, call Catholic priests and Hindu *pujaris* and Jewish rabbis (and rebbes and kohenim) and Siberian shamans and all medicine men and witch doctors clerics.

Nevertheless, we have seen that many scholars would argue for two distinctly separate subcategories of clerics: priests, who are to be observed in stratified, literate (in other words, "complex") societies and who do not engage in trances or other altered states of consciousness; and shamans, who are to be found in nonstratified, nonliterate (in other words, "simple") societies and who typically engage in all sorts of ecstatic and altered behavior.

Whether consciously intended or not, this does seem to imply a fundamental difference between religions (or at least religious personnel) of "complex" societies as against those of "simple" societies—so are we perhaps hearing a persistent echo of "civilized" versus "primitive" religion? Most anthropological students of religion would contest such an allegation. That issue firmly to one side, however, it would appear that many anthropologists in fact see certain significant differences between religion in stratified, literate societies and religion in nonstratified, nonliterate societies. As Marvin Harris has observed, "Full-time specialists, monumental temples, dramatic processions, and elaborate rites performed for spectator congregations are incompatible with the infrastructure and political economy of hunters and gatherers. Similarly, the complex astronomical and mathematical basis of ecclesiastical beliefs and rituals is never found among band and village peoples" (Harris 1987:282). What, then, are the implications of full-time versus part-time religious activity? To begin with, some clerics, we know, perform their duties as members of hierarchical bodies and thus according to prescribed (in fact, almost invariably *written*) sets of dogmas and instructions for ceremonies. These, of course, are the ones we feel most comfortable calling priests. Others—the ones we call shamans (or witch doctors or medicine men)—perform their duties in the absence of any superiors or of any externally prescribed body of rules or interpretations.

A priest is therefore subject to external authority: that of his present superiors

---

[3] Some may confuse *cleric* with the cognate *clerk* and assume it implies literacy or writing skills, but these were not in fact original attributes of a cleric.

[4] See, for example, the entry "clerk" in the *Encyclopaedia Britannica*, 11th ed.

in the hierarchy (where there is one) or that of the dogma written by those who have gone before him. He is not free to reinterpret or to devise new ceremonies or modify old ones. Most particularly, he is not free to seek independent divine guidance—that is, he may not jump the chain of command by communing with whatever being or power lies above or beyond the formal human organization and literature.

A shaman, however, is not part of any formal organization and lacks any corpus of written rules. He or she may occasionally accord deference to some respected colleague (or teacher) or have memorized a complex set of rules more or less shared by fellow officiants in neighboring communities. Nevertheless, the shaman is not *subject* to any outside authority, nor is he or she in danger of being unfrocked if ceremonial procedures are abridged or replaced. And if a shaman seeks information about attitudes or desires of divinities or ancestors or whatever, he or she is completely free to go directly to the source—which often means by way of some altered state of consciousness.[5]

From this perspective, then, we might argue that the absence of trance, possession, and the like on the part of priests is primarily a reflection of organizational, or hierarchical, necessity for discipline: If any priest, any time, could go into trance and come out of it claiming personal divine authority, the priestly hierarchy and literature would crumble in short order—or never have come into being.

This view, that the priest-versus-shaman distinction reflects the presence and absence of any hierarchical organization or chain of command, is useful for anthropology and anthropologists. It avoids the clearly ethnocentric civilized/primitive mode of explanation, thereby enabling us to probe further into the reasons for the presence or absence of trance, possession, and other forms of altered states of consciousness. Is the presence of hierarchy the major determining factor, or is the existence of a literary corpus diagnostically more significant? The ethnographic literature provides examples of all kinds of differences and permutations, and one can generate an endless list of questions to be pursued in the field. What, for example, of part-time clerics who do not undergo any form of altered states of consciousness? What of full-time clerics who do?

I leave such questions to others to pursue—aided, I hope, by the observation that all such are clerics, that is, religious leaders committed to guiding their flocks according to the rules of their particular belief systems. I would like, however, to touch on still another matter of contention, one reflecting what might legitimately be termed a cultural materialist issue.

Considerable anthropological attention has been drawn to the significance of energy acquisition as a factor affecting, even determining, cultural forms. Briefly, the argument has been (cf. White [1949] 1973, Harris 1959, 1987) that where the

---

[5] For further discussion of these and related issues, see Harner 1973, particularly "Shamanism and Priesthood in Light of the Campa *Ayahuesca* Ceremony" by Gerald Weiss.

amount of energy customarily acquired in a given society (i.e., in the form of food) barely exceeds the amount of energy expended in the food quest, the society will lack the resources to support full-time specialists, and therefore will not exhibit them. Full-time specialists are those who need not spend any time in the food quest but are free to attend to some alternative activity, such as warfare, artisanry, political leadership, and religion.

The issue is not that *individuals* in "simple" societies (e.g., hunting-and-gathering, horticultural, etc.) necessarily have less leisure than their counterparts in more "complex" societies (e.g., agricultural, stratified, urban, etc.). As a matter of fact, they frequently have considerably *more* leisure time (see, for example, Sahlins 1968 and 1972, on "the original affluent society"). What cultural materialists argue, however, is that the hunting-and-gathering *society*—however undemanding of individuals' time—cannot support *institutions* that require bodies of individuals to be permanently alienated from the quest for material goods. Such societies, therefore, cannot develop a body—a category—of full-time specialists in religion, as they cannot in medicine, warfare, or even governance. Without the presence of a distinct societal institution, those who engage in such activities do so as part-time specialists, however much free time a given individual may have. Or so the argument runs.

The part-time artist or artisan may be seen as being in principle as talented or skilled as his or her full-time counterpart but nevertheless likely to lack the fine edge to be derived not just from constant practice and attention but from the presence of an overarching institution, with structured procedures and complex techniques. Thus, your professional soldier is likely, all things being equal, to be a greater military threat than the man, however brave, who must learn his skills from his father or brother and who has no access to accumulated military strategy and lore.

Similarly, the part-time religious practitioner lacks all the history, dogma, and rituals available to a full-time priest: There is no institutionalized body of priestly knowledge. The part-time cleric learns from an elder, but only intermittently (in the evening or after a successful hunt has provided food for a few days) or by assisting in the performance of ceremonies.

Given the foregoing observations, then, we can expect part-time clerics to exhibit certain common characteristics. There is likely to be noticeable variation, for example, in both ritual and interpretation from band to band or village to village of even closely related groups.[6] Formal training—expressed in a body of religious knowledge and inventory of rituals—will likely be much less than that among any comparable full-time priesthood. Hierarchy is absent, and the part-time cleric may respect the skill of a colleague in another village but nevertheless

---

[6] Fredrik Barth's *Cosmologies in the Making: A Generative Approach to Cultural Variation in Inner New Guinea* (1987) is a fascinating exploration of such variations.

recognizes no one as constituting a superior authority or any kind of intermediary between the practitioner and the powers-that-be in the universe. Thus, when the part-time cleric seeks enlightenment, he or she will usually go directly to the source: the gods, the spirits, the ancestors, or whatever.

The foregoing argument is of course intrinsic to cultural materialist explanations both of the differences between energy-gathering and energy-producing societies and of the factors precipitating such evolutionary phenomena as stratification, urbanism, empire building, and so on. It does raise a potential problem for the study of religion, however, in that it directs our attention away from the clerics and solely to the issue of whether societies are "simple" or "complex." Thus, although it may be true that for the most part so-called simple societies are characterized by part-time clerics, it is certainly necessary to note that so-called complex societies *also* exhibit part-time religious leaders in addition to full-time ones.

Complex societies, after all, are characterized by stratification, and in such societies the full-time priesthood caters primarily to those at the top of the socio-economic system, those who control the sources of wealth and the concomitant leisure necessary for full-time specialization. At the bottom of such a society, however—in the poorest villages or the urban slums—where *no one* has wealth or leisure, where *all* must scrabble without end for daily sustenance, we quite often find part-time clerics serving their communities much as their counterparts do in so-called simple societies.

The terms we use are different; we speak of backwoods preachers, hedge priests, storefront pastors, and so on. A common characteristic of such part-time practitioners is a lack of education, and particularly of religious training. Frequently, they begin their careers in early adolescence, announcing simply that they have received inspiration. Again, their messages, like the rituals they perform, are *similar* to those found in neighboring communities, but they may vary considerably in detail: There is no hierarchically derived and enforced standard. Perhaps the most common feature of such clerics—distinguishing them from the full-time practitioners in their society—is their propensity to seek direct divine revelation through trance, possession, and other altered states of consciousness; they are "ecstatics," "charismatics."

There are of course many variations, and some are most interesting indeed. For one thing, such part-time clerics—living as they do in literate societies—make varying use of written religious literature. In Christian Europe and European-derived societies, such religious practitioners depend primarily, frequently exclusively, on the Bible (Old and New Testaments) as translated into the vernacular; they usually have little or no knowledge of the Hebrew, Latin, and Greek versions (and associated literature) the full-time priests of their societies study.

In the villages of India, however, and among the postexilic Jewish communities of Europe and the Muslim circum-Mediterranean world, the distinction played out quite differently, perhaps because in both cases circumstances forced formerly full-time specialists into part-time roles. Writers such as Julian Steward (1949:765–767) and Henri Pirenne (1957) have discussed what Steward called "cultural deconstruction" or "degrading"—as when South American horticulturalists were forced into areas where only foraging was possible or when in Europe, from the eighth century onward, the imperial Roman economic system was destroyed by the rise of Islam and replaced by manorial feudalism.

In the case of the Jews after the exile, the earlier priesthood disappeared almost completely[7] and was replaced by the rabbinate.[8] Though the rabbi in medieval Europe was expressly a part-time practitioner (for a long time, in fact, not permitted to charge for any services), he was expected to assimilate the compendious and ever growing religious literature. To be a learned man, a repository of learning, was his primary responsibility, though at the same time he had to earn his daily bread. In prosperous communities he might if he were lucky receive relief in the form of support from his wife or his wife's father or even contributions from members of his congregation. Thus, because of the nature of his religious responsibility, he sought authority in the religious literature, recognizing no hierarchical superior but acknowledging that there were those with superior knowledge and understanding of the literature to whom he could turn for advice and counsel. Under such circumstances there was minimal variation in ritual and interpretation from region to region, and such differences as developed were addressed by a wide-ranging correspondence among rabbis.

And when times got very bad indeed among the Jews of eastern Europe, from the seventeenth century onward, a new kind of cleric emerged: the Hasidic rebbe. In the early years the rebbe spurned much of the formal learning of the rabbi, preferring ecstatic and direct communication with divinity. Over time, however, the rebbe became transformed into a full-time religious leader, and hierarchy and a renewed emphasis on studying the religious literature appeared.

In India a similar "cultural deconstruction" seems to have occurred from the eighth century onward, as Muslim conquerors took control of much of the subcontinent. The Hindu religious edifices—temples, monasteries, and so on—were either destroyed throughout northern India or collapsed in the absence of an economic and political elite interested in (and capable of) supporting them. The similar structures of Buddhism went down in the same way, and Buddhism disappeared from the subcontinent. In the case of Hinduism, the village Brahman priests were able to keep the religion alive through the ensuing centuries.

The rural Brahman priesthood was hereditary, so recruitment and training

---

[7] Their descendants continued to be honored, called first in the congregation to read from the Torah and called upon on special occasions to bless the congregation or to perform certain rituals (as at the birth of a firstborn son, etc.).

[8] Actually, of course, the rabbinate had been in existence for some time, but with the destruction of both the state and the priestly hierarchy, the role and function of the rabbi underwent considerable transformation.

took place within the family. A boy need only be taught sufficient Sanskrit to be able to read and recite the liturgy necessary for community and life-crisis ceremonies. Many village Brahmans, in fact, did not serve as religious practitioners, preferring where possible to engage in agriculture. Those Brahmans who did serve in various religious capacities (presiding at marriages and funerals, maintaining village temples, etc.) frequently specialized in one capacity or another, managing to eke out a precarious (but almost full-time) living from contributions from more prosperous villagers. Hierarchy, however, and standardization of text and ritual could not be maintained in the villages of north India after the coming of Islam: Essentially, a village Brahman priest recognized no superior and performed his rituals as his father had taught him to do.

Priests and shamans alike, it would seem, are religious practitioners, but I urge that we distinguish them primarily as full-time versus part-time clerics. And I happily leave it to others to solve such questions as whether Hasidic rebbes and Brahman village pandits are to be called *shamans* or *priests.*

10

What Kind of Shaman
Would You Want?

In the early days, so an old Eskimo told Rasmussen, there were no sha-
mans. Only sickness existed and it was the fear of sickness and suffering
that led to the development of the first official shaman.

—Paul Radin
Primitive Religion

Clerics, we have observed, appear to fall into two broad subcategories, and there
appears to be little argument among anthropologists, at least these days, that the
appropriate term for one of the subcategories (the one encompassing part-time
religious practitioners) is *shaman*. There are some negative connotations to the
term, but it is obviously far superior to the ones that anthropologists used
earlier—*witch doctors, medicine men, sorcerers*—and that are still to be encoun-
tered, unhappily, in the popular press. Let us by all means stay with *shaman*.[1]

We anthropologists must face the fact, however, that the members of the subcategory have received very bad press, particularly from us. James G. Frazer, for
example, proposed that shamans (he called them sorcerers and magicians) were
in principle all alike; they were for the most part charlatans living off the gullibil-
ity of their clients: "The pitfalls which beset the path of the professional sorcerer
are many, and as a rule only the man of coolest head and sharpest wit will be able
to steer his way through them safely. *For it must always be remembered that every*
single profession and claim put forward by the magician as such is false; not one of

---

[1] The negative connotations of the term may be partially vitiated if we remind ourselves that the
word ultimately derives from the Sanskrit *śramaṇa*, meaning "lord" or "master"—or perhaps simply
"my superior in religious matters."

them can be maintained without deception, conscious or unconscious" (Frazer [1922] 1958:53; italics mine). Why, I ask, as you no doubt expect by now, "must [it] always be remembered"? Because we *are*, after all, *scientists;* we must insist on remembering that what we are engaged in studying has no basis in objective reality. And that inevitably leads us, to conclusions like the following:

> Accordingly, the sorcerer who sincerely believes in his own extravagant pretensions is in far greater peril and is much more likely to be cut short in his career than the deliberate impostor. The honest wizard always expects that his charms and incantations will produce their supposed effect; and when they fail, not only really, as they always do, but conspicuously and disastrously, as they often do, he is taken aback: he is not, like his knavish colleague, ready with a plausible excuse to account for the failure, and before he can find one he may be knocked on the head by his disappointed and angry employers.
>
> The general result is that at this stage of social evolution the supreme power tends to fall into the hands of men of the keenest intelligence and most unscrupulous character. (Frazer [1922] 1958:53)

The scientistic argument is, as ever, powerful and straightforward: If, as we "scientists" *know,* religion (and all its essentially meaningless or contentless subdivisions, such as magic and sacrifice and prayer) are without basis in reality, then it follows that religious activities are without instrumental utility. That is, they don't accomplish anything—a "fact" that should be apparent to any reasonably intelligent person.

But something is wrong. Our scientistic prediction does not hold: We observe that societies continue—over centuries, over millennia—to perform the practices and to maintain the beliefs of religion. The fault must therefore lie with those (the sorcerers, the shamans, the clerics) who are in the best position (1) to know how worthless and false the beliefs and practices are and (2) to find ways and excuses to continue to fool their less knowledgeable congregants. It must follow, therefore, that the most successful religious practitioners are the most crooked: very intelligent and very unscrupulous.

The trouble is, of course, that ethnographic investigations have not supported Frazer's assumption that all successful shamans are consciously aware of the meaninglessness of their beliefs and activities. Anthropologists were reluctantly forced to admit that the shamans really seemed to believe in what they were doing. Robert H. Lowie, writing decades after Frazer, wrestled with this problem and proposed an alternative explanation. Shamans, he suggested, were simply weak in the head: "magic . . . is older than religion. Only gradually the leaders of thought came to realize the futility of magical procedure,[2] which they supplanted with religious rites, while the weaker intellects continued to cling at least partially to their faith in magic" (1924:139).

---

[2] The "futility," of course, reflects Lowie's own adherence to what "must always be remembered."

But what if shamans are not only sincere in their beliefs but not even weak of intellect? How can this be, given what "must always be remembered"? How are we to explain this anomaly?

It fell to Paul Radin ([1937] 1957) to find an enticing explanation of the seeming anomaly. His explanation, however, did not challenge the supposed scientific need to remember what "must always be remembered": "Throughout the world of primitive man some form of emotional instability and well-marked sensitivity has always been predicated as the essential trait of the medicine-man and shaman" ([1937] 1957:106).[3] Radin's solution: If, as we remember, religious beliefs are false and religious activities are without instrumental effect—and if religious practitioners nevertheless continue in the face of all evidence to believe sincerely in the efficacy of what they are doing but do not generally appear to be stupid—it can only follow that the religious practitioners are mentally unbalanced.

Radin offered as support of this conclusion the following: (1) religious practitioners—and particularly shamans—do tend more than anyone else to enter into altered states of consciousness, which are usually to be interpreted as forms of neurotic if not in fact psychotic behavior,[4] and (2) the people who become shamans quite often show signs of such aberrant behavior even before they are initiated into the mysteries:

> Such instability may take a large variety of forms. Throughout Siberia we know that it assumes pathological proportions and that a shaman there is preferably selected from among those suffering from *menerik*. This is a nervous affliction in which the patient falls into trances and where he is subject to fits of unconsciousness. Although manifestly *menerik* is a disease, the insistence that shamans be selected from individuals subject to it has a definite bearing on the fundamental trait of all shamans and medicine-men everywhere. *They must be disoriented and they must suffer.* ([1937] 1957:107; italics his)

I understand why Radin believes they must be "disoriented" (it is part of what he sees as "pathological instability"), but why must they "suffer"? I think it would help if we amended Radin's ringingly italicized last line to read, "They must be disoriented and they must suffer—*because that is how in those societies prospective shamans are identified.*"

After all, in all societies neophytes exhibit their fitness for the roles they hope to be allowed to adopt, the personae they wish to project, by exhibiting a propensity for the appropriate trappings and behavior. One could look in exotic places for examples, but one need not: In any American college or university, fledgling academics are easily distinguishable in dress, habits, mannerisms, and much else

---

[3] Radin takes a firm scientistic position from the very beginning: "Man . . . postulated the supernatural in order primarily to validate his workaday reality" ([1937] 1957:9). Religion (or the supernatural), in other words, may serve to validate but is nevertheless distinct from reality.

[4] After all, let us always remember, the things (spirits, gods, visions, etc.) that they encounter during their altered states do not exist, have no meaning, are not and cannot be real. . . .

from fledgling businesspeople or fledgling doctors or fledgling professional athletes. Fraternities and sororities have long been aware of this and demonstrate their awareness in their selection procedures.

All that Radin has really observed and reported in the passage cited above, therefore, is that in societies in which shamans are expected to engage in altered states of consciousness, individuals who are drawn (consciously or otherwise) to enter the profession frequently begin to exhibit the necessary propensity sometimes well in advance of formal apprenticeship.

Radin has gone on to conclude from this observation that such individuals are drawn to shamanism because (1) the individuals are neurotic or psychotic and (2) the actions of the professional shaman—such as possession and trance—express or encourage such psychological disturbance.

It will of course be argued, and legitimately, that most contemporary anthropologists question whether altered states of consciousness are indications of mental pathology. Indeed, the issue of the shaman's mental capacity, stability, or even sincerity has largely been dropped from contemporary anthropological discourse. This is not, however, because anthropologists have stopped seeing themselves as scientists but rather, according to Brian Morris, because anthropologists have adopted a different strategy for distinguishing science from religion.

Thus, in his exploration of Lévi-Strauss's *Savage Mind*, Morris argues that although science is concerned with causality, Lévi-Strauss (and, essentially, Edmund Leach) believes magic, myth, and religion to be concerned with "primitive classifications," in other words, with "different types of phenomena." Consider the difference, Morris suggests, between them and Robin Horton, who sees *both* religion and science as concerned with "putting events into a causal context wider than that provided by common sense" (B. Morris 1987:279–281).[5]

Although I salute Morris for addressing this very serious issue, I think his argument takes us too far beyond the purview of anthropology, at least for the needs of this work. I would propose an alternative approach to the issue of the behavior of shamans (and indeed of all clerics), one that reflects quite traditional anthropological theoretical concerns. Specifically, I suggest we give more attention to the interplay between a belief system and the personae of its religious officiants, an issue I began to explore in Chapter 9.

There is very frequently, if not invariably, a congruence between the behavior of a religious practitioner and the views the encompassing society holds about the nature and sources of death, misfortune, and other miseries. The Andaman Islanders, we have noted, believe that the spirits, or ghosts, of the dead wander near—and occasionally and devastatingly among—the living. When such a spirit touches a living person, whether with malice or even with affection, the person

---

[5] The reader is encouraged to pursue this controversy by consulting such works as Durkheim (1912) 1965, Lévy-Bruhl 1926, Cassirer 1944, Lévi-Strauss 1962, Leach 1970, Horton 1970, and Piaget 1971, as well as Morris's own review of the issues.

will sicken and may even die, for the touch of some invisible ghost is the source of death (Radcliffe-Brown [1932] 1964:139 et passim).

My question would therefore be: If you were an Andaman Islander, what kind of a shaman would you want to have? Wouldn't it be nice, say, to have a cleric who can move unharmed among the spirits of the dead and can then return to his fellows and advise them on the ways to cure and prevent illness and where possible avoid death?

> There are, amongst the Andamanese, certain individuals who are distinguished from their fellows by the supposed possession of supernatural powers. These specially favoured persons correspond, to some degree, with the medicine-men, magicians or shamans of other primitive societies. The name for these medicine-men in the North Andaman is *oko-jumu,* meaning literally "dreamer" or "one who speaks from dreams". . . .
>
> The powers of a dreamer, supernatural as they are, can only be acquired by supernatural means, through contact in one way or another with the spirits. . . . One way of coming into contact with the spirits is by death. If a man should, as the natives put it, die and then come back to life again, he is, by that adventure, endowed with the power that makes a medicine-man. (Radcliffe-Brown [1932] 1964:175–177)

There is a clear relationship, in Andamanese perception, between the assumptions about the cause of death and the nature of the religious practitioner.

But suppose that you are instead a Yanomamö living in the rain forest of northern Brazil and southern Venezuela. Suppose you believed that people become sick or die "because someone sent harmful spirits—*hekura*—to steal their souls, or someone blew magical charms at them from a great distance, charms that caused them to sicken and die" (Chagnon 1992:2). What kind of cleric would you want if you were a Yanomamö? Wouldn't you want someone who was a more powerful sorcerer than the person who was sending harmful spirits and magical charms? "Thus, in every village the shamans spend many hours attempting to cure sick children and sick adults, driving out the malevolent forces that have caused their illnesses, and, in turn, sending their own spirits and charms against the children in distant villages for revenge." (Chagnon 1992:2). To perform successfully, Yanomamö shamans must establish good relationships with the ubiquitous spirits, or *hekura*. This requires, first, a long period of arduous training for the novice, including fasting and abstention from sex, and then, for the adept, the snorting of hallucinogenic snuff (*ebene*) to attract the attention of the *hekura* (Chagnon 1992:107–109).

Among the Tsembaga Maring of Papua New Guinea, in contrast, although illness and death are somewhat similarly believed to derive from the activities of spirits and hostile humans, there exists an intermediary between shaman and spirits: The shaman needs only to gain the attention of the *kun kaze ambra,* the smoke woman, who "is thought to be a link between the living and the dead" (Rappaport [1966] 1984:41). This action is particularly necessary before a fight:

On the night previous to a "small" or "nothing" fight . . . the warriors convene by clans or subclans in the men's houses to inform the spirits of both the high and low ground of the next morning's encounter. As they sit chanting in a darkness illuminated only by the embers of small fires, shamans (*kun kaze yu*), of whom there are several in each clan, induce in themselves an ecstacy by inhaling deeply and rapidly the smoke of bespelled cigars made from strong native tobacco. When his *nomane* (his animated, immortal, thought stuff) departs through his nose to seek out the smoke woman . . . in high places, the shaman begins to tremble and gibber. Soon the smoke woman "strikes" him. Led by his *nomane* she enters the shaman's head. . . . Rising to his feet he dances about the embers in a low crouch, sobbing, chanting, and screaming in tongues. It is through the smoke woman that the ancestors are now being informed by the living of the fight and it is through her that they are now signifying their endorsement of the enterprise and sending assurances of their protection. (Rappaport [1966] 1984:119–120)

It is easy to see why an unsympathetic observer would conclude that such shamans are either faking the whole thing or mentally unbalanced—or possibly both. Let us note, however, that the shamans in both of the foregoing accounts are engaged in enterprises of great pith and moment: They are seeking the causes of death and illness, and they are endeavoring to protect their communities from looming disaster.

Would you turn over such a task to a feeble-minded or unstable person? Is it not obvious that far from being mentally weak or someone who has been unable to cope with the vicissitudes of fate, the shaman must be someone in whom confidence can be placed in times of extreme crisis, someone who radiates competence and trustworthiness? I would argue that whatever the seeming similarity of shamanic behavior in a given society to what in *our society* seems unbalanced or psychotic, the shaman actually represents the polar opposite phenomenon: He or she is the anchor, the crutch, the one on whose capable shoulders is piled all the woe and fear of the community.

For another example, let us return to the shaman of the Saulteaux, who must indeed deal with such woe and fear: "In Saulteaux society, it is not fear of the Gods or fear of punishment by the state that is the major sanction: it is the fear of disease" (Hallowell 1949:377–378). Thus, for the Saulteaux, we know, bad things happen because individuals do bad things. Medicines can alleviate illness, but *only* if the one who has transgressed (the ill person or sometimes a close relative) makes a public confession.

In Chapter 8 we considered a question: Suppose nobody admits to any wrongdoing, and disease or other misfortune rages as unabated as it did in ancient Thebes during the unhappy reign of Oedipus? The answer, we saw, is that this is where the Saulteaux shaman takes over: "Since it is also believed that the medicine man's guardian spirits . . . will inform him of the cause of the trouble, there is no use withholding anything" (Hallowell 1949:383).

And this brings us to the issue under consideration in this chapter: What kind of a person is this shaman? Is he a charlatan, a fool, or merely mentally unstable? I would argue that he is—and must be—a person of considerable intelligence, insight, and presence and that he must possess above-average knowledge and understanding of his people. I say "must" for two reasons. First is the degree of anxiety precipitated by illness among the Saulteaux. According to Hallowell,

> By its very nature, disease may arouse "normal" or objective anxiety, but among the Saulteaux, native theories of disease causation invest certain disease situations with a traumatic quality which is a function of the beliefs held rather than of the actual danger threatened by the illness itself. The quality of the anxiety precipitated in the individuals affected by such situations suggests neurotic rather than objective anxiety. . . . (1949:388)

If such anxiety is precipitated by such beliefs, can we imagine that the community in its collective wisdom would, in a medical emergency, put itself in the hands of someone it regards as stupid, crazy, or morally unsavory? *You* would want—and *they* would want—the person unquestionably most capable of solving the problem and saving the community. In short, they want, as the people of Thebes did, a Tiresias.

But I must confess to a second reason for believing that the Saulteaux shaman must be of above-average intelligence and perception. Bluntly, it reflects and relates to the scientistic bias of such as Frazer, Radin—and perhaps even myself. After all, we can't have it both ways. The Saulteaux may believe that there are actually guardian spirits and spirits of the dead who inform the shaman, during his trance, which members of the community have engaged in which unacceptable activities. However, if, like Frazer, *we* personally doubt the existence of such informants, then we must find some way to account for the shaman's ability—attested to by the Saulteaux and confirmed by Hallowell—to come out of trance, point to someone, and accuse him or her of misbehaving (usually specifying the misbehavior), and then receive from that individual a full confession. If the guardian spirits didn't tell the shaman, then who did? Must we not conclude that (guardian spirits uncomfortably to one side) the shaman knows his people and their proclivities better than anyone else around?

Religious practitioners of all varieties, in short, carry enormous weight on their shoulders. They must intercede for their congregants with divinities and spirits and other beings who have enormous and fearsome powers. They must find solutions to vexing problems; they must deal with death, illness, catastrophe, misfortune—chaos itself—and if they cannot always restore tranquility and order, they must at least precipitate surcease.

This is surely difficult enough even for those clerics who can spend a lifetime learning how to perform such tasks, who have books to draw upon and superiors to consult. Consider how much more difficult it must be for the part-time clerics who lack hierarchy, literature, and, all too often, even colleagues. It is not surprising, therefore, that anthropologists report from the field that such men and women are frequently among the best and brightest and most thoughtful their communities can afford.

11

Community and Conflict

Sometimes it is directed by a corps of priests, sometimes it is almost completely devoid of any official directing body. But wherever we observe the religious life, we find that it has a definite group as its foundation.

—Émile Durkheim
The Elementary Forms of the Religious Life

Earlier I suggested that there is a tendency in ethnological theory, though not in ethnographic practice, to slight the very real human beings who participate in religious events or who contribute in various ways to the understanding and practice of what religion is in their communities.

In other words we sort of nod, in passing, to Durkheim, acknowledging his observation that religion is both source and expression of *community,* and then we move on to other issues. Let us here instead go back for a moment. Who—what kind of people, with what cross-cultural similarities and differences—make up the community? And since we know (at least ever since Lévi-Strauss pointed it out) that in the midst of community there is always and everywhere opposition, dissension, contradiction, what are the structured forms of conflict to be observed in the religious expression of community?

Even when we do get down to human cases, we tend to focus primarily (as I have been doing) on the clerics, the religious leaders, those who are accepted by their communities as having special or superior knowledge and expertise. But the term *leaders* necessarily implies the existence of followers, for surely a leader without a follower is more than pathetic; he or she is a contradiction in terms.

From the perspective of the personnel of religion, we may reasonably subsume the category of followers under the term *congregation,* that body of persons who observe the actions of the religious leader and support the latter with prayers or other specific responses as the leader directs. *Congregation* is of course congruent with what Durkheim calls the "Church," "whose members are united by the fact that they think in the same way in regard to the sacred world and its relations with the profane world, and by the fact that they translate these common ideas into common practices" (Durkheim [1912] 1965:59). Durkheim does wrestle with the idea of the individual—most particularly as an exemplar of the group totem—but he gives little attention to the implications of actually perceiving "Churches" as communities or as congregations—in other words as varieties of ordered gatherings of people.

What varieties do I have in mind? To begin with I would suggest that the congregation of the priest tends to differ characteristically from that of the shaman. The antonym of *priest* is usually thought to be *layperson*—a term that emphasizes the latter's lack of knowledge and training in religious matters. The full-time cleric has acquired command over a body of religious literature (frequently written in a language different from that spoken by the layperson) and over a complex and intricate system of ritual and prayer. In such a circumstance there is little scope for the layperson beyond that of audience: The members of the congregation observe the activities of the priests and, at the direction of the latter, occasionally contribute to the event in the form of hymns, repetition of prayers, and (if they indeed have sufficient knowledge) responsive readings.

By their presence, then, such a passive congregation provides living members for the category of followers, thus validating the priest's role as leader. In addition, of course, they constitute the "Church"—the expression, according to Durkheim, of the human social organism's sense of oneness, or common identity.

The function of such a congregation can be seen to involve more than mere validation of the *role* of the priest: The existence (or presence) of the congregation also validates the *actions* of the priest, for would anyone expect divinities to attend the prayers and rituals of a lone priest without a congregation? A controversial question, perhaps, but for many religions the answer is clearly in the negative.[1]

The congregation of the shaman, in contrast, may also fully constitute a "Church" in Durkheim's terms, but the participation of such a congregation is rarely as passive as that of the priest. Renato Rosaldo in his detailed analysis of a Zinacantan (highland Maya, of Chiapas, Mexico) cargo ritual, encodes the complex, formal interactions among the participants, who include at least "two ritual advisors, three musicians, and a handful of helpers, the official's close kinsmen and neighbors" (Rosaldo 1968:525). Why so many? Rosaldo observes:

> A cargo-holder's lifelong occupation is corn-farming; he takes on his role as an official when he is an adult, with no previous formal training. Formal instruction for

---

[1] In Orthodox Judaism, for example, a *minyan*, a minimum quorum of ten men, must be present for a full religious service to be conducted; if there are fewer than that, certain prayers and rituals *must* be omitted.

ritual performance begins in the ceremonial center, where old men and musicians, experienced in the cargo ritual, serve as advisors, guiding the officials through their first month or so of service. But they cannot teach everything. . . .

　　Cargo ritual is not autonomous; it exists at once as a system in its own right and as part of a more general system of social action. (Rosaldo 1968:525–526)

In other words ritual conducted by a priest may be "a system in its own right": The priest has years to learn its intricacies. The shaman, however, needs all the help he can get, and so must perforce draw upon the "more general system of social action."

But if the congregation is to participate, they need specific roles. They typically serve as musicians and singers—but not, as at priestly functions, merely to provide a musical backdrop for the activities of the priest. Rather, they are active and integral participants, without whom the ritual cannot take place. Such musicians, in fact, may be perceived as structurally equivalent to Zuñi Shálako dancers. As Edmund Wilson reports, the Shálako dancer is not only impersonating a divinity, but, "It seems as if the dancer by his pounding were really generating energy for the Zuñis; by his discipline, strengthening their fortitude; by his endurance, guaranteeing their permanence. . . . If the Zuñis can still perform the Shálako dances, keeping it up all night . . . they know their honor and their stamina, their favor with the gods, are unimpaired" (Wilson 1956:38). Let us reiterate, however, that in addition to all that, the dancers are also impersonating divinities, indeed serving as vehicles for the divinities themselves. This does not occur in all shamanic ceremonies, of course—such a phenomenon reflects the presence of a belief in the possibility of possession of a human mind by a spirit or divinity. In societies characterized by full-time priests, trance and possession tend (for reasons discussed earlier) to be relatively rare. And where it does occur, quite often it is only the priest (or some special adept) who is likely to undergo possession, whereas in societies (whether "simple" or "complex") in which shamans officiate at religious events, it is much more likely that some or all members of the congregation may also undergo the experience.

The African-derived religions of the Caribbean and South America (Haitian Vodun, Trinidad Shango, Brazilian Candomble, etc.) constitute particularly sharp examples of shamanic congregations. In *Voodoo in Haiti* ([1959] 1972), Alfred Métraux describes in detail the complex relationships among religious leaders (*hungan* [male] and *mambo* [female]), spirits or divinities (*loa*), and congregants (*hunsi*). To begin with, "Voodoo" (or Vodun, as it is more commonly known today) is a religion of the poor: "The greater part of its adherents are recruited among the peasants who form 97 per cent of the population" (Métraux [1959] 1972:58). Such adherents obviously cannot be expected to maintain a priesthood requiring extensive training, and thus:

Most candidates for the priesthood go through a course of instruction lasting several months or even several years with a *hungan* or *mambo* who wishes to take them on. . . .

Some priests say they got their education directly from the spirits. . . . A man who has received his *asson* from the "mysteries" will pretend to be proud of it—in order to conceal a feeling of inferiority, for he who claims supernatural patronage has never had the advantage of a proper training and so tries to say as little as possible about his "knowledge." (Métraux [1959] 1972:68)

Nevertheless, such a person still functions unassailed as a religious officiant, in part because of the absence of any hierarchical control over the officiants:

Although *hungan* and *mambo* are often closely linked with each other, they are by no means part of a properly organized corps. They are the heads of autonomous sects or cult-groups, rather than members of a clerical hierarchy. Certainly the prestige of a *hungan* may spread and affect sanctuaries served by his disciples, but there is no subordination, as such, of one *hungan* to another. . . . A priest only has authority over those who voluntarily offer themselves as servants of the spirits worshipped in his sanctuary. (Métraux [1959] 1972:62)

Such a religious leader, I have argued, both permits and requires the active participation of his congregation. Métraux provides exhaustive details of this participation:[2] The *hunsi* dance, sing, beat drums, "flee" before the possessed *mambo*, and, most significantly, undergo possession themselves.

The *loa*[3] live in "Guinea," "a sort of Valhalla, not situated anywhere," but come to earth when called during a ceremony and "incarnate" themselves by entering the head of an individual and "evicting" one of the two souls of the human (Métraux [1959] 1972:90, 121). A *loa* may thus be summoned by and may possess a *hungan* or *mambo*, but the *loa* may, if it wishes, arbitrarily and even unexpectedly possess any congregant present during the ceremony.

It should be obvious that the complex interplay of belief system, social structure, and clerical role—along with historical factors and much else—must lead to a wide array of possible permutations rather than to simple either-or situations. Thus, for example, popular (or village-level) Hinduism in India and among populations of South Asian extraction[4] exhibits some unusual combinations of elements. The Hindu village "priest" in India, as we saw in Chapter 9, is a male member of a Brahman caste who has inherited his occupation from his father. In northern India, partly as a result of the Muslim conquest, such a cleric receives his training almost entirely from his father alone. He may be said to resemble a shaman in terms of his autonomy: Apart from his father, there is no

---

[2] See, for example, the passage from Métraux's notes on pages 125–126 in his chapter "Possession," as well as his chapter "Ritual" and others.

[3] Métraux translates *loa* as "god" but adds that "'spirit' or better, literally, 'genius', gives a more precise indication of the nature of these supernatural beings" ([1959] 1972:84).

[4] As, for example, in southern and eastern Africa, Fiji, Mauritius, Guyana, and many West Indian islands. My own research has been in Trinidad and Tobago among the people once called East Indians and now known as Indo-Trinidadians.

authority above him with the power to oversee or judge his performance or to deny him the right to practice. Yet he does draw (to a greater or lesser degree, depending upon his command of Sanskrit and his personal proclivities) upon a formal body of religious literature.

But the Brahman "priest" is by no means the only religious officiant in the Indian countryside. For one thing, his own caste rules usually forbid him to provide for the religious needs of castes considered "low" or "impure." These latter groups, who make up a substantial portion of village populations, have of necessity their own religious leaders. Quite frequently there are other religious practitioners who derive from intermediate castes (i.e., non-Brahman but by no means "polluting"). Not uncommonly, these are descendants of men who had reported to their neighbors divine visitations during which, they claimed, they had been instructed to establish shrines and to provide for what Mandelbaum terms "pragmatic" religious needs (Mandelbaum 1964; and see Marriott 1955; Srinivas 1955, 1976; Klass 1978).

All such non-Brahman religious practitioners in the Indian countryside resemble shamans rather than priests. They acquire their livelihoods primarily from other (nonreligious) occupations; they are usually completely autonomous; their knowledge and training derive not at all from written sources; and so on. Most particularly, they almost invariably undergo possession by spirits or divinities while performing their ceremonies.

And as might be expected, the members of the congregations of such clerics are much more participatory: Possession by divinities such as Kali, Mari, and Dharmôraj usually cannot take place without the strong participation of musicians and singers. Nevertheless, only the leader—that is, the adept, the initiated—actually undergoes possession (see, for example, Klass [1961] 1988:173–174, 1978:159–160).

An interesting development has occurred, however, among people of South Asian descent now residing in the South American nation of Guyana, and also among those in Trinidad and Tobago. These communities are derived from nineteenth-century indentured laborers who were brought to replace slaves on the sugar plantations after slavery ended in British possessions. Abysmally poor well into the current century, the Hindu people of these communities maintained as best as they could the village-level religion of their homeland, though even such Brahman clerics as they had among them worked in the sugar fields alongside the members of their congregations. Brahmanical Hinduism, now often administered by full-time Brahman clerics, has continued, but new religious movements have also emerged (Klass 1991a, Vertovec 1992). In the case of one in particular (known regionally as Kali-Mai) the goddess Kali is worshiped with prayer and animal sacrifice. When properly summoned, Kali will possess the officiant or his wife or indeed *any* member of the congregation!

It may well be that the Kali-Mai religion reflects borrowings from Shango or other African-derived religions. It is also possible that under the pressures of life in the West Indies, traditional village-level Indian religious practices moved a few degrees further toward the fully "shamanic" direction.

Possession is of course only one form of interaction between humans and nonhumans; in Joan of Arc's case the issue was not possession but revelation. In some belief systems individuals may also receive visions or undergo other altered states of consciousness. Indeed, it might even be argued that meditation is a form of communication with divinity or at least *otherness*. For any and all of these phenomena, belief systems may differ as to whether only leaders or anyone in the congregation may undergo the experience.

Throughout the foregoing discussion, I have used *congregation* to encompass specifically the body of followers, excluding the leader or officiant. The latter might certainly claim membership in his or her congregation, but I have tried, perhaps artificially, to distinguish the cleric—the person who conducts the event—from those people who compose Durkheim's "Church" or community. For the purposes of analysis, I have termed the latter the congregation: those who, in good standing with the officiant and under the latter's directions, participate in all the ways culturally appropriate in the religious event. This approach enables me to distinguish still a third category of participant: the sinner.

By *sinner* I mean the individual (or, better, the category of individuals—the *role*) who has violated the rules, who is (temporarily or permanently) *not* in good standing with the rest of the congregation. The sinner may be some living person or someone, real or mythical, about whom cautionary tales are told. Depending on the belief system, the sinner may be an object of mockery or ridicule, may be subject to death or heavy physical punishment, or may simply be considered polluted and in need of appropriate purification.

Most interesting about the sinner is the *need* for the category, the intrinsic inevitability of the presence of someone representing it. Not that this is surprising: One cannot have a rule system ("This is the right way; this is good; this is proper") without a category for those who break the rules. One might, for example, similarly say that the *indigent* is an artifact of a monetary economic system; if money did not exist, who could be in debt or be bankrupt? In the same way one of the inevitable artifacts of any belief system is the category of transgressor: If we take this perspective, we may say religion (not the devil, not individual inclination) creates the category of sinner.

To suggest that such a category is inevitable once you have a religion may trouble the member of a religious body, and it also presents problems for the student of religion who assumes, following Durkheim, that religion equals community. It would appear, in fact, that for many in many societies, religion implies and even promotes as much conflict (or at least separation) as it does community.

Nevertheless, we all know that there are in many belief systems categories of individuals (in addition to that of sinner) who are intrinsically *outside* the community. Except in the most isolated and homogeneous societies, for example, there are usually people who—specifically because they are nonbelievers (or "other" believers)—are excluded from membership in the communities in which they live out their lives.

My point is that the traditional focus upon religion as *community* tends to blind us to the extent to which actual belief systems divide actual communities. There are of course studies of conflict between adherents of different religious bodies (Jews and Christians, Catholics and Protestants, Hindus and Muslims, and on and on and on), but certainly the issue that conflict is as intrinsic a dimension of religion as is community deserves more consideration from anthropological theorists than it has yet received.

Victor Turner has pointed a way for us to do that in his writings on liminality, anti-structure, and communitas (1969).[5] He points out, for example, that "liminality implies that the high could not be high unless the low existed" (1969:97) and that he seeks a hypothesis "to account for the attributes of such seemingly diverse phenomena as neophytes in the liminal phase of ritual, subjugated autochthones, small nations, court jesters, holy mendicants, good Samaritans, millenarian movements, 'dharma bums,' matrilaterality in patrilineal systems, patrilaterality in matrilineal systems, and monastic orders. Surely an ill-assorted bunch of social phenomena!" (1969:125) "Ill-assorted" they may be, but they are almost all examples of social and religious conflict, and Turner offers major insights into the varieties of such conflicts. He has explored, for example, the implications of "status reversal rituals" for the restoring of "unity" where there is conflict between the structurally "high" and "low" (1969:177–181), and his contributions to our understanding of the liminal dimensions of pilgrimage are of particular importance for the anthropological study of religion (Turner and Turner 1978).

Clearly, however, there remains much more to be done in what might be termed the "noncommunity" aspects of religion. Monks and nuns may be said, following Turner, to dwell in communitas if not fully in the community, but what of mendicant holy persons, hermits, and other anchorites? It may be possible to demonstrate that they, too, exhibit communitas—but if so, the communitas might be said to be in direct conflict with their fundamental religious objectives and intent.

The itinerant holy man seeking enlightenment by solitary wandering, begging bowl in hand, inevitably calls to mind the participant in the Native American "vision quest." Among the Crow, for example, a young man knew that "to become great, to make sure of success in any of life's critical situations, one must gain the blessing of some supernatural power" (Lowie 1924:3). To do this, he had to leave the community and wander off alone: "The procedure was fairly fixed. A would-be visionary would go to a lonely spot, preferably to the summit of a mountain. Naked except for a breechclout and the buffalo robe to cover him at

---

[5] See, particularly, chapter 3, "Liminality and Communitas," 94–130, and chapter 4, "Communitas: Model and Process," 131–165.

night, he abstained from food and drink for four days or more if necessary, wailing and invoking the spirits" (Lowie 1924:4).

According to Turner, "communitas has an existential quality; it involves the whole man in his relation to other whole men" (1969:127). No doubt an argument can be made for the Crow visionary's "relation to other whole men," but it could also be argued that what is important about his experience—like that of a mendicant holy man—is precisely that it was important to *separate* himself as fully as possible from all other human beings and thus to contemplate the divine as an unattached *individual*. Is this community, or even communitas?

There are further problems. The seeker after a vision may achieve, as the young Crow Lowie referred to hopes, some measure of divine blessing and success, but sometimes the vision may lead to misfortune:

> The berdache . . . or "hermaphrodite" of popular speech was a familiar figure in not a few American Indian tribes. According to all accounts anatomically a genuine male, he nevertheless affected the garb of a woman, mastered feminine accomplishments, in which he often excelled, and indulged in homosexual intercourse. . . . The Omaha believed that berdaches became such as a result of their first puberty quest of a vision. . . . "In such a case he could not help acting the woman, speaking, dressing and working just as Indian women used to do." Miss Fletcher tells of a case in which a man tried to resist the implications of his experience but found the conflict unbearable and committed suicide. (Lowie 1924:243–244)

The berdache phenomenon obviously lends itself to many areas of investigation and interpretation. Some would argue that young men with conscious or unconscious homosexual preferences or desires would be the ones to experience the appropriate validating vision. The unhappy young man referred to in the last citation would no doubt fervently disagree.

Sexual proclivities to one side, it might also be argued that the berdache phenomenon is a response to pressures to conform to difficult, culturally derived gender roles. The only acceptable male role for societies such as the Crow and Omaha was that of warrior. The only available outlet for the young man for whom such a role was a threatening or otherwise uncomfortable prospect was to become a berdache, thereby living out his life as a woman, though not always or necessarily as a homosexual.

Whatever the more accurate, or more acceptable, explanation, the phenomenon of berdache introduces us to still another arena of religious conflict, that between male and female or, perhaps more to the point, between gender roles. The notion of community, after all, as Durkheim has used it, reflects a supposition that the members of the group see themselves as one. Did Durkheim believe that in principle men and women are so united, or was he in fact thinking exclusively of the *males* as constituting the community?

Anthropologists have certainly long known that in many, if not most, societies men and women are in conflict or at least in opposition, and it should not be surprising to find this opposition expressed in the area of religion. A female priest, we observed earlier, is most emphatically not a priestess. In many stratified societies in particular, religious offices are closed to women, and where they are open, as in the case of the classic Hindu *devi-dasi*, the primary role of the woman may only be to provide sexual services for the priests or other men.

Perhaps, then, the true underlying issue addressed in this chapter is whether the scientistic view of religion has impaired our ability to understand the relationship between religion and conflict. A religion, I have argued, is a set of assumptions, beliefs, and related practices about the nature of the universe, the source and nature of death and misfortune, and the techniques for preventing or at least alleviating misfortune. In other words, religion does not *support* the status quo; it *is* the status quo.

Religion may fairly be termed the opiate of the people because it serves to maintain and buttress inequality and even persecution. And at the same time, in exactly the same way, religion supports and fosters change, even massive and revolutionary change.

Religion not only upholds the social structure, but—again, as Durkheim observed—it *is* the social structure, and that means it is both community *and* conflict.

12

On the Other Side of the Forest

Anthropological texts . . . largely focus on the religion of tribal cultures and seem to place undue emphasis on its more exotic aspects. There is invariably a chapter on magic or witchcraft.

—Brian Morris
Anthropological Studies of Religion

The subject of witchcraft has certainly long fascinated anthropologists. They are not alone in this, of course: in societies (including those of Europe) where people believe in the existence of witches and assume witchcraft as an explanation of untoward events, the topic is invariably of endless interest (and concern). People may be reluctant to tell the newly arrived ethnographer who owns which piece of land or who is secretly sleeping with whom, but just ask them why crops have been failing or the young have become so disobedient. . . .

What is somewhat surprising, therefore, is the difficulty we have experienced in delimiting *witchcraft* and defining the *witch*. Is a witch a variety of cleric? Is witchcraft a subdivision of religion, or is it significantly different? Jeffrey Burton Russell, in the *Encyclopedia of Religion,* has proposed that "three quite different phenomena have been called witchcraft. The first is simple sorcery, which is found worldwide in almost every period and every culture. The second is the alleged diabolical witchcraft of late medieval and early modern Europe. The third is the pagan revival of the twentieth century" (Russell 1987:415). I want, in these pages, to examine all three of Russell's phenomena. I am not as sure as is Russell, for example, that the recent "pagan revival" is so conceptually different and distinct from the earlier "alleged diabolical witchcraft," but I am least comfortable with his first category: "simple sorcery."

To begin with, Russell equates witchcraft with sorcery and the witch with the sorcerer. This common equation, harking back at least to James Frazer,[1] presumably reflects an assumption that witches and sorcerers engage in magic, whereas clerics engage in religious practices. For Frazer, Tylor, and other early proponents of social evolution, this distinction between magic and religion of course derives from the belief that magic emerged at some earlier evolutionary stage. At later stages religion appeared and, still later, science. I am not suggesting that Russell's use of the Frazerian dichotomy necessarily implies a belief on his part in such an evolutionary sequence, but I think that he, and any other contemporary scholar who distinguishes witchcraft and sorcery from religion, should be explicit about the basis for the distinctions.

For me, at any rate, *magic* simply refers to techniques employed by those who believe that in specific circumstances persons, powers, beings, or even events are subject to control or coercion. Magic, in other words, is a strategy in religion, as are prayer (which reflects a belief that there are beings in control who cannot be coerced but who can be influenced, moved, or propitiated) and sacrifice (which reflects a belief in beings who will, or at least may, respond to offerings).[2] Given the particular belief system, some clerics will offer prayers, some will perform sacrifices, and others will engage in magic—and some may, at different or appropriate times, do all three. Unquestionably, we do tend to associate witches with magic (or sorcery, if you prefer), but that should not inhibit us from investigating whether in specific cases witches pray or offer sacrifices.

And perhaps most importantly, if we continue to refer to witches as members of some universal category characterized, as Russell has proposed, by the employment of "simple sorcery," we need to know how and why we must distinguish them from other religious practitioners.

The problem is that this melding of so many disparate systems of belief and practice into one "worldwide" phenomenon—the "simple[3] sorcery" subdivision of witchcraft—may inhibit us from exploring not only very different varieties of witchcraft but the implications of the phenomenon itself. Why, for example, do people (in the societies that do) believe in witches? And in the societies that *do* have witches and *do* distinguish them from clerics, what are the bases or sources of this distinction?

Russell addresses this last question, at least in part: He separates "simple sorcery," or "low magic" (and those who perform it), from both "high magic" (prac-

---

[1] Note, for example: "Some people burn their loose hair to save it from falling into the hands of sorcerers. . . . The almost universal dread of witchcraft induces the West African Negroes, the Makolo of South Africa, and the Tahitians to burn or bury their shorn hair" (Frazer [1922] 1958:275).

[2] See Chapter 15 for further discussion of these and certain related issues.

[3] Russell supports the use of the term *simple* with the claim that "simple sorcery . . . is usually practiced by the uneducated and unsophisticated" (1987:415).

ticed by astrologers and alchemists) and "public religion." There are occasions, he observes, when sorcery can be considered part of religion,[4] but for the most part it is malevolent in intent ("bad magic"), "intuitive rather than analytic," and in general "dysfunctional, exacerbating and prolonging social tensions" (Russell 1987:415).

Note, however, that Russell is discussing sorcery (which for him is congruent with witchcraft). He says almost nothing about the actual witch or sorcerer, except tangentially as the performer of the witchcraft. What is there to say? Well, I would begin by raising the question whether witches are to be considered not only human participants in religion but whether they are even considered human at all. Lucy Mair has clearly concluded that witches are, at least in principle, other than human. After assessing attitudes about the nature of the witch in a number of African societies, she observes:

> What I myself would regard as the essential characteristic of a witch, the evil disposition that at least theoretically sets him outside the pale of common humanity, is lacking in the beliefs of the Zande[5] themselves. Many other peoples, including the Nyakyusa, do draw this picture of the witch as the anti-model of approved behaviour. But the Lugbara say that sorcerers—in the sense of people who use medicines—are more evil than witches who use only the emotions of anger and envy. (Mair 1969:22)

Some might want to argue that such talk of people being nonhuman or "outside the pale of common humanity" is simply hyperbole: We may not *like* witches, but we *know* they are human. I disagree: The distinctions made in given societies between those who are entitled to be called human and those individuals who are not entitled are of utmost importance for any understanding of both the social structure and the value system.

In all societies there are individuals—male, female, old, young, that is, "ordinary" humans—who perform the activities and exhibit the roles of what might be termed *basic membership* for a given community. In addition, there are of course usually individuals with special or exceptional roles involving leadership in times of danger (aggression by outsiders, illness, etc.). But even when these latter roles encompass such powers as the ability to commune with invisible beings (the dead, spirits), the individuals exhibiting them are usually perceived as human—at most, perhaps, as some sort of "enhanced" human.

In addition, however, every society recognizes the category of *aliens:* otherwise ordinary humans who are not of *us*—who are not, from our perspective, entitled to the rights we accord to ordinary humans. We may not marry them, and we may feel free to kill them or enslave them, even eat them—even when our rules

---

[4] "When such acts are performed publicly and for the public good, they are as close to religion as they are to magic and are generally considered to have a positive social function" (Russell 1987:416).

[5] Also known as the Azande—a people of southern Sudan, originally studied by E. E. Evans-Pritchard. More about them shortly.

specifically forbid murder, enslavement, and cannibalism. Without compunction, we may rape their women and take their goods, their cattle, their property; we do not manifestly consider them as human as *we* are (see Klass 1983).

However, it should be observed that we frequently also treat as aliens not only strangers but even members of our own society: In complex societies those who exhibit subcultural differences (of religion, dialect, occupation, etc.) and in many societies those who exhibit physical abnormalities and so on.

Most significantly (for this work, of course), we—the basic members of specific societies—thrust into this category of aliens those members who step over the line of permitted behavior: men and women who transgress sexually (prostitutes, unfaithful spouses, homosexuals, child molesters, those who commit incest, etc.), murderers (that is, those who kill humans)—and witches.

The terms, deriving from many languages, that we tend to gloss as *witches* appear to be applied to a wide variety of types of persons in different societies. In some societies witches may be of either sex, in others only of one; in some they are believed to enter into their state intentionally (freely, of their own desire and volition), in others they become witches willy-nilly (they are cursed or taken over by evil spirits, etc.). Whatever the circumstance, what is significant for this discussion is the transference thereby of witches from human in good standing to alien (not fully human, not in good standing).

Russell has noted, we have seen, that many religious officiants—the clerics we label *priests* and *shamans*—engage, with the approval of their society, in the same sort of practices for which witches are expelled or even killed. The priest or shaman may perform a ceremony or petition a nonhuman entity for such purposes as healing the sick, reviving the dead, ending a threat to livestock or crop, visiting misery on enemies, foretelling the future, and so on.

The significant difference is that, on the one hand, the priest or shaman functions as the representative of the community and is understood to be working for the good of the community. The witch, on the other hand—*when doing exactly the same things*—is perceived as a threat to the community: He or she fraternizes with malevolent spirits, serves as a conduit for inimical forces or powers, endangers innocent people, and so on. It would appear, therefore, that for all societies *human* has a clear Durkheimian connotation: someone (or *something?*) who is *of* and *for* the community. It might, for example, be argued that ancestors are as human (perhaps enhanced human?) as shamans, whereas ghosts, like witches, are once-human.

The line between acceptable and nonacceptable religious activity—between acceptable cleric and nonacceptable witch—is not only a fine one; it may have to be drawn through the same individual. In other words, in some societies the same individual may be at times a priest or shaman and at other times a witch or sorcerer, depending upon the nature and purpose of the activity engaged in: Is he, for example, threatening the well-being of an innocent person or only of a malefactor?

Some societies, particularly those that are homogeneous, lacking stratification, may be so structured that the issue is irrelevant; witches are disapproved, whereas clerics have the approval of the group. In other societies (more complex, hetero-geneous, stratified), however, we observe a still further complication: *Some* members of the society disapprove of yet *others* approve of—and indeed traffic with—witches.

In Chapter 9 I pointed out that in some stratified societies priests provide for the religious needs of the higher-ranked and more prosperous segment of the population, whereas the shamans serve the humbler folk. In such cases the priest not uncommonly inveighs against the shaman, calling the latter a witch and de-manding his or her death or expulsion.

In some societies there may even be no true witches present—that is, no one actually practices any form of witchcraft, magic, or sorcery. Even if there are such people, their presence or absence is essentially irrelevant; any individuals who are viewed as aliens may be chosen as scapegoats. This, of course, can happen only in societies in which the belief system reflects an assumption that bad things hap-pen specifically because some person or set of persons is consciously, intention-ally *causing* them to happen.[6]

In anthropology the classic case of such a society is that of the Azande of East Africa, mentioned earlier in the citation from Mair's *Witchcraft.* E. E. Evans-Prit-chard reports that, for the Azande, "witchcraft is ubiquitous"—it is considered the source of *all* misfortune:

> If blight seizes the groundnut crop it is witchcraft; if the bush is vainly scoured for game it is witchcraft; if women laboriously bail water out of a pool and are rewarded by but a few small fish it is witchcraft; . . . if a wife is sulky and unresponsive to her husband it is witchcraft; . . . if, in fact, any failure or misfortune falls upon anyone at any time and in relation to any of the manifold activities of his life it may be due to witchcraft. (Evans-Pritchard 1937:63–64)

If Azande witchcraft is all that, says Evans-Pritchard, then in effect it is a paradox; it is *too* much: "Witches, as Azande conceive them, cannot exist" (1937:63).

All of this leads us inexorably back to Russell and his second category of witch-craft: "the alleged diabolical witchcraft of late medieval and early modern Eu-rope." Who exactly, and what, were the witches of Europe? Were they "simple" antisocial practitioners of magic, or were they shamans providing for the reli-gious needs of those so poor and benighted that they were neglected by the church? Were the witches perhaps members of a religion (or set of religions) that had preceded Christianity and that they were endeavoring to maintain against the

---

[6] There are, of course, many other possible assumptions about the sources of misfortune: angry (or merely whimsical) divinities, the remorseless degeneration of the universe, malevolent (or simply frightened) ghosts, powerful sorcerers working for enemy groups, and so on. And for some, there is always "pure chance."

attacks of the adherents of Christianity?[7] Or were they possibly not involved in religion in *any* significant way but simply different examples of innocent unfortunates, scapegoats who were seized upon and unjustly blamed for plagues and misfortunes?

The historian H. R. Trevor-Roper (1968) has argued that the European "witch-craze" reflected the emergence in European Christianity (most specifically, in Roman Catholicism) of an assumption of a universal, fundamental duality—essentially, a Manichaean belief that what happened in the world derived from the continuing war between good and evil. According to Trevor-Roper, this duality (in earlier centuries, part of the heresies of the Cathars, the Albigensians, and others) ultimately penetrated and transformed the seemingly triumphant orthodoxy and became the source of explanation for all worldly troubles and contention: "The new 'heresy' of witchcraft, as discovered in the old haunts of the Cathari and the Vaudois, rested on the same dualism of God and the Devil; it was credited with the same secret assemblies, the same promiscuous orgies; and it was described, often, by the same names" (Trevor-Roper 1968:184).

For Trevor-Roper, the Greek Orthodox church—and therefore the Slavonic peoples of eastern Europe (apart from the Roman Catholic Poles)—"built up no systematic demonology and launched no witch-craze" (1968:185). In western Europe, in contrast, this belief in duality not only fostered Catholic attacks on a wide variety of what Trevor-Roper terms "social scapegoats" (Jews under the Inquisition, witches everywhere, and nonconformists in general) but, he argues, was taken over by the very *opponents* of Catholicism—the Protestants of the Reformation!

> They might reject the Roman supremacy and go back, for their Church system, to the rudimentary organization of the apostolic age. They might pare away the incrustations of doctrine, the monasticism, the "mechanical devotions," the priest-craft of the "corrupted" medieval Church. But these were superficial disavowals. Beneath their "purified" Church discipline and Church doctrine, the Reformers retained the whole philosophic infrastructure of scholastic Catholicism. (1968:187)

Thus, according to Trevor-Roper, Protestants persecuted witches and other nonconformists not only with the same zeal the Catholics before them had shown, but—since they were imbued with the same belief in duality (the same unending war between good and evil)—they persecuted Catholics in the same way and used the same accusations as when Catholics persecuted Protestants.

There is certainly evidence to support Trevor-Roper's contentions, and I am not here challenging him. I would, however, point to two aspects of his argument that deserve additional consideration:

---

[7] This question, of course, takes us to Russell's third—and in his view distinct—category: "the pagan revival of the twentieth century."

1. his view that this western European belief reflects the penetration of a Manichaean duality first into the Cathar and other early heresies, and then into orthodox Roman Catholicism, and finally into Reformation Protestantism.

2. his conclusion that once this "medieval synthesis" was finally done away with, in the seventeenth century, the "myth" of the witch disappeared with it.

I would urge attention to another possibility: that the supposedly Manichaean belief in duality—attributed to the Cathars, and others—actually reflected a fundamental and long-standing (i.e., pre-Christian) European assumption that an organized malevolent conspiracy composed of real individuals was (and *continues to be*) responsible for major misfortunes, including times of serious anomie. After all, Christians were thrown to the lions because they were believed to have set Rome on fire. Jews were blamed for misfortunes and were accused of killing Christian children and drinking their blood long before the fifteenth century.

What I am suggesting, therefore, is that an assumption—similar to that reported by Evans-Pritchard for the Azande of East Africa—was and is present among western Europeans[8] and their descendants in other parts of the world and that this assumption fosters the belief that there is a terrible conspiracy in existence, dedicated to the destruction of all "we" hold dear. This belief has been reported for various European groups: the Cathars in southern France, the Roman Catholics in their regions, the Calvinists in theirs, the Nazis in Germany, the Puritans in colonial New England, the followers of Senator Joseph McCarthy in the United States at the middle of the twentieth century, and so on.

Trevor-Roper, however, argues that stereotypes such as these latter are different from the "stereotype of the witch" and thus, in effect, do not reflect the same underlying assumption:

> In the mid-seventeenth century . . . the medieval synthesis, which Reformation and Counter-Reformation had artificially prolonged, was at last broken, and through the cracked crust the filthy pool drained away. Thereafter society might persecute its dissidents as Huguenots or as Jews. It might discover a new stereotype, the "Jacobin," the "Red." But the stereotype of the witch had gone. (1968:192)

My point is that the "stereotype of the witch" is only a local manifestation of a pervasive and unchanging assumption: We *know* that our misfortunes are a result of conscious, organized, malevolence; the only problem we have is in pinpointing the malevolent group responsible. They may be witches, Christians, Jews, Cathars, Communists, or whatever. True, the *name* given to the group may vary,

---

[8] What of eastern Europeans? Trevor-Roper's claim that they lack this assumption is certainly open to challenge.

but (and here is where I particularly differ with Trevor-Roper) the *stereotype* remains unchanged.

Those of evil intent—those who plot to destroy us, who want to pollute our way of life—have exhibited the following stereotypical characteristics from the time of Nero to that of Adolf Hitler:

- They meet in secret, in places beyond the boundaries of the culturally normal or proper: in forests, cemeteries, and profaned churches.
- They engage in practices that violate our propriety, such as unrestrained sexual activities and violation of food restrictions (e.g., they drink blood).
- They take pleasure in profaning our religious practices and elements: If, for example, *we* are Roman Catholics, *they* will profane communion wafers.
- Their hidden, but conscious, agenda is to pervert and weaken our way of life and thus ultimately destroy it.

The foregoing are by no means solely my conclusions; Trevor-Roper himself observes, "The inquisitors ascribed to the societies which they opposed at once a more elaborate cosmology and a more debased morality than we have any reason to do. In particular, they ascribed to the Albigensians an absolute dualism between God and the Devil in nature, and orgies of sexual promiscuity—*a charge regularly made by the orthodox against dissenting societies*" (1968:183–184; italics mine). Thus, at various times and in different places, not only were Jews and witches accused of killing babies and ingesting their blood while engaged in orgies, but so were heretical sects such as Cathars and Albigensians, and so were Protestants (in Catholic areas) and Catholics (in Protestant areas). The contention that all Communists believed in "free love" withstood all evidence of Puritan-like morality in the Soviet Union and the People's Republic of China.

Such a stereotype may be viewed as a slot, a position in the social system reflecting the assumptions about the sources of anomie. The witch may be gone, but the stereotype remains, and any group may be assigned it. It is, in fact, a stereotype not just of the nonconformist alone but of any suspected source of anomie: Anyone who is not of us, anyone who is not fully human, any threatening alien.

But there is another explanation of the persecution of witches, one that Trevor-Roper seems to reject. It is that witches were more than merely scapegoats, innocent or not, but were in addition *in fact* members of a secret body, though not necessarily a malevolent one. With this observation, of course, we find ourselves entangled in the third of Russell's categories of witchcraft.

In 1921 Margaret Alice Murray published her ground-breaking book *The Witch-Cult in Western Europe*. In it she argued that witchcraft in Europe was manifested in two forms:

Under Operative Witchcraft I class all charms and spells, whether used by a professed witch or by a professed Christian, whether intended for good or for evil, for killing or curing. Such charms and spells are common to every nation and country and are practiced by the priests and people of every religion. They are part of the common heritage of the human race and are therefore of no practical value in the study of any one particular cult. . . .

Ritual Witchcraft . . . embraces the religious beliefs and rituals of the people known in late medieval times as "witches". The evidence proves that underlying the Christian religion was a cult practiced by many classes of the community, chiefly, however, by the more ignorant or those in the less thickly inhabited parts of the country. It can be traced back to pre-Christian times, and appears to be the ancient religion of Western Europe. (Murray [1921] 1967:11–12)

According to T. M. Luhrmann, Murray's proposal (that witchcraft was in fact all that remained of a pre-Christian, western European religion) inspired one Gerald Gardiner, who claimed that the old religion was still being practiced in secret in Britain and elsewhere and that he himself had been initiated into it (Luhrmann 1989:43, and see Adler 1986). Ultimately, and depending on one's view, a new religion was born or an old one was resuscitated.

In any event, whatever the roots, whatever the truth about the past, there exists today, particularly in Great Britain and the United States, a body of believers who claim to be the spiritual descendants of this ancient religion, which they call Wicca (see Luhrmann 1989, Adler 1986). However, though they consider all witches who were persecuted in earlier centuries to have been martyrs for their faith, contemporary proponents of Wicca do make a distinction between witchcraft for evil purposes ("left-handed," "satanic," "black") and true ("good," "white") Wicca.

This emergence of Wicca therefore poses a number of fascinating questions for anthropologists. Are the practitioners entitled to be called clerics, or do the witches of Wicca belong in the same category with the witches of anthropology, that is, those who engage in *unapproved,* socially condemned practices? Some might argue that whatever their avoidance of "black magic," they do belong in the witch category if indeed the society around them, in the form of the dominant religious bodies, continues to reject them as evil witches. Or, whatever they call themselves or are called, are they clerics when they engage in "white magic" and witches only when they perform "black magic"?

And before we leave the topic of witches, let us note that the witches of the European witch craze may (in addition to any or all of the foregoing) reflect still another and totally different set of issues: the consequences, in western European societies, of neolocality combined with suspicion of women who live alone.[9]

---

[9] See Luhrmann (1989:44–45, footnote 8) for a comprehensive review of proposed explanations for the witchcraft craze. The additional one I offer here derives in large measure from observations Conrad M. Arensberg made in class and in private communications—though unfortunately never in print.

Remember the story of Little Red Riding Hood, who got into such trouble with the wolf when she was crossing the forest to visit her grandmother? The anthropologist (in association with the social worker) must inquire: Why was Grandmother living alone in a cottage on the other side of the forest? Grandfather is obviously either dead or has wandered off, but why isn't Grandmother safe and protected in the home of one of her children?

The answer, of course, is that even in the mythic days of Little Red Riding Hood, much of western Europe (particularly England, Germany, Switzerland) was characterized by neolocality: Newlyweds set up new and separate households. Unlike virilocal (and matrilocal and avunculocal) societies, therefore, there would be no place for the grandparents in the homes of their children. As long as both elder parents were alive, they could be company for each other (Darby and Joan by their fireside; the grandparents in their isolated Swiss cottage in Maeterlink's *Blue Bird*, for example). But women outlive men, and so an old widow becomes Red Riding Hood's grandmother, alone in a tiny cottage on the other side of the forest. She is poor, at least partially dependent on her children, (who send her a basket via her granddaughter), so she probably forages in the forest for nuts and berries and herbs. She is lonely, so she probably has a cat for company. She has probably developed osteoporosis from calcium deficiency, so her back is humped, her teeth are mostly gone, and her nose seems to meet her chin. Do we not detect a similarity between Red Riding Hood's grandmother and the witch of Hansel and Gretel?

If, in a society characterized by neolocality and therefore by a noticeably larger number of widowed old women living alone in poverty, there is in addition an assumption that bad things happen because wicked people consciously cause them to happen, such old women are likely suspects. Don't they, in their loneliness, mutter to themselves or, even worse, to their cats? Will they not, from their foraged herbs, provide simples and cures and, if paid enough, love potions and more suspect philters? If they know how to cure a sick cow, might they not be responsible in the first place for the sickness?

Perhaps, then, there was a pre-Christian religion preserved and followed in later centuries by old women; perhaps Manichaeism came to permeate the ideology of western Europe; and perhaps there were even witches of the classic Evans-Pritchard variety. But it is also likely there were many frightened, impoverished, widowed, lonely old women who went to the stake simply because in a neolocal society they lived alone and were therefore a source of suspicion and fear for their neighbors.

Witchcraft, I would argue, is never "simple" sorcery and indeed is not reducible to three categories of phenomena, at least not the three Russell proposed. Indeed, I would oppose any effort to bound prematurely witches and witchcraft: The subject cries for continued anthropological investigation of varieties to be observed and, most of all, of the implications of the presence of witches in any society.

13

The Incorporeal Dimension

What the peasants understand by nanm *is something very vague and ill-defined. We are entitled to wonder whether the word may not have been adopted by my informants as a subterfuge which always enabled them to give an answer to my questions about the causes of natural phenomena.*

—Alfred Métraux
Voodoo in Haiti

Admittedly, the approaches to the study of religion I have championed do seem to entail a lot of worrying about words and their definitions. Words do have power over us, however, and definitions are even more tyrannical. The Haitian countryman, if we are to accept Métraux's suspicions, was pleased to have a word that provided a categorical answer to the ethnographer's unending queries. Métraux, for his part, found the same word to be an impediment to his research.

Let us therefore begin with a consideration of the term *ghosts.* In their introduction to a section on "the meaning of ghosts and ancestor worship," William Lessa and Evon Vogt observe, "Apparently basic to the institutionalized fear of ghosts is the belief that after death, though the spirit of the individual continues to exist in the afterworld, the basic 'personality' structure of the spirit undergoes a striking change—it becomes malevolent. Regardless of what the person may have been in life, his spirit is potentially dangerous to the living" (Lessa and Vogt 1979:381). This is, if you think about it, a rather surprising formulation. One can easily understand the presence of a belief that whatever remains after the death of a person who has been malevolent during life will continue to exhibit the same kind of behavior. Similarly, we should see no problem with the beliefs of those who argue that the incorporeal dimension of good and responsible people continues to manifest good and responsible behavior after their deaths. But why the belief in many different and unrelated societies that death precipitates a change in the "personality" of the deceased, so that formerly good people become "malevolent"? After all, we never hear the obverse proposed as a belief, that those who were wicked during their lifetimes become benevolent after death.

Lessa and Vogt note, in fact, that this "apparently basic" belief "is not always the case": "In many groups, ghosts may be only partially evil or dangerous, and in still others, they may be conceived of as ever-present members of the social group. . . . Sometimes repressive and harsh, at other times benign and beneficial, the ghosts or ancestral spirits coexist with the living, influencing and even determining the fortunes of the tribal members" (1979:381–382). The problem here, I would argue, results from the confusion precipitated by the absence of terminological clarity. Thus, from Lessa and Vogt's perspective, these are all "spirits of the dead"—whether ghosts or ancestors—sometimes malevolent and sometimes beneficent. All of these, Lessa and Vogt conclude, "are revered though that reverence is possibly never free from feelings of fear and awe" (1979:382).

I suggest that the fundamental issue here is the nature of the role ascribed after death to the "spirits of the dead" in a given society, and thus I insist on the need for different generic terms to distinguish the different types: They are not all simply and indistinguishably *spirits*—nor, for that matter, all *ghosts.*

In fact, they are not even all *souls,* and that certainly presents a problem. In this chapter I want to consider some of the implications and consequences of varying beliefs about an immaterial or incorporeal dimension to the human—the presence of some kind or other of soul, to use the most common term. Unhappily, like so many other of the seemingly basic terms in the anthropological study of religion, *soul* carries an enormous amount of baggage, and I find the term as potentially distorting as I find *ghost* or *spirit* (or as Métraux found the Haitian term *nanm* to be).

Raymond Firth, for example, setting out to explore the different ways human societies deal with the issue of "the fate of the soul," begins with what he hopes is the most basic, the most universally applicable definition of *soul:* "By soul . . . I mean a symbolic extension of the human personality, believed to be responsible for supra-physical activity and for the most part to be capable of survival after physical death" (Firth 1955:8–9). This simple-seeming definition, he immediately realizes, actually encompasses some very distinct and distinctive types, and so in a footnote he proposes the following "distinctions": "*soul* for an immaterial entity which represents the survival personality of the human being both before and after death of the body; . . . *ghost* for the survival personality of the human being after death, in apparitional or manifestational form" (1955:9).

Thus, for Firth, *soul* refers to something ("survival personality," a "symbolic extension of the human personality") existing both before and after death of the physical body, whereas *ghost* is that same something, but (1) only after death and (2) only if it "appears" or in some other way "manifests" itself to the living.

But Firth's definition obscures other important distinctions Firth himself recognizes. Thus, sometimes soul is singular and multiple; in some societies, as

Firth notes, it undergoes a "radical transformation" after death, and in other societies there is no difference in the nature of the soul before and after death. For some societies, he goes on, the soul may precipitate fear or horror in the living (as we observed earlier in the case of the Andamanese); in others "it is looked upon with respect, even affection" (1955:10). With these last, of course, Firth's *soul* has merged with Lessa and Vogt's *ghost*.

We need a better starting point. I suggest we should begin by observing that all this discussion about the term *soul* reflects the presence of a fundamental and widely held assumption: *There is an incorporeal dimension to the living, observable, corporeal entity.*

Once we detect the presence of this assumption in a given society's belief system,[1] we can go on to seek the details of its manifestation in the form of specific beliefs. For example: Are all humans in the given society believed to have such an incorporeal dimension, or is the phenomenon limited to particular social or behavioral categories? Is it limited to humans, or do animals—or all things corporeal or even material—exhibit a similar dimension? Is there more than one type—within an individual or within a human population or within the larger universe? Is it located in some specific part of the corporeal anatomy, or is it free floating? Has it had a previous existence, or does it come into existence uniquely with the birth of its present physical body? Will it exist forever, or can it cease to exist? Can it leave the body before death; can it return; can it enter some other body? Is it conscious, sentient, aware? Does it have volition—are its fields of activity or concern in any way limited or constrained?

We need a term to denote this *something* that is assumed to exist in addition to, but significantly different and separate from, corporeality. The tendency (among those who write in English, of course) is to use the word *soul* as the encompassing term for what I have called the incorporeal dimension. Those who write in other languages understandably feel no compunction about replacing it with the appropriate term of their own language: *âme, Seele, alma,* and so on. But do all these mean exactly the same thing, even deriving as they do from similar cultures and similar (even identical) formal religious systems? And what of terms from more remote cultures and traditions? Is *soul* the same as Sanskrit *atman,* as Hebrew *nefesh,* as Haitian *nanm*?

Spirit is of course a possible generic term, but it, too, raises a number of problems, as Robert Lowie has observed: "Tylor, who gave currency to the term 'animism,' defined it as the belief in spiritual beings, and only in that sense shall it henceforth be used in this book. But what is meant by 'spiritual'? A spirit, accord-

---

[1] Some might argue, and not without reason, that this assumption is in fact universal, that there is no known human society in which it is not present. Nevertheless, unless and until the assumption is demonstrated to be a structural necessity (e.g., that without it no human belief system can be generated), such an argument is really only a statistical observation. In each new field situation, therefore, one must determine the actual presence (or absence) of such an assumption.

ing to the dictionaries, may be identified with any supernatural being" (1924:99). Lowie's primary objection was to Tylor's view that belief in divinities derives (or evolves) from a prior belief in spirits, which in turn derives from a prior belief in ghosts or souls—so that soul, spirit, and divinity all share some intrinsic sequential commonality. My concern, however, is with the implications of his observation that *soul/ghost* is conceptually distinct from *divinity/spirit*. Obviously, *spirit* comes with its own baggage, and raises as many problems as *soul*.

But if neither *soul* nor *spirit* is sufficiently neutral for our definitional needs, what term *can* we use? Traditionally, at least in European scholarship, when we need a term, we draw it from Latin or Greek. The Latin term would be *anima*, the Greek *psyche*. Unhappily, both of these present problems. The Greek word for soul, *psyche*, has been taken over by psychology, psychiatry, and related fields and has come to stand for mind rather than for any form of soul. The Latin term, *anima*, is of course used by the various Christian churches (when the communication is in Latin) and is also the contemporary Italian word for soul. Both terms are therefore burdened[2]—indeed, any term drawn from any normal human language would, as we have seen, be similarly burdened.

In desperation, therefore, I propose to draw the term from an *abnormal* human language—a constructed, artificial one: Esperanto. The advantage Esperanto has over all other languages, in this case at least, is that it lacks a voluminous and pedantic theological literature, a history of contending beliefs, or indeed any tradition of firm religious beliefs and practices. There is a word, a noun—*animo* (pronounced "anímo")—that serves as a translation for any word in any language equivalent to the English word *soul*. I propose, therefore, that we let *animo* be the term that indicates the presence in a given belief system of an assumption that there is (for some or all humans, for some or all living things, for some or all material entities) an incorporeal dimension.

If that is acceptable, I would go on to delineate the following subdivisions or varieties of animo:

Soul: an animo that has no previous or future earthly existence; it is coterminous with a single living, corporeal body. Thus, if the soul existed at all before the birth of the body, it was in some divine vault or part of some divine but noncorporeal being or whatever, but it never experienced any previous life on earth. After the death of its corporeal body, the soul may disappear or remove to some divine existence (heaven or plane or whatever), but it never returns to meld with a living body, human or otherwise. As examples, the various subdivisions of Christian, Muslim, and Jewish belief systems all may be described as assuming the existence of animo as represented by soul in some form.

Atman: an animo that has a previous and/or future earthly existence; in principle it was (or could have been) associated, from birth to death, with an endless

---

[2] In Latin, for example, *anima* (soul) is the feminine of *animus* (mind), at least according to some dictionaries.

series of corporeal entities in the past and will (or could be) in the future. Although the atman is distinct from the corporeal body, there is usually a processual relationship between the two: most commonly, that the experiences undergone during the life of the present body reflect behavior during a previous existence or existences. The term *atman* is therefore appropriate for the varieties of animo to be found in Hinduism, Jainism, Buddhism, and many other belief systems deriving from South Asia—again despite differences in specific local terminology, orthography, or pronunciation (*atma, āttio, jiva,* etc.) and in religious explanations and details.

Ghost: an animo that continues some form of noncorporeal existence on earth after the death of the (usually human) body with which it has been associated in life, thereby affecting the living. It may be invisible (as among the Andamanese) or observable (as Firth notes) as an apparition of some sort. What is most significant about the ghost is that it has its own agenda; it may be good, evil, or neither, but it does not respond to the concerns of the living unless (as in some belief systems) it can be controlled by individuals with special powers.

Ancestor: an animo that continues to exist (somewhere, somehow) as a responsible member of the family to which it belonged and continues to belong after the death of the human body. Unlike a soul (but like a ghost), the ancestor continues, after death, to be involved in the lives and events of the world of humans. Unlike a ghost (but like an atman), an ancestor is concerned with, and usually constrained by, the moral and ethical problems that face the living. A particularly sharp delineation of ancestors is to be found in Meyer Fortes's work on the Tallensi belief system (see Fortes 1981, as well as Fortes 1987), and I have tried above to hew closely to Fortes's own definition:

> An ancestor is a named, dead forebear who has living descendants of a designated genealogical class representing his continued structural relevance. In ancestor worship such an ancestor receives ritual service and tendance directed specifically to him by the proper class of his descendants. Being identified by name means that he is invested with attributes distinctive of a kind of person. (Fortes 1987:68)

The foregoing definitions and distinctions, I hope it is understood, are not set forth as an exercise in terminological niceties. My point is that an ancestor is not a ghost, and a ghost is not a soul, and so on. Still, if my distinctions do not contribute to clarification and understanding, they are a waste of time. I propose, therefore, first to explicate some of the distinctions and then to explore some of the relevant anthropological literature on ghosts and ancestors and such in an effort to see whether my suggested distinctions in fact provide additional illumination.

The ghost has its own agenda—and that it does is, I suggest, unsettling, threatening, and therefore usually viewed as inherently dangerous for the living, whatever the personality of the animo before death.

The ancestor—who continues to be a member of the family, effectively bound by the rules of kinship—must be treated gingerly, respectfully, with reverence. Like any other senior relative (only maybe more so), the ancestor will care for and protect us and punish us only if we transgress against or otherwise offend the ancestor.

The soul moves to another realm: Evil or good, it may be rewarded or punished, repentant or incorrigible—but it is not involved in the fortunes of the living. At most, we might want to offer help (in terms, say, of prayers of support) to the soul of a departed relative, as we would hope our souls would receive after our deaths.

The atman is *not* transported to another realm but is reborn to live another life on earth. The nature of that rebirth, the conditions of the new life, may well reflect some of the consequences, both good and bad, of the atman's previous life and behavior. Thus, it continues to be involved in the affairs of living people, but since they are some *other*—unknown and unrelated—people, the personality of the atman, once separated from its former body, is simply of no concern whatever to its former relatives and friends. Even memorial prayers usually cease after rebirth has been thought to take place.

Is it not clear, given the above, why it is the ghost, and the ghost alone, who precipitates what Lessa and Vogt refer to as an "institutionalized fear"? Consider, for example, the Nyoro ghost, which, according to J.H.M. Beattie "makes itself known to the living by causing them illness or other misfortune, and its agency can only be diagnosed by a diviner . . . whom the victim consults. For the most part ghosts are inimical, but they are not always so, and the ghost of a man's dead father, especially, is thought to retain some concern for the well-being of his sons and his other descendants" (1964a:128). We observe that Beattie, like Lessa and Vogt (who also fused *spirit* and *ghost*), has used *ghost* to encompass *ancestor*. True, he notes at this point that "the Nyoro do not have a highly developed ancestral cult" (apparently, the "ghost of a man's dead father" has reminded him of ancestors, and so he has looked for ancestor worship and could not find it), but he cannot bring himself to distinguish the two types of ghost.

In contrast, John Middleton, reporting on a society *with* a cult of the dead (i.e., one involving propitiation of ancestors), distinguishes two types of ancestors, called *a'bi* and *ori* by the Lugbara of East Africa. All "forebears" or "progenitors," *living and dead*, are referred to as *a'bi*, but some dead progenitors are referred to as *ori* "when individual shrines are placed for them by agnatic or uterine descendants" (Middleton 1987:32–33).

Middleton wrestles with the problem of translation ("I could call *a'bi* 'ancestors' and *ori* 'ancestor spirits'. . . . But I think it better to keep the word spirit to refer to manifestations of divinity," [1960] 1987:34, footnote 2) and finally elects to translate *a'bi* as "ancestor" (alive or dead) and *ori* as "ghost." But in so doing he finds it necessary to note, "This is at variance with common English usage, in which all the dead, or their spirits, are ghosts. In my usage all ghosts are ancestors but not all ancestors are ghosts" ([1960] 1987:34). Thus, in the above citation, we have *ancestor, spirit,* and *ghost,* each used in a way that violates both "common English usage" and very possibly Lugbara understanding as well.

Would it not be simpler to translate *a'bi* as "progenitor" (alive or dead)? It would then become possible to translate *ori* as "ancestor" (a progenitor who is, in Middleton's own words, "an individual ancestor who is in personal *and responsible* contact with living descendants"; [1960] 1987:33; italics mine)—and thus keep *spirit,* as Middleton prefers, for "manifestations of divinity."

Why should we translate *a'bi* as "progenitor"? Does it matter? Well, for one thing, it maintains the Lugbara distinction between, on the one hand, kinsmen, alive or dead, who deserve respect because they are forebears—that is, take precedence because they are senior in birth to ego—and, on the other hand, those dead kinsfolk whose animos are in some form of interaction with their living descendants. Equating *a'bi* with "progenitor" also maintains the Lugbara *lack* of distinction between living and dead forebears: A Lugbara *a'bi* is simply, and no other than, a senior (to me) member of my family. It may be important to Middleton to know whether that senior person is still among the living; it apparently doesn't matter to the Lugbara.

It seems to me that this last observation is of considerable importance for the anthropological study of the belief systems of people who exhibit what is usually termed *ancestor cults.* To begin with, it forces us to recognize that what is for us an awesome distinction—that between the living and the dead—is not in fact a universal one. We cannot, therefore, assume that it is present, nor can we even assume (where it seems to be present) that the contours of the distinction are everywhere the same. In short, we are forced to face up to the ethnocentric dimension of something we thought was so obvious that it *must* be universal.[3]

We are also directed to a reassessment of what we have termed *ancestor cults* or even *ancestor worship.* As Meyer Fortes has pointed out, "In the most general terms . . . the ancestor cult is the transposition to the religious plane of the relationships of parents and children; and that is what I mean by describing it as the ritualization of filial piety" ([1959] 1981:30). This suggestion cries out for more attention than it has received. If "filial piety" is what we are really talking about when we speak of ancestor worship, and if it doesn't matter to those involved whether the recipients are alive or dead, how shall we distinguish the giving of gifts on Mother's Day from propitiation of ancestors—or should we perhaps not bother to? To go a step further, is there really a meaningful "transposition" of kin relationships to some "religious plane," as Fortes suggests, or are we really dealing

---

[3] We have experienced this recognition of our own ethnocentricity elsewhere in anthropology, most frequently in the study of kinship: Is it possible for people customarily to call more than one woman "mother"? Can kinship terminology really ignore generation, so that (as in Crow and Omaha systems) I call people of my parental and grandparental generations by the same terms I use for people of my children's and grandchildren's generations? Happily, students of kinship have learned to avoid ethnocentric assumptions; surely it is time for students of religion to do the same.

with *untransposed* kinship issues that are more complicated (but only for us scientistic observers) in that some of the kin happen to be dead?

Societies exhibiting "ancestor worship" often seem to exhibit dazzling levels of complexity for the anthropological observer. Chinese popular religion is widely credited with a belief in three kinds of souls, but Myron L. Cohen has argued that there is really only one soul: Whether it undergoes reincarnation, becomes a troublesome ghost, or remains a benevolent ancestor depends upon its relationship with the living (Cohen 1988). I think the terminological distinctions I have proposed support his argument. For the Chinese, there may be only one animo to every human, but it may, after death, take one of three forms or even all three seriatim.

Elsewhere (1991a:86–89), I have suggested that it is precisely the *absence* of a clear distinction between *soul* and *atman*—in the form of a prevailing tendency to call them both *soul*—that contributes to the ease with which the claim is accepted in the West that South Asian religions are universal and seek the same ends as Christianity, Judaism, and Islam. Specifically, the claim is made that Hinduism and Buddhism, just like the religions of the West, seek to enable the "soul" to achieve "salvation." Actually, of course, the concern of the South Asian faiths is with helping the atman avoid rebirth, something very different from what is meant by salvation of the soul in the Western faiths.

This absence of precision may aid the missionary, but it surely impedes the anthropologist who would study religion.

14

Divining the Divine

Animism on the one hand, and taboos *on the other, such are the essential factors of religion. To the natural, I might almost say the physiological, action of animism are due the conceptions of those invisible genii with which nature teems, spirits of the sun and of the moon, of the trees and the waters, of thunder and lightning, of mountains and rocks, not to speak of the spirits of the dead, which are souls, and the spirit of spirits, who is God.*

—Salomon Reinach
Orpheus: A History of Religions

Given my last chapter, with its perhaps interminable terminological distinctions, one might think that I would be happy to find such an array of terms for that which is divine: *powers, fetishes, spirits, godlings, deities, divinities, gods,* and *God.* I have no objection to most of those terms, but I admit I am troubled by the definitions attached to them and even more by certain assumptions underlying those definitions.

To put it simply, but I think correctly, most of the terms in current anthropological use for other-than-human participants in religion still reflect unreconstructed, nineteenth-century, unilineal evolutionary notions. As we know, Edward B. Tylor and his contemporaries and immediate successors (Andrew Lang, R. R. Marett, James G. Frazer, Émile Durkheim, W. Robertson Smith, and others) believed that the evolutionary sequence of religious concepts could be deduced from the array of beliefs and practices to be observed among contemporary "primitives." They wrestled with such certain questions: Did *all* religion or just sacrifice derive from totemism? Did belief in nonpersonalized powers precede belief in personalized spirits? Did belief in spirits precede belief in gods, or did the belief in one universal God somehow precede beliefs in multiple spirits and gods?

If those and similar issues interest you, then the terminology still in use will be of service in your deliberations. If you feel, as I do, that those questions are everything from irrelevant to misguided, you might want to join me in my reassessment of the terms.

My concern is not with evolutionary priorities or the nature of intellectual sequence. Rather, I seek approaches that enable me most easily and most accurately to encompass, for a given belief system, views on such matters as who and/or what has created the universe and its component elements, maintained it over time, and is currently responsible for what is transpiring and what will occur. I want to understand the views held on the nature of such entities as are believed to exist: Are they considered to be predictably moral or unpredictably whimsical, or are they motivated by concerns beyond human understanding? Are their responses limited to particular issues (i.e., supply of food animals, illness in humans, natural disasters, etc.), or are their areas of interest more universal in scope? Can they be controlled or cajoled or bribed or moved to compassion?

What we need, for comparative study and analysis, are terms that will help us to understand how given belief systems respond to the above (and similar) questions, and how the belief systems vary and differ. For example, if there is a belief in overarching, even unitary, divinity, is that divinity coterminous with the universe or intrinsically separate? Is it conscious, sentient, or simply present (and thus explanatory) but without volition or agenda? Given all the possible (or recorded) answers to such questions, is the term *God* appropriate for all cases? I have doubts.

In Chapter 4 I argued against defining religion in terms of the supernatural or superhuman. Among other arguments I maintained that such definitions forced us into irremediable ethnocentrism. Now I would go further: The widespread view that God—or the gods or divinity in any form—is and must be of central concern in all religions, is another example of the same pervasive Western ethnocentrism.

The South Asian philosopher Sarvapalli Radhakrishnan was the first to alert us to this ethnocentrism: "For the Jews and the Christians,[1] God is a supreme person who reveals His will to His lawgivers and prophets," but for Hindus and Buddhists,[2] "religion is salvation. It is more a transforming experience than a notion of God" (1939:8, 21; and see Klass 1991a:83–89).

In the religions of South Asia, according to Radhakrishnan, the *primary* focus is on ending the continuous cycle of rebirths of the atman rather than on the existence and desires of some "supreme person." That doesn't mean, of course, that these South Asian faiths completely ignore or, deny the existence of such beings or powers but simply that such phenomena are not the central concern: Salvation is. Before we can delve further into this issue of the nature and signifi-

---

[1] I would add Muslims to this list; I don't understand why Radhakrishnan left them out.

[2] I would urge that Jains be added to this list.

cance of supreme persons in South Asian faiths, we should pause and clarify our terms.

At least in English, there are two terms that seem sufficiently free of connotational baggage for our purposes: *deity* and *divine*. I propose, therefore, that we assign to the category deity the presence of a belief in a personified, sentient, other-than-human entity. In other words, the presence of such a belief implies the assumption that the universe exhibits a divine dimension—though, as we shall see, there are other beliefs that are also reflective of that assumption.

To stay with generally accepted terms, therefore, by all means let us keep *God* as the term for the form of deity found in religions such as Christianity, Judaism, and Islam: personified, sentient, unitary, and separate from the universe. And in the plural and in lowercase, the term *gods* is perfectly acceptable as a representation of the view of the divine in societies that perceive *deity* as multiple but still sentient and personified.

It isn't all that simple, of course: Shall we attribute a belief in God, for example, to those Christian Unitarians and Jewish Reconstructionists who would exclude sentience and volition from any dimension of the divine? I leave the problem to the appropriate theologians (and perhaps anthropologists) concerned.

There are similar problems with the religions deriving from South Asia: Hinduism, Buddhism, and Jainism. Among all these, as we have noted, the primary focus is on ending the continual rebirth of one's atman, but beliefs about deities are to be found in the sectarian subdivisions of all three. The fundamental and shared assumption appears to be a form of pantheism: Divinity and universe are one and inseparable—except when they aren't. Thus, for those devotees at all interested in such questions,[3] there is a divine dimension to the universe: all-pervasive, immaterial, but neither sentient nor personified. Different terms for this are used in the literature: In my own writings (Klass 1991a) I have preferred to call this *Godhood* rather than *God*.

But if South Asian Godhood is not personified, it is, in many South Asian faiths, believed capable of periodically *acquiring* personification: That is, an individual will be born who is believed to be Godhood in human form. For believers, this in no way constitutes contradiction; since humans are part of the universe, and the universe and divinity are in the end one, as a matter of fact *all* humans, it can be (and often is) argued, are in principle divine.

Furthermore, for many devotees of South Asian faiths, the universe also holds an abundance of gods, that is, named, personified deities, some with widespread interests and some with more limited areas of effectiveness. There is much debate among those interested: Some see these as distinct deities in their own rights; others see them as aspects (or manifestations) of the universal Godhood whose pri-

---

[3] Theravada Buddhists take the position, at least officially, that questions about the nature of divinity belong to the category of "questions not tending toward edification."

mary function is to provide more comprehensible foci for the prayers of ordinary people. In many cases (particularly among the sects of Hinduism) these deities are arranged in hierarchies and/or categorized in terms of attributed concerns.

I am giving particular attention to South Asian religions here not only because of my personal interests but also because those religions exhibit such a complexity of beliefs about divinity. Thus, McKim Marriott has championed the term *godling* (meaning, presumably, a junior deity—one lower in the hierarchy— rather than the offspring of a god, as the term might imply for some) for what others, following in Tylor's footsteps, would have called a spirit (Marriott 1955). Marriott's godlings are other-than-human entities, local in their provenience (that is, found only in specific regions of South Asia, not throughout the subcontinent), each believed to have a narrow area of concern: intestinal illnesses, say, or snakebite or pregnancy.

Myself, I would call them gods, noting only that they have more to do with what Mandelbaum (1964) has termed the "pragmatic" dimension (immediate human problems) of religion than his "transcendent" (universe-maintaining) religious dimension. But whether one prefers to call them gods, godlings, spirits, or whatever, what is important—for me and I suspect for Marriott and Mandelbaum as well—is not the determination of their position on some continuum of developing theological perception; rather, it is the clear delineation of their role or roles in the particular community's religious universe.

To inquire into roles of deities is, inevitably, to raise the issue of whether morality is an attribute (or even a concern) of divinity. There are a number of possibilities, as the ethnographic record indicates. The Apa Tanis of the eastern Himalayas, for example, are reported to restrict morality to the human social sphere:

> Apa Tanis imagine the world peopled with Hilo deities, and that according to the nature of a disease or affliction the one or other Hilo deity is thought responsible and duly propitiated. . . . The gods Ui-Kasang and Nia-Kasang are associated with war, and before going on a raid Apa Tanis pray to these deities to give them strength and courage, and afford them protection in the fighting. . . . I can recall no other allusion to morality in connection with their beliefs in the after-life than a priest's brief statement that in the Land of the Dead good people will be good again and bad people bad.
>
> This does not mean that Apa Tanis lack any sense of moral values. . . . To attain one's end by peaceful means is considered preferable and more laudable than to resort to violence. . . . And it is the support of public opinion in the moral judgement on criminals which enables the *buliang* [council] to take punitive action against habitual offenders. (Fürer-Haimendorf 1962:135, 136, 148)

In Hinduism and the other religions of South Asia, morality is an attribute of the divine but not necessarily of deities. There is believed to be a law of the universe—the law of karma—that imposes an immutable cosmic response on all human behavior: "Bad" behavior in this lifetime will precipitate punishment in the next, whereas "good" behavior will precipitate reward. Yet Hindu gods (particularly in village-level belief systems) behave like Apa Tani gods, rewarding those who propitiate them and punishing those who don't, with little attention to the rights and wrongs of human disputes (Klass 1978:133 et passim).

Among the Tallensi of West Africa, the relationship between morality and divinity is similar to that found among the Apa Tanis, but there are significant differences:

> In this special relationship of a man with his Destiny ancestors (as in his relationships with all his ancestors) morality in the sense of righteous conduct does not count. All that matters is service and obedience. A man who is wicked by Tale standards may flourish while his virtuous brother is a failure. . . . One lives according to one's mundane lights, guided by the jural and moral sanctions of society, knowing that the ancestors dispense justice by their own standards. . . . (Fortes [1959] 1981:51, 53)

This sounds like Apa Tani beliefs, but the presence of ancestors in the belief system changes the equation, for unlike Apa Tani deities, Tale[4] ancestors *are* concerned about morality. It is the *living* Tallensi for whom the issue of "righteous conduct does not count": "For the ancestors are not considered to be wholly indifferent to moral values. On the contrary, they are the jealous guardians of the highest moral values, that is to say, the axiomatic values from which all ideal conduct is deemed to flow" and "in the last resort whatever the ancestors decree is just" (Fortes [1959] 1981:53, 64).

The title of the monograph I have been citing is *Oedipus and Job in West African Religion,* and in it Fortes is particularly interested in exploring the intricate manifestations, in Tale beliefs, of what he calls "two fundamental principles of religious thought and custom": "The Oedipal principle is best summed up in the notion of Fate or Destiny, the Jobian principle in that of Supernatural Justice" ([1959] 1981:11). The distinction, as Fortes demonstrates, turns on the specific issue of whether there is a divine entity who is in effect "bound" to reward righteous conduct. If there is, Fortes argues, "It is almost a contractual relationship, in which God is bound to act justly and mercifully, and man is free to choose between righteousness and sin. There is a known code of righteous conduct, and a man who has consistently followed the way of righteousness is entitled to wellbeing, peace of mind, happiness, and even material prosperity as a gift from the Supreme Ruler of the universe" ([1959] 1981:16).

In Judaism, then, as in Christianity and Islam, the actions of God are not—can never be—immoral or even whimsical: The devotee (such as Job) may not be able to understand the reason but knows that there *is* in fact a reason for everything that happens and that it is a moral reason. The difficulty that permeates not only the Book of Job but much of Western theology lies in trying to understand why and how—if God is all-powerful and totally moral—there should be evil in the universe.

---

[4] *Tale* is the adjectival form of *Tallensi.*

Still, the discovery that for some people God (or the gods) lacks morality is of course shocking for those raised in one of the Western religions, and when they encounter such a view, they may interpret it as evidence that their own faith is of a higher order. On their side, devotees of faiths that do *not* ascribe morality to the sphere of the divine might well retort that to do so is actually to anthropomorphize deities, for from the perspectives of such faiths, morality is a *human* attribute.

This last observation raises another set of questions for us on the subject of different views about the nature of the divine: In a given belief system, is it thought that deities resemble humans in any significant way or ways? What attributes are thought to be shared by both? What is thought to be characteristic of all humans but not of gods—and vice versa?

For example, a contemporary burning issue for many Jews and Christians is whether God is male, female, both, or neither. This can be a troubling question only among people for whom there is and can be only *one* deity; for those who believe in many deities, all four possibilities may be present in the pantheon.

But what does it mean when one says that God is male (or female)? For the ancient Romans, H. J. Rose tells us,

> The name of the deity was generally (not always, at least originally) of either masculine or feminine gender, and this was a useful guide in such matters as determining the sex of the victim to be offered. . . . It was no business of [the Romans] what their deities looked like, how they passed their time when not listening to their worshippers and attending to their wants, or punishing their offences, whether they were in any real sense male and female, and so forth. (Rose 1959:xi)

Rose contrasts Roman attitudes with those of the ancient Greeks, for whom the gods were "clear-cut figures" with "likes and dislikes, loves and hates" (1959:ix). In the case of the Greek religion, however, one might argue that maleness clearly implied an interest in having sexual intercourse with female humans as well as with female deities, and as a consequence the fathering of children who exhibited various degrees of divine nature. Zeus, Poseidon, and Apollo were particularly known for their sexual adventures with human females, but other male deities were credited with similar exploits.

Most female deities, though, were believed to confine their sexual activities and exploits to the sphere of the divine. Goddesses such as Hera and Aphrodite were said to be concerned with or to preside over sexual activity, marriage, and childbirth. It was believed that they married or had affairs with male *deities* (and thus had children by them). Compared to the adventures ascribed to male deities, allegations of female deities' having sexual relations with humans were much less frequent. Does this perhaps reflect an assumption of a divine correspondence with some human social rule such as that of the female's marrying "up" and the male's marrying "down"?

The contemporary belief system known as Wicca exhibits considerable interest in the issue of the gender of divinities. In Wiccan belief there are both male as well as female deities, but the female is usually accorded first place or major significance: "In our culture which has for so long denied and denigrated the feminine as negative, evil or, at best, small and unimportant, women (and men, too) will never understand their own creative strength and divine nature until they embrace the creative feminine, the source of inspiration, the Goddess within" (Adler 1986:ix). The followers of Wicca (or "the craft") may or may not include sexual activity among their religious rituals (there is much variation from group to group), but "the creative feminine" referred to above—"the Goddess within"—seems more to imply the *maternal,* as opposed to the *sexual,* dimension of divine femininity. Thus, Adler quotes a devotee as saying, "I relate to the Goddess every day, in one way or another. I have a little chitchat with Mommy"[5] (Adler 1986:105, and see Luhrmann 1989:46–47).

Is the Goddess of Wicca a "Mother Goddess" then? The appellation almost invariably creeps into any anthropological or other religious discussion of female deities. H. R. Ellis Davidson titles her subchapter on Scandinavian goddesses such as Frija, Frigg, and Fjorgyn "The Mother Goddess" (1964:110), and James Preston's cross-cultural study of female divinities goes under the title *Mother Worship.* Preston is aware of the distinction:

> This book is concerned with a wide variety of manifestations of female sacred images. It is recognized that not all female deities are primarily mother figures. Nevertheless, a survey of the literature on the topic reveals that even the most nonnurturant goddesses are considered "mother deities" by their devotees, because the term "mother" stands for more than simple nurturance. (Preston 1982:xi)

Yes, *mother* unquestionably implies "more than simple nurturance," and Kali and Mari in India are indeed called "mother" by their devotees. Nevertheless, I would argue that to encompass female deities (and other female divine entities) as different as Frigg and Hecate and Hera and Mari and Rangda and Brigid and Diana and the Virgin of Guadelupe under one heading—and that one *mother*—is both unnecessary and unwise.

It is unnecessary because category headings such as "worship of the feminine" or even "female deities" would be adequate and more accurate. And it is unwise because it seriously blurs important differences. Despite their conversion to Roman Catholicism, the indenture-derived people of South Asian descent living in the French Caribbean island of Martinique at midcentury continued to sacrifice sheep to *Mari-Amma* ("Mother Mari"), the south Indian female deity who is both source of and protector against smallpox and similar ills. They insisted they

---

[5] This familiarity may seem startling, but probably only to speakers of languages, such as English, without familiar pronouns and other forms of address used for intimate relationships. And that raises the question why deities *should* be addressed with pronouns and other terms (such as the above "Mommy") otherwise reserved for intimacy. How common is the practice? Has anyone looked to see?

were still good Christians, however, because *Maṛi-Amma* was in truth indistinguishable from *Marie-aimée,* Mother of God (Horowitz and Klass 1961): The names, they said, sounded alike precisely because they referred to the same divine person. It is true that both are viewed as divine mothers, but I submit that that is all they really have in common (apart from similar-sounding names); the differences are surely much more interesting.

Female deities may hold sway, as we have observed, over the hearth and childbirth. They may be thought to be the source of fertility in humans, animals, and plants, or they may be, as in the case of Maṛi and other South Asian "Mother Goddesses," apportioners of illness, snakebite, death in war, and other such misfortunes. To lump the latter with the former is not only dubious categorizing; it makes it difficult to know how then to treat the South Asian *male* deities such as Shiva and Krishna, who the same devotees believe preside over fertility.

It is not only bad anthropology; I suggest it can lead to bad archeology, as exemplified by those who would label every clay figurine that is remotely female in appearance a mother goddess. Might not some of them be memorial representations of deceased female relatives—or even just *dolls?*

There are of course human attributes other than gender that can be, and are, assigned to deities. These include but are by no means limited to anger, hate, physical injury (Hephaistos, for example, was lame), affection, remorse, vanity, and greed. Some deities have attributes of animals as well as of humans, exhibiting these either in their appearance or in their actions and interests. Very commonly, if not indeed universally, deities exhibit *hunger:* They must be fed. Their food may be exactly what people eat or simply a better (rarer or more expensive) variety of it, or they have a taste for what is forbidden to humans, including human flesh itself.

With this observation, however, we move to another topic: how one influences or even controls deities (or whoever or whatever affects all that happens). The topic is surely an important one and therefore deserves a chapter of its own.

15

Into the Land of Moriah

Take now thy son, thine only son Isaac, whom thou lovest, and get thee into the land of Moriah; and offer him there for a burnt offering upon one of the mountains which I will tell thee of.

—God
Genesis 22:2

Human sacrifice, however rare in practice, is always startling enough to draw our full attention. We will address it later in this chapter, along with similar subjects, but the underlying issue of the chapter is really the human desire to influence or control deities and events or, at minimum, to find out what is happening or about to happen. Earlier I proposed that this concern for whatever degree of control over events people perceive as possible is a crucial dimension of religion in any society. At issue, of course, is what they perceive as possible: Although the concern is universal, the perceptions of the possibility of control are many and varied.

The first question is whether anyone at all—that is, anyone sentient, anyone (or anything) capable of being influenced or coerced—is in fact in control of events. There are indeed other possibilities: The universe may manifest only non-sentient forces and/or the operation of inexorable laws. Some early anthropological subscribers to theories of unilineal evolution viewed such assumptions about the nature of the universe to be the most primitive; they constituted the phenomenon of animatism, which preceded animism (belief in spirits and other entities) in the evolution of human understanding.[1] First came animatism, the argument

---

[1] The difference of opinion was mostly between E. B. Tylor, who introduced the notion of animism as the earliest manifestation of religion ([1871] 1970), and R. R. Marett, who championed the priority of animatism (1909).

ran, followed by simple animism, then evolving religious perceptions fostered beliefs in gods, then in one all-encompassing God—until, finally, at least among civilized Europeans, religion was replaced by science.

Some might consider this a rather curious evolutionary sequence, since it actually constitutes a closed cycle: At the end, as at the beginning, the assumption is that the universe is composed of nonsentient forces (such as gravity) and laws (such as those of thermodynamics). The difference, of course, is that the scholars know that there is no such thing as mana whereas there is unquestionably such a thing as entropy.

If, however, we table the issue of which forces and laws exist and which don't, we can see certain striking similarities in the way people approach the problems of dealing with nonsentient, inexorable forces and laws. In societies that believe in such forces and laws, coercion and bribery, for example, are likely to be viewed as a waste of time. Rather, one must study the forces, learning their complexities and boundaries. Most of all, one must seek to determine whether it is ever possible to evade, channel or somehow gain control (or take advantage) of the forces, and, if so, under what conditions.

In Hinduism and Buddhism, for example, the law of karma (do evil in this life and you will be punished in the next) cannot be repealed or evaded, but one can strive so to live that the law of karma will bring only good in the incarnation to come.[2] Similarly, the laws of aerodynamics of the scientific belief system preclude the possibility of a person's constructing wings and flapping successfully into the sky. But know those laws and you can build heavier-than-air machines that will not only fly but that can even break the bonds of the planet's gravity.

The prime question, therefore (in societies characterized by such assumptions and derivative beliefs) is how most effectively to learn about the laws and forces that make up the universe. Introspection is probably the most common technique: essentially, one sits and ponders—one meditates. It isn't as easy as that, of course; one must be trained, must learn all that was discovered by those who went before. Deduction and induction are not unknown outside the boundaries of European philosophy: Neither the knowledge of syllogism nor the practice of experimentation came into existence only with the emergence of the modern scientific method. Still, like introspection, they do require training and study.

And sometimes, of course, nothing can be done: No one, we have been assured, is ever going to exceed the speed of light; no one, it is universally agreed, ultimately avoids death. Such knowledge does not foreclose speculation: What would happen to people who could not die? Would they be as miserable as Jonathan Swift's Struldbrugs? Would they shrivel away like the Sibyl of Cumae?

---

[2] Two fine collections of papers on the subject of karma are Ronald W. Neufeldt, ed., *Karma and Rebirth: Post Classical Developments* (Albany: State University of New York Press, 1986), and Charles F. Keyes and E. Valentine Daniel, eds., *Karma: An Anthropological Inquiry* (Berkeley: University of California Press, 1983).

Science-fiction writers have wrestled for decades with Einstein's dictum about the limitations on speed: What would happen to people who attained the speed of light, who tried to go faster? Can we somehow evade this restriction and travel through hyperspace or through wormholes in the fabric of the universe? We can speculate, or (depending on our temperament) we can accept with dignity the limits we perceive in what is possible to affect or change.

In all societies, however, there are some things humans *can* affect or change. For adherents of many belief systems, this is so because sentient entities are in control. The entities may be human, like witches and like the Yanomamö sorcerers who cause illness and death, or they may be once-human, like the ancestors of the Tallensi. Or they may be nonhuman deities who range in type from those narrowly concerned only about such things as who may cross a specific river safely all the way to a transcendent, solitary God with a master plan for the entire universe and everyone in it.

The question *then* becomes, How do we get the entity in control (sorcerer, ancestor, witch, god, or whatever) to manipulate events the way *we* would like?

Sorcerers and witches are among us; we must seek them out wherever they are, in our community or in some neighboring one, and overcome them with more powerful varieties of the same techniques they use. A Santal *ojha* (healer) once explained to me that illnesses ultimately are caused by witches:

> There are many men, he notes . . . with knowledge of how to combat the work of dainis [witches]. But [witches] vary in their power, and not all men can counteract the most powerful. He is, he says, one of the strongest ojhas in the district, although he has come into conflict with dainis stronger than himself. He has had, in other words, patients he could not cure, and has had to send them on to even more powerful ojhas. (Klass 1978:144)

Sorcerers and witches, however powerful, are in the end human, and though the battle may be touch-and-go at times, they can usually be defeated or controlled by other humans. The techniques for such efforts of control are usually subsumed under the headings of magic or ritual, along with the essentially similar techniques in use for controlling or coercing nonhuman entities. Suppose, however, it is assumed that the entities involved are too powerful for humans to control or coerce. What can we do when the powers running the universe are stronger than we can ever hope to be?

Both deduction and induction become weak reeds when gods can perform miracles; the most meticulous efforts at rigorous attention to detail in either a scientific experiment or a magic ritual can be vitiated at the whim of an all-powerful deity. A South Asian doctor who had received his medical training in Europe had no problem believing that Sathya Sai Baba (a south Indian holy man who claimed to be God incarnate) had once brought back to life a man who had been dead for four days: "God can do anything," he told me (Klass 1991b). And so God can—up to creating the universe with everything in it, including all your

memories, only five minutes ago. Where such a belief is present, theological studies are manifestly more important and more interesting than the study of history,
biology, geology, and astronomy put together.

In such a belief system, then, the questions to ask include: Why is the powerful
entity who is beyond our control (deity, ancestor, etc.) doing this to us? Have we
in some way, even inadvertently, angered the entity? Is there something he/she/it
wants from us? Is the entity open to gifts or bribes? Whom among us will it listen
to—what rules must be observed in attempting to establish communication?

To begin with, it does seem to be universally assumed, at least as far as I can
determine, that such powerful beings do indeed desire—or under the proper circumstances will accept—something from us. And we further assume that in return they will at least consider our petitions:

> In July of 1963 the six-year-old son of Nirmal Bauri . . . developed diarrhea and other
> signs of severe intestinal illness. He ran to Brahman para, fearing his son was dying,
> and . . . as instructed, recited the following manśik, or promise: . . . O, Mother, save
> my child and I shall give to you one lopped-head and sixteen annas. . . .
>
> The "sixteen annas" (one rupee) went to [the Brahman administrator of the
> shrine of Rôkkhô-Kali, who] also provided Nirmal with powder derived from a
> dried plant. . . . Nirmal returned home, administered the powder as directed, and
> the child recovered. The young Bauri then saved his money for months, eventually
> purchasing a young ram goat for twelve rupees (a figure he recites with pride and
> awe) in fulfillment of his manśik. (Klass 1978:152)

Nirmal offered the goat as a sacrifice at the shrine dedicated to the deity Rôkkhô-
Kali, a goddess who determines who suffers and how severely from intestinal illness. The Brahman administrator performed the sacrifice, decapitating the goat.
Rôkkhô-Kali received the life of the goat, the Brahman received the head (which
he sold to a butcher since he was a vegetarian), and Nirmal Bauri received back
the rest of the goat, with which he made a feast for his entire Bauri neighborhood
(Klass 1978:152).

No one could promise that the goddess would or definitely must heed the
prayer of the young father but soon all were convinced that she had heard it and
had been moved to respond to it, for the child did in fact recover. Such a divinity,
in other words, can never be coerced into any action but can sometimes—if one
is fortunate and if one offers enough—be charmed, bribed, or otherwise influenced into an action favorable to the human petitioner.

Prayer, let us therefore observe, means different things in different belief systems. In the theistic religions deriving from Southwest Asia (Judaism, Christianity, and Islam) the prayer most generally approved by religious leaders is one that
simply petitions the deity to help one become a better, more moral person. This
may in addition imply or specifically state a willingness to submit without challenge or reservation to whatever the deity has in store for the supplicant. The
unstated hope is that though one asks for nothing, God will be pleased by

the submission and the promise to be good and will bless the supplicant with unasked-for (but deeply desired) good fortune.

However, even devotees of these religions (with or without official sanction) quite often pray for divine aid in time of trouble, promising offerings in the event that their prayers are rewarded. The questions whether prayers may properly be petitions for assistance in times of travail[3] and whether even the offering should ideally be given freely are debated by theologians of those faiths, if not always by laypersons.

For the people of the village in West Bengal where the event described above took place, however, prayer is clearly understood to be a petition for divine assistance in a time of danger or potential disaster—a petition in the form of a plea coupled with the promise of appropriate remuneration if (and *only* if) the petition receives a favorable response. Missing entirely from the Bengali *mansik* is any moral dimension: The petitioner does not promise to be good in the future, nor does he necessarily assume that the misfortune (his child's illness) is the result of some improper action on his part or on the part of some member of his family. Rather, both he and the Brahman believe that whatever the ultimate cause of the illness, if in fact there is an ultimate cause,[4] the deity responded favorably because a proper gift (a payment, really) was specifically promised.

What kinds of things, then, do all-powerful, noncoercible entities want? Some may, as we have seen, desire submission on the part of the petitioner: an acknowledgment of the petitionee's superior power, superior righteousness, and/or superior judgment. The ancestors of the Tallensi, for example, want their living descendants to show proper respect; this may include offerings, but it is the respect of familial juniors for familial seniors that is of paramount importance.

But some want painfully more than that. Nur Yalman begins his paper "The Ascetic Buddhist Monks of Ceylon" with the observation, "*Tapas,* the mortification of the flesh, has always held considerable fascination for religiously inclined people everywhere. Asceticism, the attempt to break the link with the world of men, is one of the approaches to the world of the deities" (Yalman 1962:315). "Mortification of the flesh"—like human sacrifice—has indeed "held considerable fascination" and not only for the religiously inclined. A great deal of Frazer's *Golden Bough* is devoted to the subject, for example. One danger of such fascination, however, is that all (or too many) examples of mortification, asceticism,

---

[3] What, after all, is the true significance of the saying that there are no atheists in foxholes? Is God truly pleased with the desperate submissions of the terrified, those in the last extremities? How will God respond to the forcibly converted or to those who pray as the missionaries wish only in order to get food for starving children?

[4] If questioned, the father might speculate that he had in some way offended a *bhut* (ghost) or a witch. The Brahman might raise the issue of the father's (or the son's) karma. However, when the goddess responds favorably, as in this case, no one really cares: There was potential catastrophe, for whatever reason, and the goddess, properly petitioned, decided to avert it (see Klass 1978:182–189 and Mandelbaum 1964 for further discussion of this and related issues).

and bodily mutilation may be lumped together when in fact they may represent very different phenomena. Thus, for Frazer, the practice of circumcision and the practice of cutting off a finger during mourning could be considered together simply as examples of religious bodily mutilation. The study of society and of culture has made strides since Frazer's time, and today most anthropologists would certainly argue that circumcision, like subincision and cliterodectomy and foot binding and tooth filing, can more meaningfully be approached as a phenomenon of social structure rather than of religion.

In contrast, mourning rites, including cutting or shaving hair, tearing clothes, breaking bracelets, and mutilating of the body, certainly have a much stronger religious dimension, and bodily mutilation here must be seen as something quite different from conformation to rules for presentation of self or for becoming a gender-specific acceptable member of one's community. When in so many societies the grief-stricken mutilate themselves, rend garments and destroy ornaments, and so on, they are ceremonially expressing despair. Life, the mourner announces, has lost its meaning and savor: I relinquish all that has given me pleasure; I seek pain and even death.

And there is a third and very different reason for acts of mutilation. Consider the Crow Indian Lowie described, who would "hack off a finger joint of the left hand" before going on a vision quest. This had nothing to do with either rites of passage or the expression of despair. He performed the mutilation "as an offering to the supernatural beings" (Lowie 1924:4). The mutilation may be physically identical to that which occurs in the mourning rite; its purpose and meaning are very different—it is, like asceticism, an offering intended to draw the attention and approval of deities as one sets out to establish communication with them.

As one is "attempting to devise means of approaching the threshold between men and gods . . . the flesh ties one down to this side of the threshold (like all other worldly interests). The approach to the 'threshold' . . . requires at least a subordination of the flesh, but the crossing of the doorway must probably be paid for more painfully" (Yalman 1962:315). This underlying assumption—that communication with noncoercible deities requires an initial offering in the form of physical pain to oneself or "at least a subordination of the flesh" (i.e., asceticism)—is of course very widely held, as Yalman observes: "It is remarkable how the problems confronting *all* those groping toward the deity, or deities, are similar in essence. The many ascetic orders of Christian monks, the Trappists, the Whirling Dervishes of Islam, and the ascetic hermits and wanderers of India and Ceylon, with all the varieties of doctrinal difference between them . . ." (1962:315; italics mine). I italicized Yalman's *all* in the preceding citation because it is the only part of his observation with which I disagree. I wish he had used *many* or even *most*: The assumption is indeed widespread (shared by the Crow, as we have seen, and by many other peoples, as could easily be demonstrated), but it is definitely not universal. It is even possible in particular cases that the presence of the assumption that asceticism—at least in the form of males' sexual abstinence—is a prerequisite for "approaching the threshold" of the divine reflects not only an offering requirement but also a belief that contact with women (and especially cohabitation) precipitates pollution, a ritual uncleanness that is apparently offensive to fastidious deities.

The interplay of such assumptions can be quite complex and therefore can never be taken for granted. As Yalman observes, the whirling dervishes of Islam mortified their flesh, and there are many other examples of both mortification and asceticism in Muslim societies. Nevertheless, Mohammed was married and presumably periodically engaging in sex when he received his revelations. Some divisions of Christianity permit religious leaders to marry and engage in sex; others do not. It is not entirely clear that fear of female pollution is as much a factor in Christian religious asceticism as is the assumption that communication with divinity requires relinquishment of all pleasures of the flesh.

In traditional Judaism, in contrast, there is a clearly present belief in pollution precipitated by sexual activity, but there is also a sharp rejection of asceticism as a necessary prerequisite for communication with divinity. Thus, "When having intercourse one should think of matters of the Torah or any holy subject, and although it is forbidden to utter the words with the mouth, yet thinking is permissible, even meritorious, for as far as this is concerned thinking is not considered as utterances" (Ganzfried 1927:CL, 14). The *Code of Jewish Law* (*Kitzur Schulchan Aruch*) goes on to remind men of their "marital duty" to their wives ("And her duty of marriage shall he not diminish"). Limitations on sexual activity may be precipitated by obligations of occupation, such as travel (i.e., "Those who convey baggage on camels from distant places, should have an appointed time once in thirty days"), but barring such impediments it is a man's obligation to have sex as frequently as he can. And (particularly significant for this discussion), "The time appointed for the learned men [i.e., rabbis and other religious leaders] is from Sabbath Eve to Sabbath Eve," in other words, on any and every day in the week (Ganzfried 1927:CL, 15).

With this, let us return finally to the land of Moriah and the issue of human sacrifice. I have been arguing that (1) it is commonly assumed that noncoercible deities will respond favorably to offerings; (2) to that end people offer whatever they believe will please the deities; and (3) these offerings include promises of good behavior, respect, valuable goods, parts of one's body, and the life of an animal or even a human.

The account of Abraham's attempted sacrifice of his son is one of the most emotionally charged passages in the Bible, one that has drawn the attention of uncountable Jewish, Christian, and Muslim theologians. Discussion usually focuses, at least to begin with, on two derivative conclusions: There is a divine interdiction against human sacrifice, and there is a certainty that submission to the deity's commands will and can lead only to good fortune and never to the performance of immoral acts. Certain other implications contained in the account receive much less attention from the theologians: Why should Abraham have believed for a moment that God wanted a human sacrifice? Why did God in fact accept as a substitute for a human life the life of a ram?

Although religious leaders of all three of what are sometimes called the Abrahamic religions currently express discomfort with, even disapproval of, animal sacrifice, the practice continues to occur among fringe groups of all three. Certainly—and perhaps understandably, given the specificity of the account of Abraham, Isaac, and the ram—few voices if any are raised among the most orthodox to say that even the biblical practice of animal sacrifice deserves condemnation: The fact is indisputable that God once clearly savored the odor of burnt offerings. The best we can say, therefore, is that for the present other offerings are accepted, even preferred. It is surely understandable that some Jews, Christians, and Muslims prefer to stay with the original offering.

If the notion that the deity wants—or ever wanted—the sacrifice of a living thing is an uncomfortable one for some modern Western theologians, it appears to have blown the minds of nonreligious students of religion. It is surely astonishing that so widespread a practice (the sacrifice of animals), pervasive in the ethnographic accounts, has received such minimal attention in the ethnological literature.

One result of this inattention, perhaps, has been the distortion whereby one subdivision of the practice of sacrifice—that of human sacrifice—has received considerable attention from anthropological theorists. The debate, still ongoing, revolves particularly about the question of whether human sacrifice has an ecological base: Was Aztec human sacrifice (the most commonly discussed case) simply a way of dealing with severe protein deficiency? Much has been written for and against this conclusion, with meticulous analyses put forth about the amount of protein otherwise available or not available (see, for example, Arens 1979; Harner 1979; Harris 1985, 1987; Sanday 1986).

Myself, I do not know how important human flesh was for the Aztec diet. What interests me more is the amount of attention the issue has received. One must presume this is because of the disgust the act precipitates, but perhaps it also reflects a response to the awesomeness of killing, and possibly eating, humans for the greater glory of some deity. As I have indicated, I believe sacrifice of humans is simply a variant of the sacrifice of animals (those people sacrificed are in any event usually aliens and therefore by definition not fully human).

The practice would appear to reflect the presence of an underlying assumption that a noncoercible deity exists who can be influenced by the gift of a life. Where this assumption occurs, whether the sacrifice is of a chicken, a goat, a sheep, a pig, a dog, an ox, a horse, or a human, the residue, after the taking of the life, is almost always at the disposal of those performing the sacrifice: It is, in effect, the deity's leavings.[5]

---

[5] Has anyone thought to inquire into what Abraham and Isaac did with the ram after they sacrificed it?

According to Roscoe (1923), the Banyankole of East Africa did not permit the slaughter of cattle for food; cattle could be killed only as sacrifices. Of course, after the religious offering of the life of the animal, the carcass was consumed as meat—and, as Roscoe notes, the number of animals sacrificed equated remarkably with the number that could be killed without decimating the herds.

My point? No human practice can continue over time to be ecologically unsound, and, equally, it is not surprising that even religious practices have sound ecological bases. Neither observation, however, goes very far in enabling us to penetrate the assumptions and beliefs underlying and expressed in the religious practices. Abraham went into the land of Moriah and put his knife to the throat of his son because he believed he had been instructed to do so by a deity who demanded blind obedience, who could very well crave the death of a human, but who, Abraham also knew, would never—*could* never—in the end allow Abraham to perform such an act.

The answers lie in the subtleties and complexities of the assumptions and beliefs about the nature of divinity, and that is as true for the Aztecs and the Banyankole as it was for the ancient Hebrews or the modern practitioners of Santería.

16

A Myth Is As Good

Apart from the fact that the science of myths is still in its infancy, so that its practitioners must consider themselves fortunate to obtain even a few tentative preliminary results, we can already be certain that the ultimate state will never be attained, since were it theoretically possible, the fact still remains that there does not exist, nor ever will exist, any community or group of communities whose mythology and ethnography ... can be known in their entirety.

—Claude Lévi-Strauss
The Raw and the Cooked

What is a myth? How is it to be distinguished from all that is not myth? And having determined that (if we are lucky), what of significance can we expect to learn from the examination of myths? The literature on the meaning of myth expands yearly in richness and profundity, but it seems as if each year we grow more and more reluctant to specify just what we are talking about. Thus, Claude Lévi-Strauss gets right down to business as he begins the first volume of his monumental study of myth. His first mention of the word *myth* is as follows: "I shall take as my starting point *one* myth, originating from *one* community, and shall analyze it, referring first of all to the ethnographic context and then to other myths belonging to the same community. Gradually broadening the field of activity, I shall then move on to myths from neighboring societies" (Lévi-Strauss 1969:1; italics his). In no way do I question his proposed plan of attack (indeed, I intend to follow it myself, at least in part, in this very chapter), but I think, though he clearly does not, that the categorical subject of all this attention does require some minimum delineation at the outset.

Similarly, Ernst Cassirer, though he provides us with enormous and much-needed insight, never defines, never delineates. We may deduce from his intro-

ductory chapter that he believes *myth* relates to the universe of the improbable—
"the realm of spooks and daemons" (Cassirer 1946:3)—but that is as close to definition as he permits himself to get.

One problem, according to G. S. Kirk, is that the term *myth* no longer means
what it did at the beginning: "Etymology is a traditional point of departure, but
in this case an unhelpful one. For the Greeks *muthos* just meant a tale, or something one uttered, in a wide range of senses: a statement, a story, the plot of a
play" (Kirk 1970:8). Well, that is hardly good enough for us, is it? "Something one
uttered" would encompass my last lecture or your scholarly paper, and surely
there is nothing "mythic" about such works of modern scholarship. Many would
insist, after all, that for us today what is most fascinating about myth is that it is
something other people take seriously that we know to be false or, at minimum,
erroneous.

Dictionaries are quite clear that myths deal with the supernatural or with manifest error and usually both. Thus, for example, the *Oxford Universal Dictionary*
offers the following definition of *myth:* "1. A purely fictitious narrative usually
involving supernatural persons, actions, or events, and embodying some popular
idea concerning natural or historical phenomena. Often used vaguely to include
any narrative having fictitious elements. 2. A fictitious or imaginary person or
object" (*OUD* 1955:1306). The *American Heritage Dictionary* offers similar definitions[1] but also proposes one worth pursuing here. Before turning to it, however,
let us observe that *myth,* as usually defined, understood, and used, constitutes a
particularly sharp example of the traditional ethnocentric, scientistic approach
to religion I have been challenging in this work. It is true, of course, that the term
is used for phenomena outside of religion (the *AHD* notes such usages as "the
myth of Horatio Alger," "the myth of Anglo-Saxon superiority"). Furthermore, as
Kirk argues, myths need not always refer to the supernatural and relate to rituals.
Still, as Kirk concludes, "to return to the broader question, it would be foolish to
deny that many important myths in many cultures are associated in some degree
with *religion*" (Kirk 1970:29). I think it is possible to narrow it down even further.
As the term is used by students of mythology, a myth is a culturally specific response to questions beginning with such words as *why* and *how* and *when*. More
significantly, however, it is a response that *we* (the Western scholars) find not
only untrue but unacceptable. It is, as the dictionaries keep reminding us,
fictional.

Consider the following hypothetical interview of a native informant by a visiting anthropologist:

"When and how did your ancestors get to this island?"

"According to our genealogies, they arrived about thirty generations ago, prob-

---

[1] For example, "A traditional story originating in a preliterate society, dealing with supernatural beings, ancestors, or heroes that serve as primordial types in a primitive view of the world. . . . Any fictitious or imaginary story, explanation, person, or thing," and so on (*AHD* 1969:868–869).

ably in the same kind of boats we have now, and the word has come down to us that they were sailing due west."

That sort of response is certainly not a myth—even though it might in fact turn out to be incorrect in every particular. But suppose the answer is on the order of, "One of the gods pulled this island up out of the sea and shaped our first ancestors out of the mud of the lagoon." Now *that's* a myth!

I submit, therefore, that the issue is not the *accuracy* of the response but its *acceptability*. Victors, we know, write the history books, but so, on occasion, do sloppy historians; there are both accurate and inaccurate historical accounts. We do not, however, refer to the inaccurate ones as myths; rather, we save that term for accounts that derive, as Cassirer says, from "the realm of spooks and daemons," that is, from a discourse that is prohibited to scholars. I would argue that it is precisely because of this inescapably ethnocentric—to say nothing of judgmental—assumption about the nature of myth that we have experienced such conflict about how to deal with the subject.

A myth, we all agree, is not true history; for one thing, in the mythic narrative reality is like quicksilver, constantly flowing and changing shape. That may be. But is it not interesting, and possibly humbling, to observe that the anthropological analysis of myth may also be compared to quicksilver? After all, where are the shapes of yesteryear? Gone with the assumptions that shaped our views but the year before!

Once, with Max Müller (1878), we saw myths as a "disease of language," the compounding of linguistic change, "mythopoeic thought," and metaphoric explanations of natural phenomena. And then we (I say *we* because have we not, in assuming the mantles of those who came before us, thereby assumed the burden of both their honors and their errors?) concluded, with Andrew Lang (1898), that myths were relics or survivals from earlier stages in the sequence of cultural evolution. And so on and on: Lang's views went down in the crash of the theory of unilineal cultural evolution,[2] and myth came to be viewed variously as "charter," as psychological "projection," as the obverse of "ritual," as "narrative," as "theme," and as many other things.

Rarely, however, is myth perceived as a number of these very different things *together*. The *American Heritage Dictionary,* as I indicated earlier, points us in the right direction in at least one of its proposed definitions: "2. Any real or fictional story, recurring theme, or character type that appeals to the consciousness of a people by embodying its cultural ideals or by giving expression to deep, commonly held emotions" (*AHD* 1969:869).

An operational definition of *myth,* then, might be:

> Any account, offered in and reflective of a specific cultural system, that expresses cultural ideals, deep and commonly held emotions and values, or fundamental assumptions and perceptions about the nature of the universe and of society. Examination is necessary in each

---

[2] See Dorson 1965 for an analysis of some of these changing views.

case to determine whether the given account functions in any way, or in any combination of ways, as metaphor, history, social charter, psychological projection, obverse of ritual, or simple narrative.

What kind of accounts shall we include under myths? Which ones shall we leave out? To begin with, according to the above definition, intentional fiction is something other than myth. Again, accounts reflective of archeological research or of the study of surviving documents—whether or not they turn out ultimately to be accurate—are also other than myth.

Yet it could reasonably be argued that all religious accounts and all political manifestos (e.g., "We hold these truths to be self-evident . . ."), along with much philosophical disquisition, clearly fall within the compass of the above definition. This should not precipitate indignation if we bear firmly in mind that the operational approach has nothing to do with the question, Is it true? Rather, the sole concern is how we anthropologists may most effectively, and avoiding scientific ethnocentricity, study the accounts we receive from our informants.

Surely this task is difficult enough, particularly given the multiplicity of contending and mutually exclusive theoretical positions. In recent years, however, the voices of eclectics have been raised, mine among them (Klass [1980] 1993). We argue that no *one* approach is necessarily entirely or uniquely correct (or incorrect), but rather, that, a number of approaches, sensibly melded and even synthesized, may provide the most satisfactory explication of anthropological problems.

At any rate, the eclectic approach is the one I espouse, and what I propose now is an effort at an eclectic analysis of a myth of origin, one I collected during fieldwork in West Bengal, India. In so doing, I am among other things responding to Lévi-Strauss's charge that we encompass as much of the ethnographic context as we can. I shall also follow his example and "take as my starting point *one* myth."

*   *   *

On the morning of Thursday, February 13, 1964, I was conducting research in a village to which I have given the fictitious name of Gondogram (Klass 1978). Since, for me, the myth collector is as much part of the ethnographic context as the myth narrator, I must report that I was particularly interested that morning in learning more about the local manifestation of *gotra* (or *gotrô* in local pronunciation). *Gotra* is the exogamous patrisib[3] that is to be noted in many but not all castes in much but not all of India. Furthermore, when a caste does exhibit this structural feature, its form and functions may vary. Among some castes, for ex-

---

[3] A *sib* is a kin group whose members believe they are descended from a common ancestor but who cannot trace actual genealogical relations between individuals. Members of a *patrisib* inherit membership only from their fathers.

ample, the patrisibs are ranked, thus affecting marriage patterns, whereas among still other castes they are perceived as absolutely equal.[4]

On this morning, then, I was endeavoring to determine whether exogamous sibs of any kind were to be found among the Bauri, a caste considered to be ritually polluting by West Bengal villagers of higher-ranked castes. Indeed, in the rural communities in which they live, Bauris are usually the lowest-ranked or close to the lowest-ranked caste in the village. Almost invariably, Bauri neighborhoods are at a distance from those other castes inhabit. Bauris typically engage in the most menial of occupations: field laborers, house servants, scavengers. As to the latter occupation, however, it must be noted that Bauri scavengers absolutely refuse to touch the carcass of one animal, the dog. And additionally, for purposes of ethnographic context, let us note that Bauris, "polluting" as they are perceived to be, do not receive many of the important services available to other villagers, such as those of the barber and of the Brahman priest.

And so I was sitting in the yard of a Bauri home, interviewing an elderly man, known to his castemates for his wisdom and leadership, about the structural features of his caste. When I asked whether his Bauri people knew and used the term *gotrô*, he replied:[5]

Our *gotrô* is *dog*—do you know why this is so?	*amader gotro bote kukur—kœno hoiche ta ki jano?*
Once, our priest was actually a *Brahman.*	*amader bambhon chilen pokito*
A celebration was taking place for a wedding.	*biar karon œkti hoichilo upojuggo*
At the end of the celebration, the *Brahman* still had not come.	*upojuggo nole pore, bambhon jokhon ase nai*
Just when the marriage was about to be spoiled—then the *Brahman* arrived!	*biya tokhon losta hobar somoy hoiche— se somoy bambhon cole esechilo*
Furious at what had happened, that *Brahman* was killed . . . was stabbed . . . for that reason was he killed.	*onurag je ki hoilo, sei bambhonke meri dile . . . kati dile . . . tajonno mere dile*
When the head came off, then from somewhere a dog came, and he lapped the blood.	*jokhon mundo cole gœlo, tokhon abar kutha je kukur chilo, se roktota kheiye dile*

---

[4] For a more comprehensive review of these and related issues, see Klass 1978:62–66.

[5] In my reproduction of his reply, I have attempted to convey, even in translation, some of his emotional and cognitive shifts, as well as grammatical errors. The language he uses is of course not Standard Bengali but the dialect used (particularly by the poorest and least educated) in the Asansol district. Diacritics have been omitted as unnecessary for the purposes of this transcription.

After that, all became ashamed of themselves:	*tarpor, sokole mone ghina holo:*
"Oh! what have we done! We have damaged our own future!	*o! ja kaj torchi! nijer kajer kkhoiti hoiche!*
"We have taken *your* life—and *he* [dog] has lapped a *Brahman*'s blood!	*tomar jibon liichi—o bambhoner rokto kheiye dile!*
"We will nevermore touch it [pointing to dog]!	*ike chubo nai!*
"Even when it is dead we will not touch it!"	*morleo chubo nai!*
Therefore, from the time the dog lapped that blood,	*tai, kukure rokto kheichilo bole,*
our blood and the dog's blood have been one—	*amader rokto kukerer rokto æk hoiche—*
from that day our *gotrô* has been *dog*.	*se din thike amader gotro kuker hoiche.*

There we have the myth. Since we have put aside the question whether it is an accurate account of an actual historical event, what are we to learn from it? The answer, of course, depends upon one's approach to myth. Lévi-Strauss, for example, has opened our eyes (1967:202–208) to the inherent inescapable contradiction likely to be found at the very heart of a myth of origin, and surely such a contradiction is manifested in this account: How is it that *we*, the Bauris, the nicest, dearest people that *we* know, are treated with such cruel contempt by everyone who is not a Bauri? This problem is not an academic one for Bauris, who are faced with the contradiction every moment of their lives.

Is the myth a charter, then, as Malinowski (1954:93–148) would have it? Yes, and it is interesting to note that the myth serves *both* to validate the status quo (the function of myth as charter, according to Malinowski) *and* as a program for change and uplift, though Leach insisted (1954) that it could only be one *or* the other.

For if it explains why Bauris are forever "unclean," the myth also tells us that "we Bauris" were once a high-ranked, *non*polluting caste—and might this not inspire us to change our status? Bauris in West Bengal, in fact, are indeed on the move, and the traditional Bauri myth of origin dovetails neatly with (becomes transformed into?) a more modern one that may also exhibit some Marxist influence: that "once" the Bauri caste controlled all the land of Bengal till Brahmans took it away from them (see Klass 1978:218).[6]

---

[6] For a more comprehensive and comparative study of these and many related issues, see "The Myths of Origin of the Indian Untouchables" (Deliège 1993).

Let us continue with our pursuit of the ethnographic context. For Hindu India, this means being particularly aware of the rules governing both caste ranking and ritual pollution, with Bauris to be found at the bottom of both systems. Brahman priests, we must further note, serve only the ritually pure castes. It is also important to observe that Bengal villagers consider unclean all dead animals and even certain living ones, such as the dog, generally despised as an eater of carrion, garbage, and even human waste. Finally, we should be aware that animal sacrifice is commonly performed in this part of Bengal by castes ranked both high and low, and the sacrificial animal is customarily decapitated.

All of this is not unrelated to an inquiry into the psychological implications of the myth, the indications of sublimation and projection. A "good Hindu" in rural Bengal must express love and esteem for the Brahman (as a category if not always as an individual). We see in the account an expression of Bauri moral aspiration (once we were good Hindus) as well as an expression of proper pious horror at the murder of a Brahman. But equally clearly, the myth expresses hatred and resentment of Brahmans—who, indeed, will not come to a Bauri wedding. Thus it is interesting to note how, as the narrator dwells on the act of killing, the stabbing becomes transformed into decapitation: The Bauri ancestor is thereby transformed from a murderer into a performer of sacrifice.

And so, with a deferential nod to Müller, we see that the myth is indeed metaphor. In fact, to approach the myth as metaphor is to synthesize and expand, for there are many levels of metaphor, and they are not in conflict.

Let me introduce my first metaphoric dimension by reporting that the nineteenth century ethnographer Edward Dalton once asked some Bauris why they avoided the dog. He reported: "I was gravely informed by some of their elders that as they killed and ate cows and most other animals, they deemed it right to fix on some beast which should be as sacred to them as the cow to the Brahman, and they selected the dog because it was a useful animal while alive and not very nice to eat when dead—a neat reconciliation of the twinges of conscience and cravings of appetite" (Dalton 1960:315). Dalton's Bauri informants were obviously eclectics: Along with having certain cultural materialist perceptions, they were apparently interested in structural analysis. They understood the importance of the system in which they were enmeshed; for as the cow among Hindus is to the animal world—symbol and source of purity, inviolate, quasi-divine, generating blessings by its mere presence—so exactly is the Brahman to the human world. And as cow is to Brahman, so dog is to Bauri: Both dog and Bauri are unclean, to be kept forever at a distance, necessary but abhorrent, eaters of that which should not be eaten. Thus, in a thoroughly Durkheimian way the dog is not merely the Bauri totem;[7] it is in fact the root metaphor of and for the Bauri: "Our blood and the dog's blood are one."

For my final metaphoric dimension, I would begin by raising the question why my informant felt compelled to narrate this myth *to me*. After all, this myth is

---

[7] Obviously, *gotrô* means "totem," not "patrisib," to Bauris.

known and the facts contained within it self-evident to every Bauri above the age of infancy with whom the narrator is acquainted. Let us observe, therefore, that the narration of the myth constituted a response to certain questions, and that these questions indicated the ignorance and confusion of the ethnographer, not of any Bauri. In other words, our Bauri informant had found himself in the presence of an adult who seems not to perceive or to understand the nature of reality itself. How is one to convey reality to such a person?

The old man believed, not unreasonably, that he observed in me a profound ignorance of the social universe of the Bauri and of the Bauri's position in that universe: an ignorance of the Bauri's relations with Brahmans, of the Bauri's secret resentments and aspirations, of their sense of ultimate meaning and possible change. All these things were as apparent to my informant as they were to Dalton's, and he was faced with a similar need to communicate it all to someone who seemingly neither knew nor understood any of it.

We have seen his response: The old man takes a deep breath and delivers himself of what *we* call a myth. But this myth is not an explanation for Bauris, at least in this context; here, we observe, it is an explanation *for the ethnographer,* who apparently requires total instruction!

From this perspective, then, we see that this Bauri myth of origin is a portrayal of reality in words and images; it is in this context an all-encompassing metaphor—it is a *metaphor for reality.*

The foregoing discussion is not offered, at least primarily, as an advertisement for eclecticism in anthropology (including myth analysis), though I obviously support that theoretical stance. I intend it as an argument for taking an operational, nonethnocentric approach to myth, as indeed to all aspects of the anthropological study of religion.

A myth is an account—an account of reality—and it comes into existence, at least in the form in which we usually have it in the anthropological literature, as a response to the presence and questions of a particular ethnographer. It therefore calls for both textual and reflexive analysis, as well as for the traditional anthropological kinds of inquiry.

And by the way and given all of that, it may even exhibit *accuracy.*

17
Wondrous Portals

When, lo, as they reached the mountain-side,
A wondrous portal opened wide,
As if a cavern was suddenly hollowed;
And the Piper advanced and the children followed,
And when all were in to the very last,
The door in the mountain-side shut fast.

—Robert Browning
"The Pied Piper of Hamelin"

Every year almost, coming from everywhere and anywhere, the charismatic Pied Pipers of religion appear on the scene: Jim Jones, David Koresh, Sun Myung Moon, Rajneesh, and others captivate and seem to enslave those who hear their tune, and mystify and terrify those who hear nothing at all and who are forced to watch helplessly as their children and neighbors march off into the side of the mountain.

It is hardly surprising, therefore, that the literature on the subject of cults and cult leaders is both enormous and increasing. I turn to the topic—broadly, the emergence of alternative belief systems in complex societies—with some trepidation; I don't wish to add unnecessarily to the accumulation. What I propose to do is, first, review some aspects of the topic from the perspective of anthropology and, second, explore the advantages of an approach to the issues deriving from the insights of Victor W. Turner.

Cult, readers should expect by now, is a word I must call upon anthropology to reject. It is up there with *myth* and *supernatural:* Whatever its uses and advantages for theologians and sociologists, for anthropologists it can only and irretrievably communicate the presence of *unacceptable* beliefs and practices, because, as far as I can determine, no writer ever uses the term approvingly or ever applies it to his or her own belief system.

In an earlier work I have reviewed a number of the problems the term poses for anthropologists (Klass 1991a:10, 95–96); here I would note only that it leads those who use it to focus on the pathological rather than the structural dimensions of the subject. The questions most often asked are such as, What is wrong with the society in which cults proliferate? What psychological or social problems drive some individuals to join cults (cf. Beckford 1987)?

Again, I am not suggesting that such questions are irrelevant or should not be pursued. What I do argue is that they derive from the assumption of and concern with the pathological and unacceptable aspects of the new religious movements—all inextricably embodied in the term *cult*. Inevitably, therefore, they tend to impede the framing and the pursuit of more anthropologically oriented questions about the alternative belief systems that frequently emerge in large and complex societies, appealing with great force to some segments of the population and not at all to others.

The term *cult*, moreover, has a tendency to freeze the dimensions of time, space, and significance of the subject under consideration. Sometimes the alternative belief system appeals to a tiny number of people and/or disappears swiftly from the scene. And sometimes what starts out as an obscure "cult" attracts so much attention and so many followers that observers stop calling it a "cult" and, however reluctantly, find themselves forced to accord it the dignity of a "religion" or at least a "religious movement." They are so forced because the three most common contemporary[1] hallmarks of a "cult" are a small number of adherents, a brief existence, and of course the presence of a "charismatic" leader. None of the three is satisfactory from a definitional point of view. Elsewhere (Klass 1991a:96) I have queried, "How are we to know, except in retrospect, whether a set of religious teachings is destined to survive the test of time? Is the term only to be applied in the cemeteries of ideology?" Those who insist that *cult* is a meaningful and useful term for students of the anthropology of religion are, I think, obligated to respond to such questions.

We are fortunate that anthropologists have pointed to ways out of this ethnocentric dilemma. In my view potentially the most helpful alternative approach to the study of such religious phenomena lies in Turner's work on liminality. In a number of writings, beginning with "Betwixt and Between" (1967), Turner developed and explored the related concepts of liminality, communitas, and anti-structure (1969). He was meticulous about ascribing credit to Arnold van Gennep's *Rites of Passage* ([1908] 1960), but Turner's interests and theoretical perspectives actually took him far from van Gennep. The term *anti-structure*, indeed, alerts us that Turner was a structuralist who was striving for a way to deal

---

[1] There has been a shift: The earlier emphasis on strange, obscene, or otherwise off-putting "cultic" practices is largely missing from the contemporary literature (see Yinger 1970, Maring 1979, Beckford 1987).

with phenomena seemingly outside of structure—such as the movement of individuals from persona to persona within a social system.

Why should this be a problem for structuralists? In his 1940 lecture "On Social Structure," A. R. Radcliffe-Brown, the father of anthropological structural-functionalism, put it in no uncertain terms:

> Closely connected with this conception of social structure is the conception of "social personality" as the position occupied by a human being in a social structure, the complex formed by all his social relations with others. Every human being living in society is two things: he is an individual and also a person. . . . Human beings as individuals are objects of study for physiologists and psychologists. The human being as a person is a complex of social relationships . . . the object of study for the social anthropologist. *We cannot study persons except in terms of social structure.* . . . The failure to distinguish individual and person . . . is a source of confusion in science. (1965:193–194; italics mine)

When, therefore, an individual human being is not situated in a position but is rather transiting from one "social personality" (say, child) to another (say, adult), how is the student of social structure to deal with it? At such a time, there is no *person* to observe. Radcliffe-Brown, as we see, offers no help whatever. Turner's solution is to propose the existence of a "liminal" *period* between "structural" *states*. He goes on to explore some of the aspects of this period: Since it is outside of structure, it is characterized by anti-structure manifested in communitas, an unstructured, undifferentiated "communion of equal individuals" (1969:96).

Turner is thereby enabled to compare a number of liminal situations: rites of passage, pilgrimage, monasticism, and so on. One observation of Turner's is particularly significant for the present discussion of emergent alternative belief systems:

> Among the more striking manifestations of communitas are to be found the so-called millenarian movements. . . . Here I would merely recall some of the properties of liminality in tribal rituals that I mentioned earlier. Many of these correspond pretty closely with those of millenarian movements: homogeneity, equality, anonymity, absence of property . . . sexual continence . . . minimization of sexual distinctions . . . abolition of rank, humility . . . and so forth. (1969:111–112)

Nevertheless, and despite all the anti-structural similarities, I would argue that there is an important difference between liminal rituals and emergent religious movements. The adolescent, like others undergoing life-crisis rituals, is a visitor passing through the liminal zone; the neophyte, in contrast, often intends to *take up residence* in liminality and does not expect to leave again—neither by returning (like Omar Khayyam) "through the same door by which in [he] went," nor (like the emergent adult) by passing through some portal on the far side to a different part of the social order.

Turner is of course not unaware of this difference: He proposes the term *permanent liminality* and applies it to the case of the monastic order founded by

Saint Francis (1969:145). But *liminality*, in Turner's own words, is "betwixt and between"—it is so much a transitional and thus transitory period that the term *permanent liminality* seems almost an oxymoron. Still, Turner acknowledges that it can and does occur, and so we must ask, What will happen to communitas when people live out their lives in liminality? Turner suggests that structure will emerge over time, at least of the sort typically found in religious orders (1969:146, 149).

True enough, undoubtedly, but Turner's suggestion seems to precipitate more questions than it answers. It implies quite clearly that a passage has been effected for the neophyte—from the structured society without to the new structure within an ongoing religious order. In that case, however, how can it be called permanent *liminality*? Because, as Turner obviously perceives, the religious order is itself peripheral (or liminal) to the main body of the society. Still, are we all comfortable with the notion that liminality, peripherality, and perhaps marginality are essentially the same?

That issue put firmly to one side, what we must ponder here is how the religious order can be at one and the same time a structured unit or subdivision of a society and also a part of the liminal zone that we know to be characterized by communitas and anti-structure. Turner does not really address this issue at all and thus leaves us wondering how, and to what extent, the characteristics of *transitional* liminality are transformed into the structure-resembling characteristics of *permanent* liminality.

The foregoing should not be construed as a rejection of Turner's formulations. What I am calling for, rather, is much more anthropological attention to monasteries, armies, pilgrimages, and so on viewed specifically as situations of permanent liminality. Indeed, pilgrimage has already received attention from this perspective (Turner and Turner 1978, Greenfield 1990), and Sharon Mills (1989) utilized Turner's approach in a study of a convent. The problems are fascinating, and there remains much to investigate and interpret.

As an example, therefore, I propose to explore here some of the aspects of permanent liminality exhibited in Trinidad and Tobago by followers of the south Indian holy man Sathya Sai Baba, who is believed by his millions of disciples all over the world to be God incarnate, the One who walks the earth with the appearance of an ordinary mortal. The specific problem here, as I hope to show, derives from the need of the devotees in Trinidad to continue their regular existence in the structured, secular world while periodically visiting the liminal domain of their guru.

Elsewhere (Klass 1991a) I have written at considerable length about Sathya Sai Baba's life in India, his teachings, and some of the consequences those teachings have had for the social and political concerns of the particular segment of his followers who live in the West Indian nation of Trinidad and Tobago. Here my primary concern is to explore some of dimensions of the liminal world he has called forth—and indeed, by extension, of the liminality that seems inevitably to come into existence around any charismatic leader and his followers.

The term *charismatic* would seem a good place to begin. Despite much misuse (such as the tendency to apply it to any stirring political speaker), it still conveys its original theological gloss: one others recognize as having spiritual gifts, inspirations, or powers beyond those available to ordinary mortals. I have intentionally avoided the more customary attribution of *divine* inspiration in my definition, though of course such an attribution is encompassed, because I would not exclude those whose followers clearly perceive them as charismatic but whose belief system does not admit of a divine source for the inspiration. The Buddha, for example, should qualify as a charismatic leader whether or not Theravada Buddhism recognizes the existence of divinities. Even more, my approach will not force us to exclude founders of so-called cargo cults (revitalization movements in Melanesia) and others who may be charismatic in every significant sense even though their belief systems diverge substantially from those of the West.

And finally there are belief systems (and Hinduism provides perhaps the clearest examples) in which an emergent charismatic leader both claims and is accorded a fully divine nature (God *incarnate*) without necessarily implying any sharp disjunction between human (the follower) and divine (the charismatic leader). Sathya Sai Baba can, in the same discourse, announce not only his own absolute and overarching divinity but also the divinity that is present in any human being:

> Continue your worship of your chosen God along the lines already familiar to you. Then you will find that you are coming nearer and nearer to Me. For, all Names are Mine and all Forms are Mine. There is no need to change your chosen God and adopt a new one when you have seen Me and heard Me. . . .
>
> Everyone of you is an Avatar. You are the Divine, encarsed [*sic*] like Me in human flesh and bone! Only you are unaware of it! You have come into this prison of incarnation through the errors of many lives. But I have put on this mortal body, of My own free will. (McMartin 1982:4, 10)

Thus, Sathya Sai Baba is unquestionably a charismatic leader in that he claims to have, and is accepted by his followers as having, spiritual gifts, inspirations, and powers not ordinarily available to other people. Even more, he belongs to the subdivision of charismatic leaders composed of those who claim actual divine status: those who do not merely convey the word of God but who are themselves divine. We must remember, however, that both Sathya Sai Baba and his followers—at least those who subscribe to the tenets of Hinduism—believe that *all* humans are in principle as fully divine as he is! And, further, Hinduism enjoins all devotees to treat all gurus (spiritual guides and teachers) as avatars, that is, as true incarnations of divinity.

From this perspective, therefore, Sathya Sai Baba is indistinguishable from *any* Hindu spiritual leader. And it could even be argued that all Hindus are indistinguishable from what some would call "members of cults." After all, Sathya Sai Baba and his teachings (along with all his Hindu followers) are embedded in a pantheistic belief system in which divinity pervades the universe. The universe includes all humans, who are therefore particles of divinity but who are usually not aware of their own divinity. Religious guides (gurus) are those people with the capacity (deriving from knowledge, training, divine inspiration, divine origin, or whatever) to lead others to a spiritual awakening, to help them to realize their own divine nature and potential. In turn, the follower of the guru, the devotee, is expected to acknowledge with joyful and unquestioned submission the divinity of the guru who has provided such inspiration. Sathya Sai Baba's instructions to his devotees express a view fundamental to Hinduism in general:

> Once you have secured a Guru leave everything to Him, even the desire to achieve liberation. He knows you more than you yourself ever can. He will direct you as much as is good for you. Your duty is only to obey and to smother the tendency to drift away from Him. You may ask, how are we to earn our food, if we attach ourselves to a Guru like this? Be convinced that the Lord will not let you starve; he will give you not merely anna [money, wealth] but even Amrita, not only food but the nectar of immortality. (Kasturi 1981, vol. 4:50)

Overseas followers of Sathya Sai Baba, such as those who live in the nation of Trinidad and Tobago in the West Indies, must therefore be understood to exist in two seemingly discrete and contradictory conceptual universes. Their bodies (so they would argue) are in the secular world—specifically, on the island of Trinidad, where they participate in all the activities and events of ordinary life: They pursue professions and hold jobs, they pay bills and invest their money, they marry and raise children and in turn marry them off, they visit with relatives (in and out of the movement), they vote in national elections, and so on.

But their minds (and souls, they would claim) are ever with Sathya Sai Baba at his ashram in Puttaparthi in India. Obviously, the attention of a devotee can be distracted by events occurring in the secular world, but it is expected that as soon as possible the devotee will endeavor to redirect his or her thoughts out of space and time and back to the contemplation of God in the body of Sathya Sai Baba.

Put another way, the Sai Baba devotee simultaneously inhabits structure and permanent liminality. Whatever problems this may pose for the analyst of social systems, the devotee experiences little discomfort.

But he or she does experience some. On the one hand, the devotee must function effectively in the nonliminal, or secular, world of structure. This means, to begin with, that he or she must have a source of income. Men who are fairly wealthy, and particularly those who have businesses of their own, have a degree of advantage over their fellow devotees who must work at regular jobs under the supervision of nondevotees. During the workday the latter devotees must concentrate on the details of their employment, on the behavior that will gain the favor of their employers, and on ways that will result in promotion or the acquisition of higher wages. If their employers or fellow employees engage in what to the devotees' minds are improper actions or language—if they even occasionally mock Sathya Sai Baba—the devotee who wishes to keep his job can only turn his mind from such distractions to the private contemplation of his guru and God. But he cannot turn his mind too far; he must not be accused of inattention. One devotee who holds the position of office manager in a large firm summed up his office policies quite bluntly to me: "Frankly, I don't discuss religion with people in the office."

The wealthy businessman devotee has his problems, too. If the business is to remain successful it requires constant attention. Such a businessman may well be past middle age, and not infrequently he dreams of retiring and devoting his remaining years to his religion. A few have done just that; most, however, seem not to be able to relinquish their business activities. Sons are not yet old enough or experienced enough to take over, times are difficult, and there are economic storms to be weathered by those with experience or the entire enterprise may founder; it may even be that there are pleasures and perquisites of power and wealth that are difficult to forgo even when one sincerely wishes to do so.

Apart from the economic pressures of the secular world, there are the social pressures. Both men and women have obligations to family and old friends, even if such people have not (yet) seen the light and become devotees of Sai Baba, and devotees must spend time at homes and at social events that are far removed from those of the liminal Sai Baba universe. Children must be raised, which involves a special set of problems, as they must be reared as devotees of Sathya Sai Baba but must also be properly prepared to function effectively in the secular world: "It make a big, big difference in our life. Before [we knew of Sai Baba], we used to go to Carnival, and all that. Now, the children don't know anything about 'party' or this or that. No outside life, except—well—when they used to go to school. Now they working" (Klass 1991a:146).

And so the devotee wanders continually in two universes, that of the secular, structural world of his neighbors and workmates, with all its worries and concerns, and that of the liminal world of Sathya Sai Baba, where the devotee may mentally sit forever at the feet of God, singing *bhajans* (hymns) and contemplating a living avatar. Sometimes the devotee attempts to inhabit both universes simultaneously; sometimes he or she must switch back and forth. For if one must temporarily shut one's mind to Sai Baba to cope with office or school, one can, at the *satsang* (service) at the local Sai Centre, sever all ties with the secular world and, in the company of other devotees but mentally alone, seek full communion with Sathya Sai Baba.

Even then—even deep in prayer and meditation as a member of a movement specifically dedicated to remaining in liminality—as Turner suspected, permanent liminality generates structure, and the structure conflicts with anti-structure. Sathya Sai Baba permits no one to speak for him or interpret his message; socializing at *satsangs* is considered inappropriate. As we have observed, people attending the *satsang* have entered a liminal zone. In their view Sathya Sai Baba himself is present among them, so no explication of his views is needed; at most, someone may read aloud from a collection of his sermons. Socializing—discussing business, asking after family, gossiping—is clearly an intrusion into liminality, as is serving and sharing food. At a *satsang* one is in principle both alone and simultaneously part of a group[2] communing with God: The things of the secular world, of structure, have no place here.

But this is not a transitory liminality; it is at least episodically permanent. Devotees spend hours each week at such religious services, and in addition many manage to enter the liminal zone even while engaged in secular and mundane activities,[3] for this is true reality—where one *should* be. And the reverse also becomes true: Secular interests intrude on the world of liminality. Women find it impossible to meet together regularly without providing refreshments; men find it impossible to sit with friends and associates without mentioning business affairs and occurrences. There is an awareness of impropriety about such activities, but not enough to prevent them from occurring (Klass 1991a:140–141).

For many people, one of the attractions of Sai Baba's teachings is that, unlike many other South Asian gurus, he does not require his devotees to leave the secular world and retire to his ashram. As we have noted, wherever they may be in the world, they may in effect enter his ashram and sit at his feet whenever they engage in prayer. Thus, the entire worldwide Sai Baba movement is a liminal, anti-structural universe. All devotees are equal; no membership lists are kept or dues collected, for such would violate communitas. And yet the movement, however anti-structural *internally*, exists in the structured secular world. There are inevitable expenses, such as bills for repair of meeting places, and there are necessary activities to be performed, such as preparations for ceremonies and cleaning up after services.

"How, one might well inquire, are Sai Centres and the larger organization maintained, in the absence of dues and assessments? Solely, it is everywhere asserted, by the free and unsolicited actions of devotees who feel moved to reach into their pockets when bills arrive" (Klass 1991a:126). It works: The Trinidad Sai Centres pay their bills and through this system even manage to build temples and provide funds for education of children and aid to the needy. But such a system appears to lead inevitably to domination by the wealthy, and this in turn leads to seepage from structural community into anti-structural communitas. In principle, for example, all participants at *satsangs* are equal and undifferentiated (apart from the separation of men and women). In practice there are leaders and movers who sit in the front of the congregation and less important (poorer, more peripheral) devotees who sit in the rear.

What we are seeing here, it may be argued, is the fragility of the liminality of "permanent liminality." Might we say that structure abhors communitas—that,

---

[2] Might this not be an essential aspect of communitas?

[3] Such as, for example, accompanying Sai Baba (on tape) in singing a *bhajan* while driving one's taxi (Klass 1991a:148).

given time, community will permeate and drive out anti-structure? I offer it as a hypothesis; further research (in monasteries, pilgrimages, armies, and other nontransitory liminalities) is obviously needed to test its validity and detail its manifestations.

In addition, there is a need for the application of Turner's insights (as well as the critical assessment of those insights) to millenarian and revitalization movements both in the present and in the archives. The liminality of the Native American Ghost Dance is potentially as fascinating, at least for the insights to be derived, as is the communitas exhibited by the followers of the Reverend Jim Jones—who followed their Pied Piper into the mountainside through a portal opened not by music but by Kool-Aid.[4]

---

[4] For scholarly assessments of the Jonestown mass suicide, see Weightman 1983 and Moore and McGehee 1989.

18

When Worldviews Collide

But, it would seem, religion at times is unable to patch up the dissonant cognitions of members of societies structurally riven by internal strain. Societies are not, after all, forever stable; political revolutions and civil wars tear them apart, culture changes turn them over, invasion and acculturation undermine them.

—Anthony F.C. Wallace
Religion: An Anthropological View

We have, throughout this book, been concerned primarily with the ways religion provides coherence and order for the members of a cultural system in what is naturally a chaotic, confusing, and therefore frightening universe. In so doing, of course, I inevitably replicate that very phenomenon—by focusing on coherence and order in belief systems themselves. But as Wallace reminds us, this state of order and coherence (the ideal, if you will) is not always to be observed, and even when it is true of a particular belief system, it is subject to change without notice as a result of either internal or external factors or both.

In the previous chapter we explored new religious movements, but primarily in such terms as how they may be perceived by the larger society or how they may engender communitas among those who turn to them. But what of the impact of an alien belief system—whether intrinsically or extrinsically derived—upon those who still adhere to the culture's original system? How do they deal with the presence of a different "ordered universe"? Variously, we may hypothesize, they may reject the intrusive doctrine (by ignoring it, by debating it, by killing those who adhere to it, etc.), or they may knowingly or unknowingly absorb elements of the new belief system into the old, or they may adopt the new either in toto or to a significant extent but still bring with them substantial portions of the old.

All of the above responses lead of course to legitimate areas of inquiry for students of the anthropology of religion. Given contemporary assumptions and perspectives, however, we must observe that any variety of merger of elements from two different belief systems raises potentially enormous theoretical problems. I have argued, as have most contemporary anthropologists who have addressed the subject, that the elements of a belief system form a coherent and interrelated whole: the nature and purpose of the universe, the nature of divinity, the interrelationship of human and divine, the source of illness and death, the role of the religious officiant, the degree of control possible, and so on. By definition, therefore, a different belief system implies different assumptions about all these—and indeed other—issues.

Obviously, there are many theoretical questions one could pose and many topics to engage the attention of the anthropologist. This is, for example, a pregnant arena for the exploration of culture conflict, for examination of violence in the clash of ideological systems, for study of the underpinnings of class, ethnic, or gender confrontations and of the sources and culminations of hegemonic and colonial dislocations. I have touched on some of these elsewhere in this text, and in the final chapter I intend to explore one particular and contemporary ideological conflict, that among fundamentalists, those of the mainstream, and proponents of the "New Age."

It seems to me appropriate to focus first, however, on the nature of the collision itself: For example, when two systems collide, how is it *possible* for elements to travel between the two? Must not such transposition inevitably precipitate ambiguity, confusion, conflict? Sometimes, but apparently not always. The anthropologist or other external observer may see contradiction in, say, two simultaneously held beliefs about what happens after death (your soul goes to heaven; some souls are reborn and undergo new lives), but the people who hold the conflicting beliefs rarely seem particularly perturbed.

One classic explanation of this astonishing state of affairs is that the new or intrusive belief is "reinterpreted." Thus, for Melville J. Herskovits, *syncretism* was "one form of reinterpretation," which in turn he perceived as "the process by which old meanings are ascribed to new elements or by which new values change the cultural significance of old forms" (Herskovits 1949:553). He does not further define *syncretism* itself, but by his usage and examples it is clear that he means the term to signify reinterpretation in the case of conjoined or fused elements deriving from disparate sources once unrelated to each other but now somehow "reconciled" (1949:553).

Herskovits provides a number of examples of reinterpretation in language and in other cultural domains, but he appears to have reserved the term *syncretism* for religion—a decision very much in accord with accepted usage: The primary definition of the term in the *American Heritage Dictionary* is "the attempt or tendency to combine or reconcile differing beliefs, as in religion or philosophy" (*AHD* 1969:1304).

Is his explanation still tenable today? Some might argue that it is not. After all, the terms Herskovits used (such as *reinterpretation* and *syncretism*) reflect a very specific theoretical approach in anthropology, one about which he was very explicit in his writings. Herskovits, like other anthropologists of his time, particularly in the United States, saw culture as the manifestation—the observable presentation—of a particular accumulation of discrete elements usually referred to as *traits*.

A trait might be a technological skill (e.g., pottery making) or an artistic tradition (e.g., particular designs on pots) or a social convention (e.g., only women may make pots) or an ideological perception (e.g., offerings to deities should be enclosed in pots). Any and all of these are traits; and any and all lend themselves equally to the investigation of which elements are of ancient or "native" origin, which recently introduced from outside, which recently or spontaneously developed. In such a perception of culture, the term *retention* obviously becomes important: How much (how many traits) of their "original" culture has a particular human group "retained"? How many traits (which ones) have they "lost"? What new ones have they "acquired"? And if there has in fact been considerable loss and retention, the next question inevitably becomes: What reinterpretations of new or old traits have taken place?

The work of Herskovits and his colleagues is of great importance in the history of anthropology, but there are problems for those trained in contemporary theoretical approaches who would employ the terms and concepts of an earlier period. As we have seen, for example, Turner, a structuralist, was captivated by van Gennep's notion of liminality, but Turner's usage is very different from that of van Gennep. How are we, therefore, who tend today to approach culture as symbolic or structural systems, to encompass the terms and categories of trait analysis? Herskovits (1949:43) seemed to think that *institution* and *trait-complex* were interchangeable terms; would we agree? Dare we, for example, associate Herskovits's *reinterpretation* with Lévi-Strauss's *transformation*?

I do not propose to attempt to answer such questions here; I raise them to help explain some of my difficulty in working with the concept of syncretism. One problem I have derives from the somewhat static nature of the "trait" approach: For Herskovits, relatively little culture change could occur as long as the original "trait list" was undisturbed. For the most part, only when traits were lost, or new ones introduced was change likely to occur, and most particularly because at such times reinterpretation of old or new traits could take place. Thus, from this perspective, syncretism serves as a concrete expression of culture change. Specifically, the conclusion would be that a community has lost many traits of its "original" (?) belief system and has acquired a substantial number of traits from an alien belief system—after which a reinterpretation (reconciliation, conjunction) of new and old traits has taken place, especially in the sense that both sets of traits continue to exist but are now understood to complement each other or even to represent the same thing.

The classic example, of course, is that of Afro-Catholic belief systems in the

Caribbean and Latin America. The argument offered is that people were brought from Africa carrying with them their natal religions: names and attributes of deities, details of rituals, explanations of the universe. They were stripped (often forcibly) of some of these religious elements and acquired (again, often forcibly) a new set deriving from European (usually Roman Catholic) Christianity. The result in many cases was the emergence of a new and syncretic religion (such as Haitian Vodun, Trinidad Shango, and Brazilian Candomble) in which the various traits are sufficiently discrete that provenience is easily determinable. Thus, as George E. Simpson informs us for Trinidad Shango, the power known as Ogun is on the one hand derived from the West African deity of that name but is also equivalent to Saint Michael of the Roman Catholic hagiology (1965:19).

It is interesting (and for the purposes of this book, enlightening) to compare the foregoing approach to syncretism with that of Edmund R. Leach in his paper "Pulleyar and the Lord Buddha: An Aspect of Religious Syncretism in Ceylon" (1962). Leach reports that Sinhalese Buddhists have borrowed a divinity from neighboring Tamil Hindus, that of Ganesha, the elephant-headed son of the high god Shiva. Ganesha, known in Tamil as Pillaiyar ("the son"), was converted into Pulleyar, "an elephant Lord of the Forest" now somewhat contradictorily worshiped by members of a religion (Sinhalese Theravada Buddhism) that *au fond* denies the existence of *any* divinity and accords even to the Buddha only the status of "a supremely enlightened human being" (Leach 1962:94).

As Leach notes, Pulleyar worship therefore seemingly lends itself to identification as a syncretism, but after a wide-ranging structural comparative analysis of Hinduism, Sinhalese village Buddhism, and Roman Catholicism, he challenges the identification and, by implication, the very theoretical approach: "Is this usefully considered a situation of syncretism at all? Are we concerned here with a merging of different religious ideas or is it just one particular manifestation of a complex of ideas which appears in a great variety of religious systems . . . ?" (1962:101).

The difficulty for me in all this is that Leach has gone beyond the question of the applicability of syncretism: There are, he indicates and attempts to demonstrate, structural issues or concerns in many religious systems (a concern for the affirmation of life, a concern for the inevitability of death) that are dealt with or manifested in terms of whatever specific elements are at hand. Thus, he argues, the Roman Catholic "God the Father (potent)" and "Christ the Son (sexless)" are equivalent to the Hindu "Shiva (potent)" and "Ganesha his son (sexless)" and even to the seemingly reversed Sinhalese Buddhist "Lord Buddha (sexless)" and his "servant Pulleyar (potent)."

Now all of that is most interesting, but it certainly does not come to grips with the problem implicit in the term *syncretism:* How may a belief system emerge from the blending or fusion of elements from disparate systems? Leach sidesteps that question completely, implying, rather, that the issue of syncretism is irrelevant, at least in this case. What is important is that a way is found in any belief system—and with whatever elements are at hand from whatever source—to deal with universal structural needs.

Another approach, again somewhat dismissive of the entire issue of syncretism, is to note how difficult it often is to determine the origin or source of what seems superficially to be an intrusive or syncretic element. I. M. Lewis takes this approach in his examination of the supposed presence of "pre-Islamic survivals" in contemporary Islam:

> A characteristic example of this widespread view is found in a contemporary account of Tunisian popular Islam entitled "Survivances mystiques et culte de possession dans le maraboutisme Tunisien." The author, a Tunisian sociologist, presents maraboutism (the north African cult of saints and holy men) as the embodiment of two "systems of different values: asceticism and animism." Maraboutism, we are told, derives from pre-Islamic north African roots, and its associated cult of possession is the means by which "ancient animist beliefs are perpetuated. . . . In contact with Islam, the traditional 'spirits' are simply confounded with Muslim jinns and the veneration paid to sorcerers transferred to saints." (Lewis 1986:94–95)

This sounds remarkably like interpretations of Afro-American religious beliefs and practices; for example, "In fact—what is Voodoo? Nothing more than a conglomeration of beliefs and rites of African origin, which, having been closely mixed with Catholic practice, has come to be the religion of the greater part of the peasants and the urban proletariat of the black republic of Haiti" (Métraux [1959] 1972:15). Lewis challenges the traditional syncretic interpretation of maraboutism—that it derives from pre-Islamic roots. There is in Islam, he observes, a "fierce and constantly recharged theological debate" about the "mediatory power of saints." Thus,

> What fundamentalist theologians, and their unconscious sociological hagiologists, stereotypically represent as potentially heretical and certain marginal—superstitious "pre-Islamic survivals"—possess a highly problematic quality. . . . Phenomena characterized as "fringe" or "marginal" Islam are, on closer inspection, sometimes so intimately connected with "core" Islam that they seem part of a single complex. (Lewis 1986:96)

Thus, again, the issue of syncretism does not obtain because (at least in this case) it is possible to argue that the elements in question may not in fact derive from a non-Islamic source but are instead intrinsic to Islam itself.

Still another way of avoiding the problems posed by syncretism is that of David G. Mandelbaum in his "Introduction: Process and Structure in South Asian Religion" (1964). Mandelbaum, as we have earlier observed, turned his attention to the seemingly contradictory or conflicting practices and beliefs observed among Hindu villagers throughout South Asia. Some of these are concerned with transcendent deities to be approached only through meditation and prayer, and some are concerned with locally known deities capable of being swayed by material offerings. Other anthropologists (see, for example, Marriott

1955) have interpreted this state of affairs as reflecting the presence of two systems: "Great Tradition" Hinduism on the one hand and some "tribal" or other local "Little Traditions" on the other.

The latter interpretation of course implies (even if it does not pursue) the occurrence of syncretism: Mandelbaum simply ignores questions of origin or source of the elements, preferring to demonstrate how each system serves a different religious concern. Thus, he argues, there is a transcendental set of beliefs, practices, and religious officiants concerned with "maintenance of the universe," and there is at the same time a set of pragmatic beliefs, practices, along with appropriate practitioners having to do with the day-to-day problems of people, such as illness, poor crops, and so on.

I do not derogate any of the three approaches delineated above; in my view they are contributions not only to the study of religion but even to the issues posed by the presence of seemingly contradictory elements in a belief system. They do not, however, directly challenge or debate the notion of syncretism itself, but simply evade it.

The questions remain, therefore: Is there ever such a thing as true syncretism? Are dissonant elements reinterpreted and melded? How are people able to accept without apparent conflict what—to the anthropologist—clearly seem to be contradictory assumptions and beliefs? I don't pretend to have satisfactory answers to these questions; it is important, however, that we raise the questions and begin to wrestle with them.

One argument, from a structuralist perspective, would be that the mere arrival and introduction of alien elements, even in massive amounts, do not necessarily precipitate the emergence of a syncretic religion. Rather, the resultant system will usually be clearly recognizable as a descendant or development of *one and only one* of its supposed ancestors—just as English, despite the incorporation of large amounts of French (and other) linguistic elements (phonological, grammatical, lexical), remains indisputably a Germanic and not, as was once thought, a "bastard language" without proper parentage.

One sees this quite explicitly in the case of Haitian Vodun—supposedly, since the time of Herskovits, the classic example of a truly syncretic religion. For, so we have been told, Vodun (or Voodoo) "mixes together, in almost equal proportions, African rites and Christian observances" (Métraux [1959] 1972:324).[1] Indeed, Métraux begins his chapter "Voodoo and Christianity": 'To serve the *loa* [who are of West African derivation] you have to be a Catholic. . . .' These words—of a Marbial peasant—deserve to stand as epigraph to this chapter for they express, very precisely, the paradoxical ties between Voodoo and Christianity" ([1959] 1972:323). But are they in fact "very precise"? Métraux devotes

---

[1] Why does Métraux feel the need to draw such a sharp distinction? Why not call them both *rites* or both *observances*?

much of the chapter to the history of Christian-Voodoo relations in Haiti, and it is, overwhelmingly, an account of persecution and other efforts by the Catholic church to eradicate Voodoo. Might not the underlying message of the Marbial peasant therefore also be, "You cannot (or dare not) serve the *loa* without at least pretending to be a Catholic?" I would not say that this is definitely what his comment means, but it is a reasonable alternative—given the relationship between Vodun and Catholicism in Haiti—to the interpretation Métraux and others accept, that is, that it expresses the syncretic nature of the belief system.

It is of course clear from the accounts of Métraux, Herskovits, Simpson, and others that Vodun and its sibling faiths elsewhere in the Caribbean and South America are not identical to the religions of West Africa. Apart from all other divergences, most of the devotees of the Afro-Catholic faiths are in fact born, baptized, married, and buried according to the observances of Roman Catholicism, and that is certainly not true in West Africa. One might therefore legitimately apply the approach Mandelbaum pioneered, that Catholic beliefs and practices relate to transcendent concerns and Vodun beliefs and practices to pragmatic concerns. Indeed, Métraux cites George E. Simpson's reference (1945) to an informant who "explained to him that because God is too busy to listen to the prayers of men, *loa* and saints have fallen into the habit of meeting each other half-way between heaven and earth. There the *loa* inform the saints of the wishes of the faithful. The saints then transmit the requests to God who grants them or not, as He chooses" (Métraux, [1959] 1972:327). From my eclectic perspective, however, I would suggest that the applicability of one approach does not necessarily invalidate all others. It is clear that Mandelbaum's insights are as applicable in Haiti as they are in India, and one could as easily analyze religion in the former place as in the latter without worrying over the provenience of the elements. Nevertheless, it happens to be indisputable that in Haiti (unlike in the Indian and North African cases) some religious elements derive from African religions and some from European religions. Is Haitian Vodun then, as Métraux and Herskovits would have it, a syncretic religion?

I would argue that on the basis of Métraux's own observations and despite his personal theoretical perspectives, it is *not*:

> Even while scrupulously observing Catholic rites, the Haitian peasant has remained little touched by the spirit and doctrine of Catholicism; chiefly out of ignorance, since such religious instruction as he may have received is rudimentary to say the least. He knows little of the lives of Jesus or the saints. Besides, he feels more at ease with gods and spirits which maintain friendly or hostile relationships with him, in the same way as he does with his neighbours. Voodoo is for him a familiar personal religion whereas Catholicism often shares the cold nature of the cement chapels which crown the crests of the hills. (Métraux [1959] 1972:323)

Métraux's metaphoric use of "cement chapels" is a pregnant one. For theological reasons, the Catholic priest may insist that the soul of any person who has been baptized is thenceforth Christian, but we must ask where the individual's heart and mind actually reside; it is clear from Métraux's account that the Haitian "peasant" resides religiously in the Vodun *humfo* (sanctuary) even when he or she is physically in a "cement chapel" attending a Catholic mass.

How, then, does structural absorption, such as that by which Vodun encompasses Catholic elements, take place? Perhaps the best explanation we have is that proposed by Anthony F.C. Wallace as the way in which a "revitalization movement" comes into existence:

> When there are too many elements present in the cultural "solution," when behavior is minimally predictable and approaches randomness, then to increase order it is necessary to eliminate some behavioral elements and to codify the residue in such a way that when one event occurs, it is possible to predict the next with reasonable confidence. ... When too many possibilities are already in the field, and when the orderliness of events diminishes, the only possibility for improvement lies in simultaneously simplifying the repertoire and insisting on regularity of performance. Such a procedure, often carried out under the auspices of religion, constitutes a revitalization movement. (1966:214–215)

If we take Wallace's observation only a short distance further, we may argue that much the same circumstances obtain when elements from two different belief systems coexist; most of all orderliness and prediction, in the sense of confidence about why events are occurring and what may be done to influence them, diminish substantially. The solution, according to Wallace, is "simplification of the repertoire": Some elements are eliminated, others are fused (e.g., the *loa* are the same as the Catholic saints), and some, perhaps, as Herskovits suggested, are reinterpreted. Thus, a new "ordered universe" has emerged, whether in the form of a "revitalization movement" or a "syncretic religion."

My only problem with Wallace's formula is that it is not invariable: Sometimes the repertoire is simplified, and sometimes two sets of fundamentally different and even conflicting assumptions, beliefs, and practices continue to be exhibited, not only in the same cultural system but even in the same individual!

We see this most clearly in contemporary Western society: How can one person be a fundamentalist Christian or Jew, certain that the Bible is the inerrant word of God, and at the same time be a chemist or physicist who subscribes to the tenets of science?

Elsewhere (Klass 1991b) I have suggested that such a conflict may be resolved by the belief that "God can do anything": A doctor may fully understand the implications and consequences of physical death for the tissues and organs and still believe that a divinity (or official representative) may bring back to life a person who has been dead for days. In such a case, "simplification of repertoire" is not necessary because (again) we are not dealing, as it might superficially seem, with syncretism but with one integrated belief system (the fundamentalist one) in which the elements of the other system are simply subordinated. What is happening, I suggest, might be termed repertoire *accommodation* rather than *simplification*.

If these observations in fact have any merit, might they be of help in analyzing other varieties of the science-religion interplay? Might the approach be helpful in studies of revitalization and millenarian movements where repertoire simplification seems *not* to have occurred? I pursue some of these questions in the next chapter.

Still another area for possible investigation in terms of both simplification and accommodation might well be that of political ideological movements: What are the fundamental assumptions and from what belief system do such as these derive, however unknowingly? Do you believe, for example, that progress is not only a good thing but is inevitable? Are you convinced that just ahead lies a golden age when the history of inhumanity will finally end and either "the lion will lie down with the lamb" or "the earth will have a new foundation"—or both?

But, you say, you do not believe in God; your convictions about the future derive not from any religion or set of supernatural beliefs but from simple and secular rationalism?

Once again we have come full circle: Clearly, much depends on how you define *religion*.

19

The Modern Hosts of Heaven

Anthropology, then, appears to be involved in definitions of the West while Western projects are transforming the ... peoples that ethnographers claim to represent. Both processes need to be studied systematically. ... To do that will include attempting to grasp its peculiar historicity, the mobile powers that have constructed its structures, projects, and desires. I argue that religion, in its positive and negative senses, is an essential part of that construction.

—Talal Asad
Genealogies of Religion

In this final chapter I propose to turn from the usual purviews of the anthropological study of religion—shamans and witch doctors in the more obscure recesses of Siberia and Africa and Oceania and "native America" and so on—to another larger and more contemporary arena: the world community, the global context that is neither "primitive" nor "civilized" but always both, neither "East" nor "West" but only *human*. It is my hope that my endeavor provides support for the objectives proposed by Talal Asad (1993).

I also offer this chapter as a culmination of my efforts throughout this book to escape—for the purposes of the anthropological study of religion—from what I have argued are the inhibiting propensities of traditional scientistic approaches.

The underlying question here will be seen to be: What insights into the ideological trends and conflicts of the contemporary West can be derived from an anthropological approach to religion? I am not promising blindingly new revelations or wonderful solutions; I will be more than satisfied if I have provided some modicum of additional illumination for the darkness in which we all stumble.

In particular, I want to expand upon a number of issues glossed over lightly in the preceding pages. What kinds of ideological accommodation, for example, are in fact developing between science and religion? Why do some observers perceive a contemporary movement away from rationality and toward antirationality? Why are so many of our children following Pied Pipers into strange mountainsides? What are the implications when *scientists* say, "God can do anything"? What is the attraction of fundamentalism to so many different kinds of people in so many different parts of the world?

Let us begin with the last question. Who could doubt that if H. L. Mencken were alive today, he would, as the classic bull had it, be turning over in his grave? After all, by the middle of the third decade of the twentieth century (at the time Mencken was covering the Scopes "monkey trial"), the situation in regard to religious belief and scientific knowledge was clear-cut and obvious, and the outlook for the future seemed easily predictable. Only the ignorant and illiterate, it was thought, considered the Bible an accurate and believable account of how the universe came into existence; all *civilized* people—the ones who were reading Mencken's hilarious dispatches from Tennessee—understood that science, particularly in the fields of physics, geology, and biology, had forever superseded the Bible. Education and understanding must inevitably soon penetrate even the benighted valleys of Appalachia, where the children of the God-possessed fundamentalists would eventually join the rest of us as we contentedly watched Science and its handmaiden, Technology, inexorably create a better world for all the inhabitants of our planet.

Instead, look what happened. The fundamentalists are not only still with us, they are stronger and more self-assured than ever. Science and Technology have given us such goodies as hydrogen bombs and dioxin; if we manage to avoid destroying all life on the planet, we will just drown slowly in our own wastes.

Worst of all, perhaps, many young people in recent years have seemingly wandered away from reason and rationality. A lot of them, even in the "best" universities, have joined Bible classes or taken to consulting astrologers. And those are the ones their parents and teachers can almost understand; others shave their heads and sit at the feet of orange-robed gurus or spend their time communing with crystals.

I would argue that we should stop approaching these as unconnected phenomena. Oh, we know that dissatisfaction with society's efforts to deal with war and pollution have caused some people to turn in desperation to strange "cults," but what has that to do with the resurgence of "creationism"? And putting both of those issues to one side, how, we demand to know, can an educated, intelligent person *in this day and age* really believe that if modern medicine in all its glory cannot cure arthritis, then a copper bracelet might?

Our fragmented approach is most apparent in our consideration of what many of us on the outside pejoratively refer to as *new religions* and *cults* but what the participants, from the Wicca adepts to the crystallographers, have tended in recent years to refer to as the *New Age*.

Let me begin by turning to what is in fact a superbly definitive examination of the commonly accepted scholarly approaches to the analysis of "new religions and cults": James A. Beckford's entry "New Religions: An Overview," in the *Encyclopedia of Religion* (1987). Beckford observes that "religious innovation has been associated with the disruptions of social structures," noting that those who approach the problem from this perspective wrestle with such questions as whether new religious movements "can serve as an apprenticeship for modern living" or instead tend to constitute "escapism, irrationality, or withdrawal from socioeconomic realities" (1987:391).

A somewhat different approach, he goes on, is that of viewing the new religions as responses to *cultural* disruptions—that is, as examples of revitalization and reinterpretation occurring as, on the one hand, consequences of the destructive effects of colonialism and imperialism in the non-Western world or, on the other hand, as efforts in the "West" to construct a "new self-identity" in response to "moral ambiguity, confusion, and conflict" (Beckford 1987:392).

I have no quarrel with Beckford's "Overview"—nor indeed with any of the approaches he mentions. The proponents of some may dispute with others about which approach is more important or more insightful, but I am satisfied that all contribute to our understanding of "new religious movements." What does trouble me, however, is the lack of attention not just Beckford but most writers on the subject accord to the relationship between these new phenomena and the older faiths and philosophies of our society. Must we assume that the new beliefs are sui generis, a result of some ideological spontaneous generation? Put another way, my question becomes: Are the phenomena that are subsumed under the rubrics *new religions* and *cults* simply isolated (if repetitive) responses to local instances of social, cultural, or personal stress, or is there a larger ideological event occurring somewhere at the interface of religion and science?

I think there is such an event taking place and therefore suggest that we seek to understand the New Age phenomena[1] as reflections of continuing conflict and change within the overarching context of belief and meaning. In different places and in seemingly different ways, people appear to be lining up on one or another side in this ongoing conflict. In Europe and in European-derived societies, this conflict may well have been going on for a long time (perhaps since the Renaissance), but it has certainly intensified in the last century or so.

Though I am focusing here primarily on the Western dimensions of the conflict, it is certainly by no means limited to the "West," to Europe and European-derived societies. Agehananda Bharati, for example, has argued (1970) that a Hindu Renaissance has emerged within the last century, and so it may well be that India and Hinduism must be considered as having been drawn into this conflict. There are indeed clear signs that Western colonialism and imperialism, combined with the spread of Western-derived science, technology, and political

---

[1] See Gardner 1988 for a helpful discussion of these phenomena.

philosophy (all very much part of the conflict in the West) to all parts of the planet, have served to sweep most of the peoples in the world into the fray.

My concern here, however, is with the emergence of humanism and science. I suggest that this has been at the expense of earlier ideological structures and that therefore over the past century or so individuals at all intellectual, educational, and socioeconomic levels have increasingly found themselves forced to choose between ideological allegiances. This has resulted in the repeated emergence of three separate and contending ideological constituencies, and I propose that many of the so-called new movements and cults may be understood as manifestations of just one of these constituencies.

It is only within this larger context, in my view, that concerns about social, cultural, and individual stress become meaningful. Further, if I am right, both revitalization and reinterpretation must be approached, at least to begin with, as possible reactions to this ideological conflict.

Each of the three ideological perspectives I have here isolated for consideration of course inevitably encompasses many different subsets, some so much in conflict with the others of their set that their proponents would be astonished to find themselves grouped together. I do not wish to deny or obscure such differences, but I think it useful to delineate the three categories, each of which I see as a set representing an ideological commonality. Finally, since for the purposes of study things must have names, I propose to label the ideologies *scientistic, fundamentalist,* and *post-rationalist.*[2]

The Scientistic Way

Throughout this book I have expressed my discomfort with scientistic assumptions prevalent in the study of religion. Here, however, I am using the phrase *the scientistic way* to encompass a category of contemporary religious bodies. That is, I am referring neither to science nor to the domain of the scientific but rather to the system of values, assumptions, and beliefs exhibited by those who take it as given that only *through* science—that is, by scientists using the scientific

---

[2] Why *scientistic* and not *modernist?* Why *post-rationalist* and not the aforementioned *New Age?* I seek to avoid terms identifiable with one religious tradition, reflective either of the views of proponents of some position or of their opponents. Thus, I would argue that although *modernism* derives from and reflects a specific argument within Christianity (among Roman Catholics, Anglicans, and others), *scientistic* helps us to address very similar developments in very different religious systems. Similarly, *post-rationalist* avoids the time-bound dimension of *New Age* (permitting us, for example, to consider essentially similar phenomena of the nineteenth century) as well as contemporary positive and negative connotations. What I wanted, indeed, were terms equivalent to *fundamentalism,* as that term is currently used to refer to beliefs and practices of many religions. To sum up, I would argue that *scientistic* is to *modernist*—and *post-rationalist* to *New Age*—as *fundamentalist* is to *orthodox.*

method—can we penetrate the material universe and understand how it came about, of what it is composed, how it functions, and what the future holds for the universe and for us.

Furthermore, for those of the scientistically oriented religions, it follows that the *scientist* (the only one with the necessary expertise) alone determines the areas or questions science can investigate—and once that determination has been made, all other (by definition nonscientific) explanations take a backseat: They have no credence unless they fortuitously happen to be validated by actual *scientific* studies.[3] Of course not everyone who adheres to a scientistic ideology is a scientist or even necessarily understands much about scientific methodology or findings. In this context the scientistic person is simply one who believes in the primacy of science as the source of all true or at least dependable knowledge.

Thus, by *a scientistic religion* I do not mean science itself (though, as a belief system it could of course be so approached). Rather, I refer to: (1) those contemporary denominations of Christianity and Judaism (and other faiths) that accept the aforementioned primacy of science and (2) any form of supposedly secular belief systems such as humanism or Ethical Culture—in short, any belief system in which science is perceived not as a threat or in any way an alien or uncomfortable element but rather as supportive of and integrated with the beliefs held by the followers of the particular system.

The belief systems of the scientistic way may and do vary in many other respects. Some groups, for example, may deny the existence of any divinity, whereas others believe deeply and sincerely in the existence of a sentient and purposeful God. Still other groups, such as Jewish Reconstructionists or Christian Unitarians, accept God—though often only as a kind of Durkheimian evocation of community structure and needs.

But even when the members of a scientistic faith consider God to exist and to be sentient, nevertheless all agree that belief in a divine personage does not entail any hint of the Faustian dilemma: There are no questions that humans may not ask, no avenues that humans may not explore. And further, and most important, if any conflict develops between the new findings of science and the traditional texts of the faith, then the *texts* are inevitably in error. They need not be revised, but they must be understood to have only "sentimental value" or at best "symbolic content."

How can God be wrong or have supplied us with erroneous information? One obvious solution, for many scientistic faiths, is to accept that all the texts were *written* by humans (whatever the extent or nature of possible divine *inspiration*) and therefore reflect earlier human error or the ignorance and parochialism of ancient times. Thus, within a scientistic belief system, the findings of science can-

---

[3] This of course is why scholars might legitimately argue that there was no evidence for the existence of the cities of Troy and Jericho, despite the respective accounts in *The Iliad* and the Bible, until archeologists provided acceptable "proof."

not be challenged (except according to the rules of scientific procedure) and must therefore take precedence over any statements to be found in the canons of the belief system about the nature of the universe.

Furthermore, the deity—however transcendent, however omniscient—can no longer be termed omnipotent: God does not (or, depending on your preference, *will* not or *can* not) perform miracles, if by that term one means violating or otherwise interfering with a law of nature or of the universe. Even for those who believe that God created the universe, the scientistic way requires that God be no more than a sleeping creator. Thus, one can be a follower of Darwin and yet contentedly believe that God created the primal spark of life on earth. Having once accomplished that, however, God of necessity made no further contribution, relinquishing all further developments, without interference, to the interplay of mutation and natural selection.

It should go without saying that this state of affairs did not come about easily: For advancing even minimal forms of such views Michael Servetus was incinerated, Galileo was threatened with death, Spinoza was excommunicated, and Darwin was calumniated.

Today, however, the battle is over. Not that everyone has accepted the scientistic view; there are indeed powerful dissenting voices, and we shall turn to some of these in a moment. Nevertheless, the most prestigious denominations of the formerly antagonistic (to science) Western religions, as well as prestigious formal and informal new belief systems, today accept in principle the authority of science to describe and interpret the nature of the universe. In Europe and European-derived societies, the scientistic view is considered the mainstream, the educated, the establishment, position, and any challenge to it is viewed as coming from the ideological periphery.

But if science takes absolute precedence in describing and interpreting all aspects of the physical universe—from its beginnings to its possible endings, from the microcosmic to the macrocosmic, from the nature and workings of the human mind to the limitations and possibilities of societal forms—what, then, is left for religion?

To this there is no one answer: Each of the very different scientistic belief systems can and does offer different and sometimes contending replies. For some, religion provides comfort and surcease in times of physical, mental, or social travail—or simply the restful comfort of familiar tradition and ritual. For others (or for the same people), the belief system provides guidelines for human behavior: ethical and moral directives. These guidelines may be derived from the traditional texts; that is, though the Book of Genesis, for example, may be accorded only "symbolic content," the Ten Commandments may nevertheless be accepted as unchanged and unchanging divine prescript exactly as they were considered to be throughout the ages. Again, the guidelines may eschew holy writ and be based on such things as the felt need to support and maintain the human species.

There are those, of course, who, faced with the implications of science, have opted to reject all forms of religion as outdated and irrelevant, but many even of these people could be shown to be adhering to a set of underlying beliefs not too far removed from what I have here termed scientistic. By scientistic *religions,* however, I am referring to those belief systems whose adherents manage to accept the implications of science but nevertheless continue to participate within an encompassing formal religious framework (a Durkheimian "Church")—and such people, it would seem, continue to make up a substantial, perhaps overwhelming, segment of all those who subscribe to the authority of science.

Then again, there are those who profoundly reject that authority.

The Fundamentalist Way

The assumptions of those who adhere to fundamentalist persuasions are very different from those who have chosen the scientistic ones—even though in some denominatons a fundamentalist might well be seated next to a scientistic fellow congregant. What distinguishes the fundamentalist, despite all variations and differences, is the conviction that there is a deity not only sentient and purposeful but also *omnipotent* in the sense of being both able and willing to interfere at any time in the workings of the material universe. In other words, "God can do anything" is the slogan of the fundamentalist way.

With this conviction, one could never depend entirely on the findings of scientists. Are there fossils under the ground? They may be the remains of creatures who lived millions of years ago, but it is equally possible that the bones we find were created five minutes earlier by Divinity for Divinity's impenetrable purposes. And a replication of a scientific experiment, with all variables under control, *may* duplicate the results of the first, but only, of course, if God wills it.

Fundamentalists may therefore disagree with one another about how much credence to give to scientific reports, but they all agree that science alone can *never* provide final answers nor reliable interpretations of observations, nor predictive certainty. For that sort of thing, fundamentalists agree, one must turn to the religious literature, though they may disagree on exactly *which* religious literature one should consult and how the divinely inspired writings are to be understood.

It follows, therefore, that fundamentalists all share one profound conviction: Ultimate truths are to be found in religious literature. Just as they reject or doubt the ever growing body of scientific explanation, they equally reject all scholarly modification or correction of their particular group's sacred texts. As they see it, all-powerful and all-knowing Divinity has, sometime in the past, provided humans with true explanations and instructions, and these are not subject to later emendation or reinterpretation, whatever new information is acquired or whatever changes have occurred in human affairs or in the nature of human relationships in their societies.

What this means, specifically, is that fundamentalists believe it may be possible for science to *confirm* (if one is at all interested in such confirmation) statements in the holy texts, but it is impossible for science (or historical scholarship or anybody or anything) to *invalidate* any unequivocal statement in the text. If, therefore, there is an apparent conflict or contradiction between the text and any other source of information, then the other source is wrong: Somebody, but not the sacred text, has made a mistake.

This brings us to a curious observation: Though scientistics and fundamentalists obviously derive from very different basic assumptions, there is one assumption they share with each other—but not with those of the third category, the post-rationalists. Scientistics and fundamentalists alike believe *there is a source of dependable, accurate information about the nature and workings of the universe:* In one case the source is scientific research, in the other holy writ. For both groups, therefore, because both derive from what each perceives as a dependable source of information, rational conclusions and decisions may be arrived at and irrational ones discarded.

This last observation may surprise some readers. Ever since Mencken described the antics of the supposedly unwashed and ignorant countryfolk who opposed the teachings of evolution in Tennessee in 1925, the image evoked by the term *fundamentalist* has been—in the educated milieus of the United States— that of red-necked and semiliterate hillbillies content with the Bible alone and otherwise prepared to let the rest of the world and its works go by unregarded.

In recent years the term *fundamentalist* has been used to encompass certain sects of Jews (the Neturai Karta, the Hasidim, etc.) and even of Muslims (the Muslim Brotherhood, the followers of the Ayatollah Khomeini, etc.). It is generally understood that these very different groups have in common a rejection of all literature of a theological nature apart from their own most basic holy texts, and most of all their rejection of science and all extrareligious scholarship or similar intellectual enterprises.

Consequently, it often comes as something of a shock to those who so view fundamentalism to discover that there are fundamentalists (in all of the above religions) who have doctorates in the natural and even the social sciences: There are engineers, geologists, chemists, physicians, and even psychologists and physicists who nevertheless proudly and firmly consider themselves members of what the scientistically inclined would unhesitatingly label fundamentalist faiths.[4]

Fundamentalists of the many religious persuasions continue to be steadfast in

---

[4] Consider, for example, H. M. Morris's *Scientific Creationism* (1981). Not only is it edited by "Henry M. Morris, Ph.D.," but, we are told, it is "the result of a cooperative project undertaken by the scientific staff of the Institute for Creation Research, the members of the Technical Advisory Board of the Institute, and a number of other scientists and teachers who assisted in various ways." The names of twenty-three of these "writers and consultants" are then listed; all but eight have Ph.D.'s, the rest have M.D.'s, Ed.D.'s, D.Sc.'s, and so on (1981:i–ii).

their rejection of science as *authority,* but many have come to welcome it as a *tool.* "Scientific creationists," for example, study geology, physics, and chemistry in order to work at such occupations as building bridges and searching for oil but nevertheless reject scientific interpretations and explanations about such matters as how and when and why the oil got into the ground in the first place or the implications of the half-life of radioactive substances for the age of our planet or universe: "In attempting to determine the real age of the earth, it should always be remembered,[5] of course, that recorded history began only several thousand years ago. Not even uranium dating is capable of experimental verification, since no one could actually watch uranium decaying for millions of years to see what happens" (H. M. Morris 1981:137).

Fundamentalists do not deny the presence of fossils in the ground; they do challenge nonbiblical explanations of how the fossils got there. They consider as far-fetched and unconvincing any notion of relationships between the creatures whose bones we find and actual living creatures, particularly humans:

> Even in terms of the standard chronology, and accepting the fossil evidence at face value, we have shown that there is no objective evidence that man evolved from an ape or any other kind of animal ancestry. As far as the actual fossil evidence is concerned, man has always been man, and the ape has always been an ape. There are no intermediate or transitional forms leading up to man, any more than there were transitional forms between any of the other basic kinds of animals in the fossil records. (H. M. Morris 1981:137).

Thus, fundamentalism is not necessarily characterized today by isolated and remnant pockets of ignorance and illiteracy, soon to disappear as modern education invincibly penetrates the dark corners. Rather, in all branches of Christianity, Judaism, and Islam (among other world religions), it represents healthy, confident, and growing bodies whose members believe that their faiths are strong enough to absorb science and take advantage of it without being destroyed by it. For them, their holy writ is not "symbolic" but the unchanging word of God, and God is not "bound" but free to perform any miracle, from placing oil in the ground thousands of years ago for the use of unborn generations to bringing the universe to a complete end in a moment.

And, let us observe, fundamentalism is attracting *new* adherents, even (or particularly) from the ranks of the scientistic faiths and even from among those who have rejected all faiths. One could indeed argue that contemporary resurgent fundamentalism in the United States represents not just revitalization in general but even more specifically *nativistic* revitalization. Just as some versions of the Native American Ghost Dance espoused a return to the time before the coming of the Europeans—to a world without alien domination but *with* guns and horses—so modern fundamentalism looks forward to a return to "that old-time

---

[5] A very different "it should always be remembered" from that of scientists!

religion" and to a world no longer dominated by the ideology of science, but a world nevertheless still enjoying the fruits of science and technology.

Contemporary resurgent fundamentalism is confident, ebullient, and aggressive in the face of what it perceives as scientistic opponents who have lost their confidence and their way.

The Post-Rationalist Way

Post-rationalists, who also exhibit a multitude of variant subsystems, nevertheless collectively reject the assumption that there is a single sure source of knowledge. Science may have some answers, but it can never have all, and it is as liable to error and ignorance as are the holy texts of any religion—though, again, to the post-rationalist, none of the holy texts of *any* religion can ever be dismissed as totally without merit.

Indeed, a common though not necessarily universal characteristic of post-rationalists is that they have earlier given thought and attention to either scientistic or fundamentalist faiths (and sometimes to both) and have in the end turned away unsatisfied. Post-rationalist ideologies, therefore, often reflect awareness and acceptance of science-derived criticisms of traditional Western religion (such as substantial error about the nature, age, and origin of the physical universe) along with a rejection of the scientistic premise that *only* through science can we hope to penetrate and understand the nature of things:

> Magicians [i.e., practitioners of Wicca] may be drawn to the practice because they see the freedom with which they can believe, rationalize and interpret their involvement. But I suspect that many of them are also confused about the so-called serious intellectual standards of logic, objectivity and demonstrability, and that their magic is an expression of their ambivalence. They are as hesitant about the value of scientific insight and rationalism as they are about the magic. (Luhrmann 1989:343)

Post-rationalists appear to wrestle—frequently quite explicitly—with the jointly held assumption of scientistics and fundamentalists that there is or can ever be *one* source of true or dependable knowledge about the universe. If science has forever destroyed the right of any set of sacred texts to the claim of exclusive and divinely inspired "truth," science has nevertheless failed to convince the post-rationalist that it has a significantly better claim.

My point is not simply that post-rationalists may have rejected scientistic or fundamentalist interpretations but that post-rationalists are often *aware* that they are doing it. Margot Adler, for example, begins her sympathetic portrayal of what she calls contemporary "Neo-Paganism" by citing the scholar Harriet Whitehead on exactly these issues:

> Harriet Whitehead, in an article on scientology, science-fiction, and the occult, makes the point that, contrary to the popular assumption, most occultists have an

intellectual style, "a process of sorting, surveying, analysing and abstracting." One of the hallmarks of that style is lack of dogmatism. "The occult world," she writes, offers to the individual a 'free marketplace' of ideas. . . ." What this resembles, "and not by coincidence, is the intellectual democracy of the scientific and academic communities." She writes that the difference between these two communities and the occult world is that occultists refuse "contentment with the finite" (the phrase comes from William James). Occultists continually affirm that "certain experiences do not cease to exist simply because there is no place for them in our customary order." Occultists display an extraordinary ability to shift from one dimension of reality to another with ease, feeling that the whole world "hangs together in one unified piece." While some Neo-Pagans consider themselves occultists and others do not, Whitehead's characteristics seem to hold true for the groups I've observed. (Adler 1986:12–13)[6]

For some observers (see Beckford 1987), the faiths we associate with the New Age first emerged in the 1960s and, most particularly in the United States, in response to the Vietnam conflict and attendant social issues. Although it is true that some new movements unquestionably emerged during that particular period, it can certainly be argued that many, perhaps most, of the fundamental ideological concerns and perceptions go back much further. Indeed, I suggest that the post-rationalist ideological perspective has its true origins in the nineteenth century (at the latest, and probably earlier) and thus is very much a contender in the ideological dispute precipitated by the emergence of science and humanism.

Specifically, I would list among its formative movements such nineteenth-century emergences as the Baha'i religion (see Smith 1987), Theosophy (see Blavatsky 1889, [1887] 1976), and Spiritualism (see Bednarowski 1973, Isaacs 1975, Moore 1977). Modern witchcraft comes onto the scene only a little later, in the first decades of the twentieth century, but nevertheless belongs among the forerunners of the New Age (see Luhrmann 1989, Adler 1986).

What do such seemingly disparate belief systems have in common? As I have indicated, I see post-rationalists as sharing a number of perceptions and conclusions. In my own words (not necessarily theirs) some of these commonalities are:

1. A conviction that the findings of science have destroyed the reliability of the assertions of the Bible-based religions: The world was clearly not created, developed, and maintained as the Bible asserts. They therefore agree that a literate and intelligent person can no longer accept the Scriptures on faith; the fundamentalist way is thus closed to them.

2. A discomfort with the scientistic way as profound as it is for fundamentalists. Where science calls the tune, as post-rationalists see it, there is no God in

---

[6] The Whitehead citations are from her paper "Reasonably Fantastic: Some Perspectives on Scientology, Science Fiction and Occultism" (1974); the William James reference is to *The Varieties of Religious Experience* ([1902] 1985).

charge, there is no one to pray to, and no reason to pray: There is no meaning to events and so no purpose to life and no hope for anything after death. They find emotionally unsatisfying such tactical principles as that found in humanism (protect your own species) and in the Kantian kind of moral imperative (if everyone is antisocial, we are all going to suffer).

3. A strong awareness that the world is larger than Europe and older than European culture—along with a feeling that European society and faiths are intrinsically unable to come to grips with the significance of the age of the planet and the varieties of its cultural systems. Post-rationalists believe that scientific research has shown us that our ancestral faiths are embarrassingly parochial in scope. Thus, if science ultimately lacks the power to give us comfort—but at the same time has convinced us of the errors and inadequacies of our ancestral faiths—we must of necessity turn elsewhere on the planet for faith and comfort.

Consider, for example, the Baha'i movement from the above perspective. It was perhaps the first New Age faith in that its founder, Baha'u'llah (the leader from 1866 to 1892), advocated not just toleration of other faiths but much more:

> Beyond this general attitude of tolerance which the Baha'i leaders sought to inculcate in their followers were the specifically universalistic statements and claims made by Baha'u'llah. . . . His followers were exhorted to "Close your eyes to racial differences, and welcome all with the light of oneness." . . . True religion was the surest means to establish world unity and amity. . . . Baha'u'llah specifically addressed the "people of the world" in his writings, referring in particular passages to the clergy of the Zoroastrian, Jewish, Christian, and Islamic faiths and to the rulers and kings of the world. (Smith 1987:83)

Similar calls for unity and universalism have emanated from South Asia from the time of Kabir (late fifteenth century), and the specifically universalistic and all-incorporating teachings of such contemporary South Asian holy men as Sathya Sai Baba continue to attract followers in the West. By the second half of the nineteenth century, Theosophy, a universalistic blending of Eastern and Western philosophy and theology, was introduced to Europe and European-derived societies by H. P. ("Madame") Blavatsky and her associates: "We hold to no religion, as to no philosophy in particular: we cull the good we find in each. . . . The members of the Theosophical Society at large are free to profess whatever religion or philosophy they like, or none if they so prefer. . . . The Fellows may be Christians or Mussulmen, Jews or Parsees, Buddhists or Brahmins, Spiritualists or Materialists, it does not matter" (Blavatsky 1889:19). For upper-class European (first British, then American and continental) men and women dissatisfied with both the scientistic and the fundamentalist religious positions, this joyously aggressive universalism was only one of the attractions of South Asian faiths. Vedantic Hinduism continues to offer, to those who can no longer believe in heaven and hell, an even more ancient but for them astonishingly new explanation of life and death. The law of karma may be of alien derivation, but it is easily absorbed by those already familiar with the laws of thermodynamics (see Penelhum 1986, Klass 1991a), and the notion of endless rebirth is more reconcilable with the age of the earth as propounded by modern geology than it is with the biblical account.

Spiritualism (or, variously, Modern Spiritualism, Spiritism, etc.) took many forms as it developed and changed during the nineteenth and early twentieth centuries. In much of the world outside of the United States and Britain, it developed into a distinctive religious movement reflective of the writings of Allan Kardec (the pseudonym of Hippolyte Rivail). In the English-speaking world, the proponents of Spiritualism tended to focus more on the single issue of communication with spirits of the dead rather than on more comprehensive philosophical or theological dimensions (Sidgewick 1911).

Even in Britain and the United States, however, Spiritualism was affected by the ongoing conflict between science and religion. Arthur Conan Doyle—writer, doctor, and earnest researcher of Spiritualist phenomena—offered the following observations about himself:

> When I had finished my medical education in 1882, I found myself, like many young medical men, a convinced materialist as regards our personal destiny. I had never ceased to be an earnest theist. . . . To say that the Universe was made by immutable laws only put the question one degree further back as to who made the laws. I did not, *of course,* believe in an anthropomorphic God, but I believed then, as I believe now, in an intelligent Force behind all the operations of Nature. . . . and I was convinced that death did indeed end all. . . . (1918:15–16; italics mine)

Doyle's perceptions and concerns appear to have reflected those of others— including Americans—who turned to Spiritualism:

> Spiritualism was a religious response to the crisis of faith experienced by Americans at mid-century. Based on the view that contact with the spirits of the dead provided empirical proof of the immortality of the soul, Spiritualism appealed to people in search of a new justification for a wavering faith. For those no longer convinced by the "evidences" of Christianity, Spiritualism provided "scientific" evidence of religious truth. . . . It provided a way to remain religious for those disaffected from Calvinism or evangelicalism in the antebellum years and for those disillusioned by Darwinism, biblical criticism, and the rise of science later in the century. (Braude 1989:4)

There are other post-rationalist movements. Some have turned to what they believe is the oldest and most tenacious of Western faiths, that of witchcraft. Others have preferred to turn for the source of their New Age beliefs to what scientists investigating the human mind can tell them. In recent years offshoots of psychoanalysis and psychology (Scientology, EST, and many more) have proliferated in the borderlands between religion and medicine. Still others have sought meaning and explanation in astrology and have sought health in copper bracelets and crystals (see Gardner 1988 for a scientifically oriented critique of all such forays). The post-rationalist directions and movements are seemingly legion, and yet, I would argue, they continue to have in common the conviction that both science and traditional Western faiths are inadequate, though not necessarily completely wrong.

For, from the post-rationalist perspective (unlike those of fundamentalism and scientism) *nothing* is ever *completely* wrong. I have argued that universalism is the touchstone of all the post-rationalist movements, and certainly in any of the New Age publications there are references about all of the above interests and concerns, and more. One post-rationalist may prefer to follow a guru who advocates a variety of Hinduism, a second may be a member of a Wicca coven, whereas a third concentrates on macrobiotic food and crystal therapy: None of the three completely rejects the other two and is often quite interested in the others' perceptions and experiences.

Post-rationalists are therefore free to move without guilt from faith to faith, to accept any elements of the faiths of their parents, or even of science, without feeling any necessity to accept anything else or to worry about mutual exclusivity of beliefs. What is significant, therefore, is not the differences between all these post-rationalists, as I have labeled them, but what they have in common: their acceptance of one another—not necessarily of one another's beliefs or interests but of their common quest for meaning and comfort in a world where literally anything is possibly true and nothing can be known for certain.

Another reason for post-rationalist universalism may be advanced. The planet we live on is in serious trouble. Everyone is aware of it, of course. The scientistic faiths urge science to find solutions to the greenhouse effect, toxic waste, overpopulation, and so on. Fundamentalists suggest that science is responsible and that therefore the solution must be sought in the Holy Scriptures, where "God's will" is to be found. Post-rationalists, in contrast, are convinced that there is no one answer and are prepared to listen to all suggestions. And they believe, further, that the solution will require the triumph of universalism: Only when there is true peace and love in the world—only when the human species understands itself to be a humble component alongside worms and rocks in the unity that is the planet (and even the universe)—only then can the problems that threaten us be overcome.

Manifestly, there is much to debate and to clarify in the foregoing. Most of all, in my view, the ongoing scholarly analysis of religions and religion-related movements (particularly of those currently labeled New Age) should be broadened to encompass ideological as well as the traditional sociological and psychological factors.

I suggest we begin by noting that there is quite an ideological war going on around us and that arrayed on the battlefield are three very distinctive armies representing, inevitably, three "ordered universes."

References

Adler, Margot. 1986. *Drawing Down the Moon: Witches, Druids, Goddess-Worshippers, and Other Pagans in America Today*. Boston: Beacon Press.

AHD. 1969. *The American Heritage Dictionary of the English Language*. William Morris, ed. Boston: American Heritage and Houghton Mifflin.

Arens, W. 1979. *The Man-Eating Myth: Anthropology and Anthropophagy*. New York: Oxford University Press.

Asad, Talal. 1993. *Genealogies of Religion: Discipline and Reasons of Power in Christianity and Islam*. Baltimore: Johns Hopkins University Press.

Banton, Michael (ed.). [1966] 1971. *Anthropological Approaches to the Study of Religion*. ASA Monograph no. 3. London: Tavistock Publications.

Barbour, Ian G. 1966. *Issues in Science and Religion*. New York: Harper & Row.

Barth, Fredrik. 1987. *Cosmologies in the Making: A Generative Approach to Cultural Variation in Inner New Guinea*. Cambridge: Cambridge University Press.

Basham, A. L. 1954. *The Wonder That Was India: A Survey of the Indian Sub-continent Before the Coming of the Muslims*. New York: Grove Press.

Bateson, Gregory. [1936] 1958. *Naven*. Stanford, Calif.: Stanford University Press.

Beattie, John. 1964a "The Ghost Cult in Bunyoro." *Ethnology* 3 (2): 127–151.

———. 1964b. *Other Cultures: Aims, Methods and Achievements in Social Anthropology*. New York: Free Press.

Beckford, James A. 1987. "New Religions: An Overview." In *The Encyclopedia of Religion*, vol. 10. M. Eliade, ed. New York: Macmillan, 390–394.

Bednarowski, Mary Farrell. 1973. "Nineteenth Century American Spiritualism: An Attempt at a Scientific Religion." Ph.D. dissertation, University of Minnesota.

Benedict, Ruth. [1934] 1959. *Patterns of Culture*. Boston: Houghton Mifflin.

Bharati, Agehananda. 1970. "The Hindu Renaissance and Its Apologetic Patterns." *Journal of Asian Studies* 29 (2): 267–287.

Blavatsky, H. P. 1889. *The Key to Theosophy*. London: Theosophical Publishing Society.

———. [1877] 1976. *Isis Unveiled: A Master-Key to Mysteries of Ancient and Modern Science and Theology*. 2 vols. Pasadena, Calif.: Theosophical University Press.

Bloom, Allan. 1987. *The Closing of the American Mind*. New York: Simon & Schuster.

Boas, Franz. [1888] 1940. "The Aims of Ethnology." In *Race, Language and Culture*. New York: Free Press, 626–638.

Braude, Ann. 1989. *Radical Spirits: Spiritualism and Women's Rights in Nineteenth-Century America*. Boston: Beacon Press.

Burtt, E. A. (ed.). 1955. *The Teachings of the Compassionate Buddha*. New York: New American Library.

Cassirer, Ernst. 1944. *An Essay on Man.* New York: Bantam Books.

———. 1946. *Language and Myth.* New York: Dover.

Chagnon, Napoleon A. 1992. *Yanomamö.* 4th ed. Fort Worth: Harcourt Brace Jovanovich.

Cohen, Myron L. 1988. "Souls and Salvation: Conflicting Themes in Chinese Popular Religion." In *Death Ritual in Late Imperial and Modern China.* J. L. Watson and E. S. Rawski, eds. Berkeley: University of California Press, 180–202.

Collins, Arthur W. 1987. *The Nature of Mental Things.* Notre Dame: University of Notre Dame Press.

Cook, Scott. 1966. "The Obsolete Anti-Market Mentality: A Critique of the Substantive Approach." *American Anthropologist* 68: 323–345.

Dalton, Edward. [1872] 1960. *Descriptive Ethnology of Bengal.* Calcutta: Firma Mukhopadhyaya.

De Bary, William T., et al. (comps.). 1958. *Sources of Indian Tradition.* New York: Columbia University Press.

Deliège, Robert. 1993. "The Myths of Origin of the Indian Untouchables." *Man* (n.s.) 28 (3): 533–549.

Dorson, Edward T. 1965. "The Eclipse of Solar Mythology." In *Myth: A Symposium.* T. Sebeok, ed. Bloomington: Indiana University Press, 25–63.

Doyle, Arthur Conan. 1918. *The New Revelation.* New York: George H. Doran Company.

Dumont, Louis. 1970. *Homo Hierarchicus: An Essay on the Caste System.* Chicago: University of Chicago Press.

Durkheim, Émile. [1912] 1965. *The Elementary Forms of the Religious Life.* New York: The Free Press.

Ellis Davidson, H. R. 1964. *Gods and Myths of Northern Europe.* Harmondsworth, England: Penguin Books.

Evans-Pritchard, E. E. 1937. *Witchcraft, Oracles and Magic Among the Azande.* Oxford: Clarendon Press.

———. 1965. *Theories of Primitive Religion.* Oxford: Clarendon Press.

Firth, Raymond. 1946. *Malay Fishermen: Their Peasant Economy.* London: Routledge.

———. 1955. *The Fate of the Soul: An Interpretation of Some Primitive Concepts.* Cambridge: Cambridge University Press.

Fortes, Meyer. [1959] 1981. *Oedipus and Job in West African Religion.* New York: Octagon Books.

———. 1987. *Religion, Morality and the Person: Essays on Tallensi Religion.* Cambridge: Cambridge University Press.

Frazer, James G. [1922] 1958. *The Golden Bough: A Study in Magic and Religion.* New York: Macmillan.

Fried, Morton H. 1975. *The Notion of Tribe.* Menlo Park, Calif.: Cummings.

Fürer-Haimendorf, Christoph Von. 1962. *The Apa Tanis and Their Neighbors: A Primitive Civilization of the Eastern Himalayas.* London: Routledge & Kegan Paul.

Ganzfried, Solomon. 1927. *Code of Jewish Law (Kitzur Schulchan Aruch).* New York: Hebrew Publishing Company.

Gardner, Martin. 1988. *The New Age: Notes of a Fringe Watcher.* Buffalo, N.Y.: Prometheus Press.

Geertz, Clifford. 1971. "Religion as a Cultural System." In *Anthropological Approaches to the Study of Religion.* M. Banton, ed. ASA Monograph no. 3. London: Tavistock Publications, 1–46.

Goode, William J. [1951] 1964. *Religion Among the Primitives.* Glencoe, Ill.: Free Press.

Gough, E. Kathleen. 1962. "Caste in a Tanjore Village." In *Aspects of Caste in South India, Ceylon and North-West Pakistan.* E. R. Leach, ed. Cambridge: Cambridge University Press, 11–60.

Greenfield, Sidney M. 1990. "Turner and Anti-Turner in the Image of Christian Pilgrimage in Brazil." *Anthropology of Consciousness* 1 (3-4): 1–8.

Hallowell, A. Irving. 1949. "The Social Function of Anxiety in Primitive Society." In *Personal Character and Cultural Milieu: A Collection of Readings.* D. Haring, comp. Syracuse: Syracuse University Press, 375–388.

Harner, Michael J. 1979. "The Ecological Basis for Aztec Sacrifice." *American Ethnologist* 4: 117–135.

Harner, Michael J. (ed.). 1973. *Hallucinogens and Shamanism.* New York: Oxford University Press.

Harris, Marvin. 1959. "The Economy Has No Surplus?" *American Anthropologist* 61: 185–199.

———. 1985. *Good to Eat.* New York: Simon & Schuster.

———. 1987. *Cultural Anthropology.* 2nd ed. New York: Harper & Row.

Herodotus. 1942. *Herodotus: The Persian Wars.* Trans. George Rawlinson. New York: Modern Library.

Herskovits, Melville J. 1949. *Man and His Works: The Science of Cultural Anthropology.* New York: Alfred A. Knopf.

———. [1940] 1952. *Economic Anthropology: A Study in Comparative Economics.* (Originally published as *The Economic Life of Primitive Peoples.*) New York: Alfred A. Knopf.

Horowitz, M. M., and Morton Klass. 1961. "The Martiniquan East Indian Cult of Maldevidan." *Social and Economic Studies* 10 (1): 93–100.

Horton, Robin. 1970 "African Traditional Thought and Western Science." In *Rationality.* B. R. Wilson, ed. Oxford: Blackwell, 131–171.

Isaacs, Ernest Joseph. 1975. "A History of Nineteenth-Century American Spiritualism as a Religious and Social Movement." Ph.D. dissertation, University of Wisconsin.

James, William. [1902] 1985. *The Varieties of Religious Experience.* Cambridge: Harvard University Press.

Kasturi, N. 1981. *Sathya Sai Speaks: Discourses of Bhagavan Sri Sathya Sai Baba.* Vol. 4. Bangalore: Sri Sathya Sai Books and Publications.

Keyes, Charles F., and E. Valentine Daniel (eds.). 1983. *Karma: An Anthropological Inquiry.* Berkeley: University of California Press.

Kirk, G. S. 1970. *Myth: Its Meaning and Functions in Ancient and other Cultures.* Berkeley: University of California Press.

Klass, Morton. 1966. "Marriage Rules in Bengal." *American Anthropologist* 68: 951–970.

———. 1978. *From Field to Factory: Community Structure and Industrialization in West Bengal.* Philadelphia: Institute for the Study of Human Issues Press.

———. 1983. "The Artificial Alien: Transformations of the Robot in Science Fiction." In *Robotics: Future Factories, Future Workers.* R. J. Miller, ed. Beverly Hills, Calif.: Sage Publications, 171–179.

———. [1961] 1988. *East Indians in Trinidad: A Study of Cultural Persistence.* Prospect Heights, Ill.: Waveland Press.

———. 1990. "The Closing of 'the Bazaar of Cultures': Anthropology as Scapegoat." *Education and Urban Society* 22 (4): 356–363.

————. 1991a. *Singing with Sai Baba: The Politics of Revitalization in Trinidad.* Boulder, Colo.: Westview Press.

————. 1991b. "When 'God Can Do Anything': Belief Systems in Collision." *Anthropology of Consciousness* 2 (1-2): 32–34.

————. [1980] 1993. *Caste: The Emergence of the South Asian Social System.* New Delhi: Manohar Press.

Kroeber, Alfred A. 1909. "Classificatory Systems of Relationship." *Journal of the [Royal] Anthropological Institute* 39: 77–84.

Lang, Andrew. 1898. *The Making of Religion.* London: Longmans Green.

Langer, Suzanne K. 1960. *Philosophy in a New Key.* 4th ed. Cambridge: Harvard University Press.

Leach, E. R. 1954. *Political Systems of Highland Burma: A Study of Kachin Social Structure.* Cambridge: Harvard University Press.

————. 1962. "Pulleyar and the Lord Buddha: An Aspect of Religious Syncretism in Ceylon." *Psychoanalysis and the Psychoanalytic Review* 49 (2): 80–102.

————. 1970. *Lévi-Strauss.* London: Fontana/Collins.

Lehmann, Arthur C., and James E. Myers (eds.). 1989. *Magic, Witchcraft and Religion: An Anthropological Study of the Supernatural.* 2nd ed. Mountain View, Calif.: Mayfield.

Lessa, William A., and Evon Z. Vogt (eds.). 1979. *Reader in Comparative Religion: An Anthropological Approach.* 4th ed. New York: Harper & Row.

Lévi-Strauss, Claude. 1962. *La Pensée Sauvage.* Paris: Libraire Plon.

————. 1967. *Structural Anthropology.* Trans. Claire Jacobson and Brooke Schoepf. Garden City, N.Y.: Doubleday.

————. 1969. *The Raw and the Cooked: Introduction to a Science of Mythology.* Vol. 1. Trans. John and Doreen Weightman. New York: Harper & Row.

Lévy-Bruhl, Lucien. 1926. *How Natives Think.* London: Allen & Unwin.

Lewis, I. M. 1986. *Religion in Context: Cults and Charisma.* Cambridge: Cambridge University Press.

Lowie, Robert H. 1924. *Primitive Religion.* New York: Boni and Liveright.

————. 1937. *The History of Ethnological Theory.* New York: Rinehart.

Luhrmann, T. M. 1989. *Persuasions of the Witch's Craft: Ritual Magic in Contemporary England.* Cambridge: Harvard University Press.

Mair, Lucy. 1969. *Witchcraft.* New York: McGraw-Hill.

Malinowski, Bronislaw. [1948] 1954. *Magic, Science and Religion and Other Essays.* Garden City, N.Y.: Doubleday.

Mandelbaum, David G. 1964. "Introduction: Process and Structure in South Asian Religion." In *Aspects of Religion in South Asia.* E. B. Harper, ed. *Journal of Asian Studies* 23: 5–20.

Marett, R. R. 1909. *The Threshold of Religion.* London: Methuen.

Maring, N. H. 1979. "Cult." In *Encyclopedic Dictionary of Religion,* vol. 1. P. K. Meagher, T. C. O'Brian, and C. M. Ahearne, eds. Washington, D.C.: Corpus Publications, 958.

Marriott, McKim. 1955. "Little Communities in an Indigenous Civilization." In *Village India: Studies in the Little Community.* M. Marriott, ed. American Anthropological Association Memoir 83, 171–222.

McMartin, Grace J. (ed.). 1982. *A Recapitulation of Satya Sai Baba's Divine Teaching.* Hyderabad: Avon Printing Works.

Métraux, Alfred. [1959] 1972. *Voodoo in Haiti.* New York: Schocken Books.

Middleton, John. [1960] 1987. *Lugbara Religion: Ritual and Authority Among an East African People.* Washington, D.C.: Smithsonian Institution Press.

Middleton, John (ed.). 1967a. *Gods and Rituals: Readings in Religious Beliefs and Practices.* American Museum Sourcebooks in Anthropology. Garden City, N.Y.: Natural History Press.

————. 1967b. *Magic, Witchcraft, and Curing.* American Museum Sourcebooks in Anthropology. Garden City, N.Y.: Natural History Press.

————. 1967c. *Myth and Cosmos: Readings in Mythology and Symbolism.* American Museum Sourcebooks in Anthropology. Garden City, N.Y.: Natural History Press.

Mills, Sharon G. 1989. "The Social Construction of Contemplation." Ph.D. dissertation, Columbia University.

Moore, R. Lawrence. 1977. *In Search of White Crows: Spiritualism, Parapsychology, and American Culture.* New York: Oxford University Press.

Moore, Rebecca, and Fielding M. McGehee (eds.). 1989. *New Religious Movements, Mass Suicide, and Peoples Temple: Scholarly Perspectives on a Tragedy.* New York: E. Mellen Press.

Morgan, L. H. 1870. *Systems of Consanguinity and Affinity of the Human Family.* Smithsonian Contributions to Knowledge 17. [Washington, D.C.: Smithsonian Institution.]

Morris, Brian. 1987. *Anthropological Studies of Religion: An Introductory Text.* Cambridge: Cambridge University Press.

Morris, Henry M., 1981. *Scientific Creationism.* San Diego: CLP Publishers.

Müller, Max. 1878. *Lectures on the Origin and Growth of Religion.* London: Longmans Green.

Murray, Margaret Alice. [1921] 1967. *The Witch-Cult in Western Europe.* Oxford: Clarendon Press.

Neufeldt, Ronald W. (ed.). 1986. *Karma and Rebirth: Post Classical Developments.* Albany: State University of New York Press.

Norbeck, Edward. 1961. *Religion in Primitive Society.* New York: Harper & Row.

OED. 1989. *The Oxford English Dictionary,* vol. 13. 2nd ed. J. A. Simpson and E.S.C. Weiner, eds.. Oxford: Clarendon Press.

OUD. 1955. *The Oxford Universal Dictionary on Historical Principles.* 3rd ed. C. T. Onions, ed. Oxford: Clarendon Press.

Penelhum, Terence. 1986 "Critical Response." In *Karma and Rebirth: Post Classical Developments.* R. W. Neufeldt, ed. Albany: State University of New York Press, 339–345.

Pepper, Stephen. 1942. *World Hypotheses: A Study in Evidence.* Berkeley: University of California Press.

Piaget, Jean. 1971. *Structuralism.* London: Routledge & Kegan Paul.

Pirenne, Henri. 1959. *Mohammed and Charlemagne.* New York: Meridian Books.

Polanyi, Karl. 1957. "The Economy as Instituted Process." In *Trade and Market in the Early Empires: Economies in History and Theory.* K. Polanyi, C. M. Arensberg, and H. W. Pearson, eds. Glencoe, Ill.: Free Press, 243–270.

Polanyi, Karl, C. M. Arensberg, and H. W. Pearson (eds.). 1957. *Trade and Market in the Early Empires: Economies in History and Theory.* Glencoe, Ill.: Free Press.

Preston, James J. (ed.). 1982. *Mother Worship: Themes and Variations.* Chapel Hill: University of North Carolina Press.

Putnam, Carleton. 1961. *Race and Reason: A Yankee View.* Washington, D.C.: Public Affairs Press.

Radcliffe-Brown, A. R. [1932] 1964. *The Andaman Islanders*. New York: Free Press.

———. 1965. *Structure and Function in Primitive Society: Essays and Addresses*. New York: Free Press.

Radhakrishnan, Sarvapalli. 1939. *Eastern Religions and Western Thought*. Oxford: Clarendon Press.

Radin, Paul. [1937] 1957. *Primitive Religion: Its Nature and Origin*. New York: Dover.

Rappaport, Roy. [1966] 1984. *Pigs for the Ancestors: Ritual in the Ecology of a New Guinea People*. New Haven: Yale University Press.

Rosaldo, Renato I. 1968. "Metaphors of Hierarchy in a Mayan Ritual." *American Anthropologist* 70: 524–536.

Roscoe, J. 1923. *The Banyankole*. Cambridge: Cambridge University Press.

Rose, H. J. 1959. *Religion in Greece and Rome*. New York: Harper & Row.

Russell, Jeffrey Burton. 1987. "Witchcraft: Conceptions of Witchcraft." In *The Encyclopedia of Religion*, vol. 15. M. Eliade, ed. New York: Macmillan, 415–423.

Sacks, Sheldon (ed.). 1979. *On Metaphor*. Chicago: University of Chicago Press.

Sahlins, Marshall. 1968. "Notes on the Original Affluent Society." In *Man the Hunter*. R. Lee and I. DeVore, eds. Chicago: Aldine, 85–89.

———. 1972. *Stone Age Economics*. Chicago: Aldine.

Sanday, Peggy Reeves. 1986. *Divine Hunger: Cannibalism as a Cultural System*. New York: Cambridge University Press.

Sapir, J. David, and J. Christopher Crocker (eds.). 1977. *The Social Use of Metaphor: Essays on the Anthropology of Rhetoric*. Philadelphia: University of Pennsylvania Press.

Schmidt, Wilhelm. [1908] 1954. *Der Ursprung der Gottesidee*. Münster: Aschendorf.

Sidgewick, Eleanor Mildred. 1911. "Spiritualism." *The Encyclopaedia Britannica*. 11th ed. New York: Encyclopaedia Britannica Company.

Simpson, George Eaton. 1945. "The Belief System of Haitian Vodun." *American Anthropologist* 47 (1): 35–59.

———. 1965. *The Shango Cult in Trinidad*. n.p.: Institute of Caribbean Studies, University of Puerto Rico.

Smith, Peter. 1987. *The Babi and Baha'i Religions: From Messianic Shi'ism to a World Religion*. Cambridge: Cambridge University Press.

Spiro, Melford E. 1971. "Religion: Problems of Definition and Explanation." In *Anthropological Approaches to the Study of Religion*. M. Banton, ed. ASA Monograph no. 3. London: Tavistock Publications, 85–126.

Srinivas, M. N. 1955. "The Social System of a Mysore Village." In *Village India: Studies in the Little Community*. M. Marriott, ed. American Anthropological Association Memoir 83, 1–35.

———. 1976. *The Remembered Village*. Berkeley: University of California Press.

Steward, Julian H. 1949. "South American Cultures: An Interpretive Summary." In *Handbook of South American Indians*, vol. 5. J. H. Steward, ed. Washington, D.C.: United States Government Printing Office, 669–772.

Trevor-Roper, H. R. 1968. "The European Witch-craze of the Sixteenth and Seventeenth Centuries." In H. R. Trevor-Roper, *The Crisis of the Seventeeth Century*. New York: Harper & Row, 90–192.

Turnbull, Colin. 1972. *The Mountain People*. New York: Simon & Schuster.

Turner, Victor W. 1967. "Betwixt and Between: The Liminal Period in *Rites de Passage*." In V. W. Turner, *The Forest of Symbols*. Ithaca, N.Y.: Cornell University Press, 93–111.

————. 1969. *The Ritual Process: Structure and Anti-Structure.* Chicago: Aldine.

————. 1973. "Symbols in African Ritual." *Science* 179, 1100–1105.

Turner, Victor W., and Edith Turner. 1978. *Image and Pilgrimage in Christian Culture.* New York: Columbia University Press.

Tylor, Edward Burnett. [1871] 1970. *Religion in Primitive Society.* (First published as part of *Primitive Culture.*) Gloucester, Mass.: Peter Smith.

van Gennep, Arnold. [1908] 1960. *The Rites of Passage.* Chicago: University of Chicago Press.

Vertovec, Steven. 1992. *Hindu Trinidad: Religion, Ethnicity and Socio-Economic Change.* London: Macmillan.

Wallace, Anthony F.C. 1966. *Religion: An Anthropological View.* New York: Random House.

Weber, Max. [1922] 1963. *The Sociology of Religion.* Boston: Beacon Press.

Weightman, Judith Mary. 1983. *Making Sense of the Jonestown Suicides: A Sociological History of Peoples Temple.* New York: E. Mellen Press.

Weinreich, Uriel. 1968. *Modern English-Yiddish/Yiddish-English Dictionary.* New York: McGraw-Hill.

Weiss, Gerald. 1973. "Shamanism and Priesthood in Light of the Campa *Ayahuasca* Ceremony." In *Hallucinogens and Shamanism.* M. J. Harner, ed. New York: Oxford University Press, 40–47.

White, Leslie A. [1949] 1973. *The Science of Culture: A Study of Man and Civilization.* New York: Farrar, Straus and Giroux.

Whitehead, Harriet. 1974. "Reasonably Fantastic: Some Perspectives on Scientology, Science Fiction and Occultism." In *Religious Movements in Contemporary America.* I. Zaretsky and M. Leone, eds. Princeton: Princeton University Press, 547–587.

Wilson, Edmund. 1956. *Red, Black, Blond and Olive; Studies in Four Civilizations: Zuñi, Haiti, Soviet Russia, Israel.* New York: Oxford University Press.

Yalman, Nur. 1962. "The Ascetic Buddhist Monks of Ceylon." *Ethnology* 1: 315–328.

Yinger, J. Milton. 1970. *The Scientific Study of Religion.* London: Macmillan.

About the Book and Author

This innovative introduction to the anthropological study of religion challenges traditional categories and assumptions, arguing that too many of them reflect ethnocentric perspectives long discarded by contemporary anthropologists. The continued use of such terms as "supernatural" and "cult" inescapably communicates that what is under study in not as real or true as the beliefs of the observer. This conflict between the axioms of science and Western scholarship and those of the belief systems under study can be avoided with careful attention to terminology and underlying assumptions.

Ordered Universes introduces and explores important anthropological issues, concerns, and findings about the institution of religion approached as a human cultural universal. Klass applies a non-ethnocentric perspective to each topic, relying on contemporary anthropological theories and using approaches deriving from other subdivisions of the discipline. Offering operational, non-judgmental definitions that avoid taking a position on whether the belief under study is "true" and providing examples from ethnographic (and other) literature on religion, Klass explores values, beliefs, witchcraft, shamans, sacrifice, ghosts, revitalization, and many other concepts. In the final chapters, he considers the emergence of new religious movements and leaders and evaluates the continuing ideological conflict between proponents of scientistic, fundamental, and post-rationalist systems of thought.

Morton Klass is professor of anthropology at Barnard College.

Index

Printed in the United States
40342LVS00006B/7